The BEATLES WHITE ALBUM
and the Launch of APPLE

Compiled by Bruce Spizer

With additional contributions by

Bill King,

Al Sussman,

Frank Daniels,

Piers Hemmingsen

and other Beatles fans

www.imagineandwonder.com

YOUR GUARANTEE OF QUALITY

As publishers, we strive to produce every book to the highest commercial standards. The printing and binding have been planned to ensure a sturdy, attractive publication which should give years of enjoyment. If your copy fails to meet our high standards, please inform us and we will gladly replace it. admin@imagineandwonder.com

www.beatle.net
498 Productions, L.L.C.
935 Gravier Street, Suite 707
New Orleans, Louisiana 70112
Fax: 504-299-1964
email: 498@beatle.net

Scan these QR codes with your phone camera for more titles from Imagine and Wonder and 498 Productions.

Copyright ©2018 by 498 Productions, LLC
This paperback edition first published 2021 by Imagine & Wonder under agreement with 498 Productions, LLC.
This book is not an official product of Capitol Records, Inc., Universal Music Group, Inc. or Apple Corps, Ltd.

The Billboard, Cash Box and Record World chart data used in this book was taken from books published by Record Research, including Billboard Pop Album Charts 1965- 1969 and The Comparison Book 1954- 1982. Photo credits: Alamy Stock Photo (pages 101, 133, 142 top); Beatles Book Photo Library (pages 63, 135, 145); Tony Bramwell (page 165); Eric Cash (page 175 drawing); Paul Goresh Collection (page 3); Colin Harrison- www.avico.co.uk page 139); Mark Hayward (page 154); Tom Murray (pages 149, 163 bottom left); Rex Features/Shutterstock (page 11); Paul Saltzman (page 141); and Cathy Sarver (page 113). The Canadian images (pages 79- 85) were provided by Piers Hemmingsen and Stan Klees. The KFRC chart (page 45) is from the collection of Chris Stinson. The lyrics (pages 151, 163) are from Jim Berkenstadt. Most of the other items are from the collections of Bruce Spizer, Frank Daniels, Jeff Augsburger and Gary Hein.

MIX
Paper from responsible sources
FSC® C017606
www.fsc.org

Paperback edition ISBN 9781637610039
Library of Congress Control Number 2021906718
Printed in China by Hung Hing Off-set Printing Co. Ltd.
1 2 3 4 5 6 7 8 9

PRINTED WITH SOY INK
Trademark of American Soybean Association

Those Were The Days

It was a cool Sunday August night in the summer of 1968, the last night of camp. I was in my bunk at Camp Zakelo in Harrison, Maine, trying to listen on my transistor radio to WABC out of New York. The reception faded in and out, but this evening there was magic in the air. The disc jockey introduced a new song by the Beatles called "Hey Jude." At first, it was only Paul's voice and piano, but then the others joined in. After a few minutes, when I was certain the song was about to end, I heard a glorious sing-along that stretched out for several minutes. And when it was over, I couldn't get that "Na, na na na na na na, na na na na, Hey Jude" out of my head.

On the plane ride back to my home in New Orleans, that ending hook kept playing over and over in my mind. The next morning I had my mother drive me to the neighborhood record store, Studio A. I quickly went to the Beatles album section, looking for the group's new LP containing "Hey Jude," but there were only albums I already owned. I asked the store's owner, Bill, if he had the new Beatles album. Bill told me there was no new album, but that a single would be released in a few days. That surprised me because the song I had heard on the radio was too long to be a single. It had to be seven minutes long. But Bill insisted that the next Beatles disc was a 45 containing two songs. "Hey Jude" and "Revolution." I called the store every day until the record arrived. That Friday, my mother rushed me there so I could buy the group's incredible new single.

Even before I got home I was impressed. The record came in a classy-looking black sleeve with a simple message — "The Beatles on Apple." And the labels, visible through the sleeve's die cut center hole, were different, too. A bright green apple on one side and a white sliced apple on the other. And yes, I was right about the length of the song. The label listed the running time for "Hey Jude" at 7:11. Upon reaching home, I raced to my room and played the record over and over again. Of course, "Hey Jude" was fabulous, but so was the flip side, the powerful rocker "Revolution." Both songs not only had great music, but also had lyrics I could relate to. At the time I didn't know anything about Apple, but I knew the label had given me my money's worth. For less than a dollar I had purchased what had to be ten to eleven minutes of the greatest music ever recorded.

A few months later it happened again. On the evening of Friday, November 15, 1968, I began hearing songs from the Beatles new album on New Orleans radio station WTIX. The variety in the music was incredible. I heard bits of rock, folk, heavy metal, calypso and country. There were parodies of the Beach Boys and Bob Dylan. There were raunchy rockers and lush ballads. And there was a long sound collage that sounded unlike anything I had ever heard before.

In 1968, WTIX played the top ten requested songs at 10:00 p.m. each evening. By Wednesday night, all of the top ten songs were from the new Beatles album. Unfortunately I did not write down the names of the ten songs played that evening, but I do remember "Back In The U.S.S.R.," "Cry Baby Cry," "Bungalow Bill" and "Ob-La-Di, Ob-La-Da" were in that number.

Once again, it was time for me to start bugging Bill to make sure I got my copy of the album as soon as it was available. Bill informed me that he would be getting a small number of discs on Friday, with more to come the following Monday. He assured me that he would hold a copy for me from the first shipment delivered to his store.

That Friday I ran from the school bus stop to get home as quickly as possible so my mother could drive me to Studio A to purchase the record, which was simply titled *The Beatles*. Upon returning home, I played the double album straight through three times on the family stereo, breaking only to eat dinner. I studied the photo collage on the album's poster and read the lyrics as the songs played. It took over ninety minutes to play all four sides. Before going to bed, I taped the four portraits that came with the album on my bedroom wall. Although the double album wiped out my allowance, the Beatles had once again given me tremendous value for my money. I still have the LP, number ● **0687809**.

Had Apple only released those records, דַּיֵּנוּ — dayenu! (that would have been enough). They were at the time and still are my favorite Beatles single and album to this day. There were other releases to follow. And while every record did not capture the magic of the first two Beatles releases, there were many fine moments on those Granny Smith Apple labels.

I remember buying "Those Were The Days" within a few weeks of its release. The Mary Hopkin single was getting saturation air play on WTIX. Upon examining its label at Studio A, I noticed that the song was produced by Paul. That clinched it for me. I had to own the disc.

My other big Apple moment was seeing the Beatles perform "Hey Jude" and "Revolution" in color on The Smothers Brothers Comedy Hour. From the close up of Paul to the sing-swaying crowd at the end, that performance of "Hey Jude" was forever burned into my brain.

Those were the days. I will never forget the magic I felt when I first removed my copy of "Hey Jude" from its black sleeve. I remember placing the needle on the edge of the spinning black disc and hearing Paul's voice come out of the tiny speaker to my record player, which was built into a curved carrying case covered with red and black plaid cloth. My old record player was thrown out in the early seventies, but my original copy of that magical single with the Granny Smith Apple label remains and is pictured above. I still can't get that "Na, na na na na na na, na na na na, Hey Jude" out of my head.

You Know We're As Close As Can Be, Man

Depending on how you count it, this is either my ninth or tenth book on the Beatles. If you go by actual books published, this is the tenth. But if you consider the separate tomes on Capitol Records to be one book, then this is Number 9, Number 9, Number 9. Either way, it is a landmark book to me as *The White Album* is my favorite Beatles album.

This year, 2018, marks my twentieth anniversary as a Beatles author. Accordingly, it is appropriate for me to look back and thank those close to me in the production of those books.

Beatles record and memorabilia dealer Perry Cox got me started by asking me to write an article on the Beatles records on Vee-Jay for his upcoming price guide. After reading my proposed prose, he casually suggested that I could do a book on the topic. And off I went. Perry helped me get information and images of what seemed like hundreds of label variations. As scanning was then restricted to the tech-savvy with money to buy the equipment, he and others would send me the actual records for me to get scanned. And, of course, I bought tons of Vee-Jay discs from him for my collection. Also helpful from the start were Gary Hein of Hein's Rare Collectibles, Gary Johnson and Wayne Johnson of Rockaway Records, Jim Hansen of Blue Jay Way Galleries and other well-informed Beatles dealers.

Along the way, I have met many wonderful fellow Beatles fans and collectors, many of whom I consider close friends although I may only see them once or twice a year at the Fest for Beatles Fans and other Beatles events. I haven't the space on this page to thank them all, but I am sure they know who they are.

Many of their names can be found in the acknowledgments to my previous books. Once again, I re-thank all who have helped me on my prior books.

British author Mark Lewisohn set the standard for well-researched books on the Beatles. My goal from the start was to match his excellence.

As was the case with my previous book on *Sgt. Pepper*, I turned to fellow Beatles writers and authors Bill King and Al Sussman of Beatlefan magazine. Bill provided me with a time capsule piece that originally ran in Beatlefan, while Al contributed a new article weaving the turbulent events of 1968 with news of the Beatles lives in and out of the studio. Piers Hemmingsen came through again with the story from a Canadian point of view. Frank Daniels has been along for most of my 20-year run. As I've said before, having him on board a project is like adding a scholar, historian, music lover and detective all in one. And, of course, thanks to all of the fans who shared their special *White Album* recollections with me and the readers of this book.

Diana Thornton has served as my art director, graphic designer, prepress, IT advisor and so much more from day one! She is truly another one of those "you know we're as close as can be, man" friends. Kaye Alexander coordinated matters with our printer. The book was proofed by Diana, Frank, Al and Beatle Tom Frangione. In the tradition, my thanks to my family, Sarah, Eloise, Barbara, Trish, Big Puppy and others too numerous and crazy to name.

It's been an incredible 20 years. And, who knows, maybe I'll be sitting behind my computer a decade from now writing about my 30 years as a Beatles author!

Words About Author

Bruce Spizer is a lifelong native of New Orleans, Louisiana, who was eight years old when the Beatles invaded America. He began listening to the radio at age two and was a die-hard fan of WTIX, a top forty AM station that played a blend of New Orleans R&B music and top pop and rock hits. His first two albums were *The Coasters' Greatest Hits*, which he permanently "borrowed" from his older sisters, and *Meet The Beatles!*, which he still occasionally plays on his vintage 1964 Beatles record player.

During his high school and college days, Bruce played guitar in various bands that primarily covered hits of the sixties, including several Beatles songs. He wrote numerous album and concert reviews for his high school and college newspapers, including a review of *Abbey Road* that didn't claim Paul was dead. He received his B.A., M.B.A. and law degrees from Tulane University. His legal and accounting background have proved valuable in researching and writing his books.

Bruce is considered one of the world's leading experts on the Beatles. A "taxman" by day, Bruce is a Board Certified Tax Attorney with his own practice. A "paperback writer" by night, Bruce is the author of ten critically acclaimed books on the Beatles, including *The Beatles Are Coming! The Birth of Beatlemania in America*, a series of six books on the group's American record releases, *Beatles For Sale on Parlophone Records*, which covers all of the Beatles records issued in the U.K. from 1962 - 1970, and *The Beatles and Sgt. Pepper: A Fans' Perspective*. His articles have appeared in Beatlefan, Goldmine and American History magazines. He was selected to write the questions for the special Beatles edition of Trivial Pursuit. He maintains the popular website www.beatle.net.

Bruce has been a guest speaker at numerous Beatles conventions and at the Grammy Museum, the American Film Institute, New York's Lincoln Center and the Rock 'N' Roll Hall of Fame & Museum. He has appeared on Fox National News, CNN, ABC's Good Morning America and Nightline, CBS's The Early Show and morning shows in New York, Chicago, Los Angeles, New Orleans and other cities, and is a frequent guest on radio shows, including NPR, BBC and Beatle Brunch.

Bruce serves as a consultant to Capitol Records, Universal Music Group and Apple Corps Ltd. on Beatles projects. He has an extensive Beatles collection, concentrating on American, Canadian and British first issue records, promotional items and concert posters.

contents

We've got this thing called Apple...

On Tuesday evening, May 14, 1968, John Lennon and Paul McCartney were guests on NBC TV's Tonight Show. The plan was for the pair (shown in the photo seated next to announcer Ed McMahon) to promote the Beatles homegrown business venture, Apple Corps. Unfortunately, guest host Joe Garagiola (a former baseball player subbing for Johnny Carson) and guest Tellulah Bankhead (an actress past her prime) (both shown behind the desk) did little to facilitate discussion about the business. It wasn't until after a commercial break that Garagiola got around to asking, "How about this new organization, Apple?"

John explained that their accountant told them they could give their money to the government or do something with it. "So we decided to play businessmen for a bit, because we've got to run our own affairs now. So we've got this thing called Apple, which is going to be records, films and electronics, which all tie up. And to make a sort of an umbrella so people who want to make films about ... grass ... don't have to go on their knees in an office, you know, begging for a break. We'll try and do it like that. That's the idea. I mean we'll find out what happens, but that's what we're trying to do."

Lennon's remarks summarize how Apple came about and why the Beatles became businessmen. The company was not created for Utopian reasons. It was formed to shelter the Beatles sizable income from British taxes. As for the Beatles running their own affairs, this was necessitated by the death of manager Brian Epstein in August 1967.

John and Paul told the TV audience what their company planned to do. It was to be a place where people with talent could go, rather than begging for a break from big business. Paul explained that "Big companies are so big that if you're little and good it takes you like 60 years to make it. And so people miss out on these little good people." John provided a metaphor based on George saying he was "sick of being told to keep out of the park." According to John, "That's what it's all about, you know. We're trying to make a park for people to come in and do what they want."

So that explained what the Beatles were trying to do. It wouldn't take long for the Beatles to "find out what happens." But on that idealistic evening in May 1968, it sounded like a noble venture that the Beatles could pull off. After all, they were the Beatles.

John and Paul had arrived in New York three days earlier on May 11, joined by publicist Derek Taylor, Neil Aspinall, Mal Evans and Alexis Mardas a.k.a. Magic Alex, a self-proclaimed electronic genius. John and Paul stayed at the New York apartment of their attorney, Nat Weiss. The next day they held an Apple directors' meeting on a Chinese junk sailing around New York Harbor and the Statue of Liberty.

On May 13, John and Paul gave a series of interviews in a suite at the St. Regis Hotel in Manhattan. They answered questions from Time, Newsweek, Business Week and Fortune magazines, The New York Times and Larry Kane, a radio newsman who had accompanied the group on their American tours. When asked by Kane what they would do in the year ahead, John replied: "Apple. Try and set it up and see where it goes. It's like a top. And we set it going and hope for the best."

On the day of their Tonight Show appearance, Derek Taylor presided over a press conference at New York's American Hotel where John and Paul did their best to explain Apple, which John called "a business concerning records, films, electronics and, as a sideline, manufacturing or whatever it is called." He talked about doing things in a "business-like way, but business and pleasure might be feasible." John confirmed that the four Beatles would own 100% of Apple and that they would be equal partners. When asked about the capitalization of Apple, John replied, "We can only use our common sense and have the right people to handle things like capitalization." As for how much money they were putting in, both said they didn't know, with Paul adding "We'll do the details some other time." A running theme of the press conference was the lack of a specific plan, even as to whether the Beatles would come back to New York as a group. John responded: "We don't plan...Now we haven't a manager, and there's no planning at all." Paul added, "This is chaos." The Apple name was explained by Paul as "A is for Apple; it's very simple, you know." John added, "An apple for the teacher." Mission accomplished, they returned to London's Heathrow Airport on May 16.

LOOK WHO'S JOINED THE APPLE CLUB NOW!

END A MEAL WITH AN APPLE
IT'S NATURE'S TOOTHBRUSH

Although the Beatles did not begin calling their company Apple until 1967, the seeds for the Apple brand name had been planted long before as evidenced by an advert with the group plugging the dental benefits of eating apples produced during the height of Beatlemania. During the group's first U.S. visit, George was filmed eating an apple and singing "An apple for the teacher."

On June 20, 1963, The Beatles Limited was incorporated in the United Kingdom and assigned Company No. 764797. The corporation's shareholders were John Winston Lennon, George Harrison, James Paul McCartney and Richard Starkey, each owning 25 of the company's 100 ordinary £1 shares. In a move to reduce the huge tax burden facing the individual members of the group, a partnership named Beatles and Co. was established on April 19, 1967. Under the Deed of Partnership, each Beatle owed a 5% interest in the company, with the remaining 80% owned by The Beatles Limited. The partnership agreement provided that all of the income earned by the Beatles, with the exception of songwriting royalties, would be paid into The Beatles Limited. This substantially reduced taxes as the British corporate tax rates were significantly lower than the individual tax rates. Furthermore, income flowing into the corporation could be offset by corporate expenses, further lowering the tax liability. At the time this arrangement was set up, the Beatles had no idea how big those expenses would become.

By resolution dated November 17, 1967, the members of The Beatles Limited (John, George, Paul and Ringo) voted to change the corporation's name to Apple Music Limited, which took effect on December 4, 1967, with the filing of the corporate documents. A special resolution adopted by the members on January 12, 1968, changed the name again, this time to Apple Corps Limited, the company's current name. This change took effect on February 9, 1968.

Paul is credited for naming the company Apple. In an Apple press release, managing director Neil Aspinall stated: "Paul came up with the idea of calling it Apple, which he got from René Magritte...[who] painted a lot of green apples. I know Paul bought some of his paintings in 1966 or early 1967." Art dealer Robert Fraser delivered Magritte's *Le Jeu de mourre* (translated from the French as The Game of Morra) to McCartney in the summer of 1966. The painting was one of Magritte's last works and features a large green apple with "Au revoir" (translated from the French as goodbye until we meet again) written across its midsection in white script letters. Alistair Taylor, who at the time was with Brian Epstein's NEMS Enterprises, recalls McCartney telling him in 1967 that the Beatles company was going to be called Apple. According to Taylor, Paul explained that "A is for Apple" is one of the first things a child learns. Apple Music quickly developed into Apple Corps, which is a pun blending apple core and Apple Corporation. When Ken Mansfield asked Paul why the company was named Apple, McCartney replied "Have you ever heard anyone say anything bad about an apple?"

The first widespread appearance of the Apple name came in June 1967 with the release of *Sgt. Pepper's Lonely Hearts Club Band*. The back of the album's jacket contains the following credit: "Cover by M C Productions and The Apple." This reference gave no clue as to what Apple was or hint that the Beatles would soon be operating as Apple. The Apple name returned in December 1967. An Apple logo surrounded by the phrase "apple presents" appears above the group's name on the inside gatefold cover to the *Magical Mystery Tour* album and EP. The accompanying booklets list Neil Aspinall and Mal Evans as "Editorial Consultants (for Apple)." The sleeve to the 1967 Beatles Christmas record refers to the company in its production credit, which reads "Another little bite of the Apple: Produced by George (Is Here Again) Martin."

As early as Spring 1967, the group began meeting regularly with their advisors to discuss ways of spending their money to defer immediate recognition of income. Initial plans for the business followed traditional investment ideas associated with tax shelters, such as real estate, including a four-story building at 94 Baker Street that would later serve as Apple's first office. Other ideas, such as establishing a chain of card shops, were shot down by the group because they didn't want their name associated with "bloody greeting cards." Consideration was given to setting up a chain of record stores, but this idea was abandoned.

After rejecting a series of investment suggestions made by their accountants and other advisors, the group decided to enter into an area promoted by Paul — music publishing. Due to the numerous recordings and performances of Lennon-McCartney songs, Paul was well aware of how much money music publishers could make with hit tunes. Years later, Paul would increase his own massive fortune by obtaining the publishing rights to several songs, including the Buddy Holly catalog. But in 1967, the idea was for the Beatles company to develop new songwriting talent.

Although Beatles manager Brian Epstein had little involvement with Apple, his death on August 27, 1967, changed everything. John was the one who best understood the serious effect that Brian's death would have on the group. Shortly thereafter, Lennon confided in Alistair Taylor, "We've fookin' had it now." The first changes came within Brian's management company, NEMS Enterprises. Brian's younger brother, Clive Epstein, was quickly appointed head of the company. Robert Stigwood, who had brought in new bands such as Cream and the Bee-Gees, left NEMS and took his acts with him, forming his own company, Robert Stigwood Organization. Stigwood's departure was prompted by the Beatles informing him that they would not accept him as their manager.

Unlike Brian and Stigwood, Clive had little interest in developing new talent, an idea embraced by the Beatles. In response to rumors that the Beatles would be leaving NEMS, the company's press officer, Tony Barrow, issued a statement in October that "NEMS continues to handle the management, agency and other business interests of the Beatles." The relationship would not last much longer.

The first Apple project was *Magical Mystery Tour,* a psychedelic fantasy film featuring the Beatles. The movie was shot in segments without benefit of a script during September, October and November of 1967. Although the film was savagely panned by the critics upon its black and white BBC debut on December 26, 1967, it is now regarded as an interesting period piece depicting the free-wheeling spirit of the sixties.

Paul had pitched his idea for the movie in April 1967 to Brian Epstein, who would have coordinated the project had he been alive. With Brian gone, Paul took charge to ensure that his idea would become reality. Many of the logistical details were handled by Beatles road manager Neil Aspinall. His successful handling of this chore influenced the Beatles decision to hire Aspinall as Managing Director of Apple. This action was not made based upon his experience or qualifications. It was based on his loyalty and the total faith and trust that each of the Beatles had in Aspinall. The group hired Alistair Taylor away from NEMS to serve as Apple's General Manager.

Meanwhile, the Beatles were anxious to get their publishing company going. They hired former NEMS employee, Terry Doran, to head Apple Music Publishing. Although Doran had no experience in the music publishing business, he had contacts and knew young and upcoming songwriters. Doran quickly signed George Alexander to a songwriting contract with Apple. Shortly thereafter, Alexander and three other musicians formed a band. John Lennon named the group Grapefruit in recognition of Yoko Ono's concept book of instructions and drawings. As Apple had not yet established its record division, the group had to look elsewhere for a recording contract. Apple Music Publishing signed other songwriters, including Jackie Lomax, who would later record for Apple Records.

The Beatles also ventured into electronics, placing their faith and money with a 27-year-old Greek television repairman, Alexis Mardas. John was particularly infatuated by Mardas and his inventions and dubbed him "Magic Alex." At first, they formed a company with him named Fiftyshapes Ltd. It was later renamed Apple Electronics and became part of Apple. Magic Alex impressed the boys with his electronic toys. Some had potential, such as a device that enabled a person to listen to a record player through a portable transistor radio, while others had absolutely no practical value, such as a small metal box with 12 small lights that did nothing and was appropriately called a "nothing-box."

Mardas was always coming up with ideas. He claimed he could invent a force field that would cause a house to hover above the ground. Alistair Taylor recalls Magic Alex creating a device that enabled a person to reach another person by phone merely by saying the individual's name. This was an early form of voice-recognition technology. He also remembers Mardas demonstrating wallpaper that could serve as a stereo system's speakers. He attracted the attention of record companies by working on a method to prevent home taping of vinyl records. The Beatles faith in Magic Alex led to them having him build a recording studio in the basement of Apple headquarters. Mardas boasted that his studio would have a 72-track recorder when 16 tracks was state-of-the-art. The result was a total disaster.

Apple Retail's first endeavor, a clothing store called "Apple," was located on the ground floor of the group's Baker Street building. It was initially run by Pete Shotton, who had no retail experience, but who had played with John in the Quarrymen. He was quickly replaced by the more-experienced John Lyndon in early 1968. The bulk of the boutique's clothing was designed by a trio of Dutch fashion designers, Simon Posthuma, Marijke Koger and Josje Leeger, who hooked up with British publicist Barry Finch and began calling themselves The Fool. The Beatles became aware of The Fool through their costume designs for productions held at Brian Epstein's Savile Theatre. This led to The Fool designing outfits for the band's Our World TV broadcast of "All You Need Is Love." When The Fool approached the Beatles about setting up a boutique using the Beatles money, the Beatles eagerly agreed, fronting them £100,000 to stock and design the shop. The Fool hired 30 art students to paint an elaborate mural over the outside walls of the Baker Street building. The Apple shop was launched with a splashy party on December 5, 1967, attended by John and George. Employees quickly noticed the lack of controls and began raiding the cash registers. Customers came by to look at the beautiful clothes and the beautiful people, browse and shoplift. When neighboring businesses complained about the building's mural, Apple was forced to paint over it. The new image was pure white with a script "apple" on both panels above the first-floor windows. The combination of The Fool's excessive spending, employee pilferage, shoplifting and sluggish sales led to losses approaching £200,000 in six months. The Beatles decided to end the financial bleeding by closing the shop. At John's suggestion, the store opened its doors one last time on July 30, 1968, inviting the public to take what they wanted in a free-for-all orgy of legal shoplifting.

Having set up film, publishing, electronics and retail divisions, the Beatles finally turned their attention to what they did best – making records. Apple Records was set up with the same philosophy as the company's other divisions. It would discover and develop new talent. In addition, the Beatles hoped that many of their musician friends would switch labels and sign with Apple when their existing contracts expired.

Apple hired Ron Kass, an American who headed Liberty Records' British operations, to be president of Apple Records. Peter Asher, who had gained fame in the mid-sixties as half of Peter and Gordon, was brought in by Paul McCartney to serve as Apple's A&R (artists and repertoire) man. His job was to discover and develop recording artists for the label. His first significant signing was James Taylor.

Rather than hire an expensive ad agency, Paul decided that he could fashion a campaign to launch Apple Records. One evening he dropped by Alistair Taylor's home to kick around ideas. Paul came up with the concept of a one-man band who would be touted as an Apple success story. McCartney convinced Alistair that he would be perfect for the role. Later that week, the pair went to a photography studio to shoot the ad. Alistair sat on a stool with a bass drum strapped on his back. He wore a harmonica around his neck and strummed a guitar. He was surrounded by a microphone, tape recorder, washboard tub, brass instruments and books. And, for the crowning touch, Paul purchased a bowler hat for Alistair. To add to the authenticity, McCartney insisted that Taylor sing. When Alistair protested that he was a lousy singer, Paul reminded him that he was being photographed, not recorded. As the photographer shot away, Alistair crooned "When Irish Eyes Are Smiling."

The completed ad was placed in a number of music magazines and distributed as a handbill poster throughout London and surrounding provinces. In America, the ad ran in the May 25, 1968, issue of Rolling Stone. Apple received over 400 tapes in two weeks. Hundreds more arrived in the following months. Although many tapes were ignored, Peter Asher did hire a staff to listen to them. According to Asher, "None of it was much good unfortunately. Out of the myriad of tapes we got in the mail, we didn't sign anyone."

This man has talent...

One day he sang his songs to a tape recorder (borrowed from
the man next door). In his neatest handwriting he wrote an
explanatory note (giving his name and address) and, remembering
to enclose a picture of himself, sent the tape, letter and
photograph to *apple* music, 94 Baker Street, London, W.1.
If you were thinking of doing the same thing yourself–do it now!
This man now owns a Bentley!

H.P.Co.

Although Apple Records would be signing and recording its own artists, the company did not have the resources to manufacture or distribute singles and albums. An agreement was reached with EMI, the owner of Parlophone Records, to handle these important functions in the U.K. Capitol Records successfully bid for the American rights. On June 22, 1968, Paul McCartney attended a Capitol sales conference in Beverly Hills as a surprise guest. He talked briefly about Apple and its new relationship with Capitol and introduced a promo film about Apple. A Capitol press release proudly proclaimed: "Beatle Paul McCartney and Ronald S. Kass, Head of Apple Corps Music, today jointly announced with Alan W. Livingston, President, Capitol Industries, Inc., and Stanley M. Gortikov, President, Capitol Records, Inc., the completion of negotiations and the signing of an agreement whereby Capitol Records will manufacture and distribute all Apple Records product for the United States and Canada." The press release went on to say that "The Beatles themselves will in the future be released on their Apple label." Another press release stated that Apple Music would be a "fully functional record company with facilities planned for all major countries of the world," and that Apple was "pledged to seek out, produce and promote young unknown talents to star status."

Other announcements dealt with record and film releases. The George Harrison score for the film *Wonderwall* would be the first Apple LP, followed by the Beatles next album and an LP featuring the voice, guitar and songs of James Taylor. The first Apple single would feature a young Welsh singer, Mary Hopkin, and would be produced by McCartney. Apple hoped to have four major films in production by the end of the year, plus another Beatles picture and film versions of John Lennon's two books. Many of these details were reported in the June 29 Billboard.

At the request of the Beatles, Capitol Records executive Ken Mansfield was given the title of U.S. Manager of Apple Records. He had met the group during their 1965 visit to Los Angeles, which included a visit to the Capitol Tower and two concerts at the Hollywood Bowl. Under the arrangement set up in the summer of 1968, Capitol continued to pay Mansfield's salary. Although his duties included the oversight of all independent labels distributed by Capitol, Apple took up nearly all of his time. Mansfield became the Beatles and Apple's liaison in America. He was in charge of all aspects of the American operation, including release dates, promotion, mastering and art work. This was quite a responsibility, as America was the Beatles biggest and most important market.

The above picture was taken at an Apple/Capitol meeting held in Suite 1727 at the Royal Lancaster Hotel off Hyde Park in London on August 11, 1968. From left to right: George Harrison (back of head), Ron Kass (President of Apple), Paul McCartney, Ker Mansfield (U.S. Manager of Apple), Ringo Starr and Stan Gortikov (President of Capitol). John Lennon is off-camera to the right

The August 17 Billboard reported that the Beatles Apple project was set to roll in America on August 25 with the release, through Capitol, of five records. The initial releases would be George Harrison's *Wonderwall* album and four singles, including a new Beatles disc featuring "two new songs written by them, 'Revolution' and 'Hey Judge.'" (The latter song was really titled "Hey Jude," and the release of *Wonderwall* was pushed back to the year's end.) The article reported that the Beatles were deeply involved in all of Apple's divisions, namely music, films, electronics and merchandising, and that a recording studio was being built in Apple's new London headquarters.

Apple Records got off to a tremendous start propelled by the huge sales of the Beatles "Hey Jude" single and new double LP (later known as *The White Album*), as well as Mary Hopkin's hit single "Those Were The Days." All three of these discs were awarded gold record status by the Recording Industry Association of America (RIAA). The February 1, 1969, Billboard reported that Capitol presented the Beatles with $2,500,000 in royalties for the last three months of 1968.

While the success of Apple's initial releases was cause for celebration, the business side of things were a different matter. At an executive board meeting at Apple, Alistair Taylor gave the Beatles a heavy dose of reality. He informed the group that Apple was losing about £50,000 a week. The group's substantial revenue could not keep pace with the company's out-of-control spending. Salaries were too high, and employees were ordering expensive art and furniture for their offices and running up outrageous expense accounts. The Beatles were also guilty of excessive spending. And then there was the outright theft. People were stealing records, office equipment and even the copper stripping off the roof of Apple's Savile Row headquarters.

Alistair warned the group that if things continued as they were, the Beatles would lose all their money within a year. He admitted that he and Neil Aspinall were not up to the task of running a complicated business such as Apple and told them that the company needed an experienced businessman such as Lord Beeching, the former head of British Railways, to take over and set things right.

DISC and MUSIC ECHO 1s

JANUARY 18, 1969   USA 20c

LENNON BARED!

· Exclusive interview: page 8

Alistair got through to John, who, in a brutally frank interview with Ray Coleman in Disc and Music Echo magazine (January 18, 1969), spilled the beans. Lennon stated that Apple needed streamlining and that if things carried on, "all of us will be broke in six months." He elaborated, "[W]e can't let Apple go on like this. We started off with loads of ideas of what we wanted to do...it didn't work out because we aren't practical and we weren't quick enough to realize we needed a businessman's brain to run the whole thing."

Although Alistair's naming of Lord Beeching as someone who could run Apple was only an example and not a suggestion, John met with him just the same. Beeching was not interested in sorting out the mess and advised Lennon that the group should get back to what they were good at – making music.

Paul was also looking for answers. He was now seriously involved with Linda Eastman and discussed the problems at Apple with her father, Lee Eastman. Contrary to erroneous stories published over the years, Lee Eastman had no connection with the Eastman Kodak company. He had changed his last name from Epstein to Eastman in his early twenties. Lee Eastman was a successful attorney and expert in international copyright law. He owned some valuable music publishing copyrights and was an art collector. He brought his son John into his law practice, which was known as Eastman and Eastman. When Paul asked Lee Eastman who he would recommend to fix Apple, Lee suggested his son John.

With Paul's blessings, John Eastman flew to London to survey the situation. He made some tax suggestions and advised the Beatles to buy NEMS, which was now owned primarily by Brian's estate. Eastman explained to the group that under their contract with EMI, 25% of their royalties were paid directly to NEMS. By purchasing the company, the Beatles would in effect receive their full royalties from EMI. Clive Epstein, who was handling Brian's estate and serving as chairman of NEMS, was interested in selling the company to obtain cash needed for payment of the substantial estate taxes due at the end of March. Eastman began negotiations with Clive, suggesting a purchase price of one million pounds. The transaction was to be financed by advance royalty payments from EMI.

Meanwhile, Allen Klein was getting ready to make his play to become the Beatles manager. Klein was an accountant who got his start in the music industry by auditing the books of record companies on behalf of musicians. Klein was aware that record labels consistently underreported royalties owed to their acts. He became an expert at finding money already owed to artists. After successfully aiding Bobby Darin, Klein began picking up other clients. He became Sam Cooke's manager. This led to him securing the music publishing of Cooke's catalog for his management company, Abkco.

Although Klein had a questionable reputation, he got results. Not only was he getting his clients the royalties they were owed, he was negotiating new recording contracts with higher royalty rates. Klein became the manager of British acts such as the Rolling Stones and Herman's Hermits. While he got the Stones a higher royalty rate than the Beatles, his acquisition of the American publishing of the band and other dealings left a sour taste with Mick Jagger and the other Stones. They parted ways, but not until Abkco had locked up the Stones sixties catalog.

Although Allen Klein had fantasized about managing the Beatles when the group first made its mark in America, he was a realist and knew nothing could happen as long as Brian Epstein was in charge. After Brian's death, he began his quest by meeting with Clive Epstein and Peter Brown. In his memoirs, *The Love You Make*, Brown found Klein "so foul-mouthed and abusive that I ended the meeting in a few moments and had him shown the door."

After hearing reports from London of John's claim that the Beatles were going broke, Klein renewed his efforts, this time going for the direct approach by securing a meeting with Lennon, which took place at the Dorchester Hotel in London on the night of January 27, 1969. Allen Klein made the most of his time with John and Yoko, impressing them both with his knowledge of the music industry, the Beatles music and Yoko's art. John immediately hired Klein to handle his financial affairs and informed the other Beatles of his decision the next day. He sent the following letter to Sir Joseph Lockwood, head of EMI: "Dear Sir Joe: I've asked Allen Klein to look after my things. Please give him any information he wants and full cooperation. Love, John Lennon." Similar letters, dated January 29, 1969, were sent to Clive Epstein, music publisher Dick James and the Beatles accountants.

After completing the *Get Back* sessions, the Beatles met to decide who would manage their affairs. John convinced Ringo and George that Allen Klein was the man for the job. On February 3, 1969, the Beatles hired Klein to review their finances. Although Paul was against this decision, he chose not to fight the others, recognizing that the group needed to hire someone to straighten things out. McCartney was able to get Eastman and Eastman hired as counsel for the group. The February 15 Billboard reported that Klein had taken over the business affairs of the Beatles and Apple, and that his function was to review and negotiate various business activities of the group.

In addition to reviewing Apple's finances, Klein became involved with the proposed purchase of NEMS. Although Clive Epstein most likely found Klein distasteful, it was John Eastman who caused the greater friction by insinuating that Brian had acted improperly by arranging for NEMS to receive 25% of the Beatles royalties from EMI. Clive grew tired of the conditions that Eastman wanted attached to the proposed sale and abruptly sold the NEMS stock to a group of investors known as the Triumph Trust. When Klein tried playing hardball with Triumph by instructing EMI to pay all royalties directly to Apple, EMI wisely froze the Beatles royalty payments until the parties settled their differences. A series of tough negotiations between Klein and Triumph eventually led to a settlement under which the Beatles paid approximately £1,100,000. In return, the 25% share of royalties was reduced to 5% and the Beatles obtained full ownership of their film company, Subafilms, and an option to buy NEMS' 4.5% ownership in Northern Songs at a below market rate. The Beatles exchanged their 10% interest in NEMS for 226,000 shares of

Triumph. On March 21, 1969, Allen Klein was officially hired as Apple's business manager. He immediately cleaned house, firing nearly everyone. Among the casualties were long-time Beatles confidant Alistair Taylor, Apple Records president Ron Kass and Magic Alex. Neil Aspinall was also on Klein's hit list, but the Beatles insisted that Aspinall keep his job. Derek Taylor was spared, apparently as a reward for helping set up Klein's initial meeting with John and Yoko. Although Klein tried to keep Ken Mansfield as U.S. manager of Apple Records by offering to triple his salary, Mansfield accepted an offer from Ron Kass to work for him at his new place of employment, MGM Records. Klein filled the void from within by assigning the running of Apple's day-to-day affairs to Abkco's Alan Steckler.

Although Paul had reluctantly gone along with the decision to have Klein look into the group's financial affairs, he had yet to sign a management contract with Abkco. On Friday evening, May 9, 1969, the group met at Olympic Studios for what was intended to be a recording session. The other Beatles told Paul he needed to sign the agreement because Klein was heading back to New York the next day. Paul told the others that the Beatles were the biggest act in the world and therefore Klein would take 15% rather than the 20% management fee called for in the contract Klein presented to the group. He wanted to have his lawyer review the agreement on Monday. The others accused Paul of stalling and stormed out of the studio. Paul ventured over to another room at Olympic where Steve Miller was recording. After telling Miller of his battle with the others, he asked if he could take out his frustrations on the drums. Miller readily agreed and he and Paul completed a track for Miller's new album. After laying down the drums, McCartney added bass, guitar and backing vocals. The song was appropriately titled *My Dark Hour*.

The May 31, 1969, Billboard reported that Abkco, headed by Allen Klein, had signed a three-year contract to manage Apple and the Beatles. The article failed to mention that Paul refused to sign the agreement.

Klein's first major accomplishment was the renegotiation of the Beatles contract with the Gramophone Company Limited ("EMI"), which ran from January 26, 1967, through January 26, 1976. After months of tough negotiations, a new agreement was reached. Under the 1967 contract, the Beatles were getting 39 cents per album. The new contract provided for 58 cents per album through 1972 and 72 cents per album for the remainder of the term.

As part of the agreement, EMI granted Apple Records, as licensee, EMI's rights to the Beatles for the United States, Canada and Mexico. This exclusive license covered all recordings made by the Beatles (either as a group or as individuals) during the term of the contract, as well as all records previously made by the Beatles owned by and available to EMI. Apple then entered into an agreement with Capitol under which Capitol manufactured and distributed the records and tapes for Apple. This brought significant revenue to Apple Records, who previously did not receive any income from the sales of Beatles records and tapes.

Although Paul was pleased with the new recording contract negotiated by Klein, he never accepted Klein as his manager. By 1973, the other Beatles became dissatisfied with Klein, and their business relationship ended. They battled each other in court for many years, but those lurid stories are beyond the scope of this book.

Throughout all the craziness, Neil Aspinall remained. He served as Apple's Managing Director through 2007. Under his care, Apple made a triumphant return in the nineties, releasing six new albums, five of which sold in the millions. Aspinall died on March 24, 2008.

Apple continues to oversee the Beatles legacy under the guidance of CEO Jeff Jones, who replaced Aspinall. The company's marketing, merchandising and music and video projects are designed not only to appeal to the group's aging fan base, but also to attract new fans.

John's quote from 50 years ago that "we've got this thing called Apple, which is going to be records, films and electronics, which all tie up" came true, but not how the Beatles intended. It was another corporation named Apple Inc. (whose name was suggested by co-founder Steve Jobs after returning from a visit to an apple orchid) that made John's vision become reality by combining music, video and electronics in products such as computers, iPods, iPhones and iPads. "This thing called Apple" may not have worked out the way the Beatles intended, but Apple has ensured that the legacy of the Beatles music will be preserved for generations to come.

Apple's First Four

On August 22, 1968, employees of Capitol Records sent press kits to radio station program directors across the United States. The kits were packaged in white envelopes with an Apple logo in the upper left corner serving as the return address. The logo was a solid green circle with a white apple in the center with the word "Apple" in white script letters above the stem. The lucky recipients of these envelopes would be among the first people in America to read about and, more importantly, hear the initial offerings of the Beatles new venture, Apple Records.

For those disc jockeys who had been monitoring Apple's progress by reading trade magazine articles, the arrival of the classy looking white envelope with the Apple logo was truly a magic moment. Upon ripping open the envelope, the recipient encountered a glossy cream colored folder with a large Apple logo on its cover. Inside the folder was a treasure of sound, visuals and information.

In contrast to the white envelope and folder were four distinguished-looking black die-cut record sleeves. One proclaimed "The Beatles on Apple" in an attractive script font. The group's name was in white and "Apple" in green. The other three sleeves merely said "Apple" in the same eye-catching green script letters. Peeking out of the center of each sleeve was a record label covered with a green Granny Smith apple.

The sleeves were not the only thing different about the singles. While most records had the same label design on both sides, these discs had a full green apple on one side (the A-side) and a sliced apple with its exposed white innards on the other (the B-side). The singles also had something new to most Americans – a slip guard consisting of 360 interlocking serrations surrounding the label. Although many people thought the tiny grooves were Apple's innovation, several British labels had been pressing discs with slip guards for years. By coincidence, Capitol had retooled its pressing plants for slip guard singles in August 1968, so the Apple singles were among the first Capitol manufactured 45s with the new look.

AIR MAIL

The Beatles

The Beatles as of now, in short... Band max...

Apple

For program directors, the most important part of the package was the first new Beatles single in over five months: "Hey Jude" b/w "Revolution." The quality of both sides of the single assured that listeners would stay put when the songs were aired. Disc jockeys were delighted to see that the running time for "Hey Jude" was an incredible 7:11. At the time the 45 was released in 1968, singles normally contained songs running between two and three minutes. This record would truly be a DJ's best friend when nature called or a groupie dropped by the station. Because the Beatles were under contract to Capitol Records, the single was assigned a record catalog number in the Capitol series, 2276. The other three singles were by artists signed to Apple Records. Unlike the Beatles disc, they have Apple catalog numbers, beginning with 1800.

The first of these, Apple 1800, is "Thingumybob" b/w "Yellow Submarine" by the John Foster and Sons Ltd. Black Dyke Mills Band. The label text on both sides of the record is printed vertically. While "Yellow Submarine" contains the usual "Lennon & McCartney" songwriting credit, "Thingumybob," which was written entirely by Paul for a non-Beatles project, is credited to "McCartney & Lennon." Both sides of the disc have a Paul McCartney production credit.

Paul also produced Apple 1801, Mary Hopkin's "Those Were The Days" b/w "Turn, Turn, Turn." All label information on this single appears horizontally.

Apple 1802 pairs "Sour Milk Sea" and "The Eagle Laughs At You" by Jackie Lomax. The record was produced by George Harrison, who is given production credit on the label. George is mistakenly listed as the writer of both songs. Although he wrote "Sour Milk Sea," the B-side was penned by Lomax.

A mere perusal of the labels of these four singles made it clear that the Beatles were heavily involved in Apple. In addition to the Beatles new single, the set included two records produced by Paul and one by George, with each of these Beatles also contributing an original composition.

The press kit also included two 8" x 10" black and white glossy photos of each artist featured on the records. The Beatles are represented by their cartoon images from the *Yellow Submarine* feature film. Because the movie had yet to be released in America, disc jockeys must have wondered why the group was being depicted as crudely drawn cartoon characters in mod clothes. A current photograph of the group would have made more sense. Paul and his sheep dog Martha are pictured with the Black Dyke Mills Band in the brass band's horizontal publicity still. Jackie Lomax and the lovely Mary Hopkin are each featured in vertical portraits. All four glossies have the artist's name printed below the picture towards the left side and the Apple logo in the lower right corner.

Recipients of the press kit learned about each artist through separate 8½" x 11" information sheets and 5½"x 8½" booklets. The text on the information sheets is credited to Apple press agent Derek Taylor. Although no credit is given in the booklets, the writing appears to be in the style of Derek Taylor as well.

The booklet on the Beatles is full of optimism and tells a story of the Beatles quite different from the tensions that sometimes surfaced during the recording of the group's first Apple album:

"The Beatles are in good health, of sound heart and willing spirit, and by the Fall the new evidence of their continuing supremacy will be spinning on the world's turntables around the symbol of their own shimmering green Apple label. At this moment they are deeply involved in the twin responsibilities of recording the album-successor to the profoundly respected Sergeant Pepper's Lonely Hearts Club Band and of administering the Happy Apple complex of companies in London. John, Paul, George and Ringo, firmly united one for all and all for one as The Beatles, growing up and outwards, phasing their expansion so as to keep a hold on which might otherwise consume their precious careers and confuse the thread of their energy sources are confident and cheerful and the human condition will be thrilled by the coming results of their willing and enduring Beatle-bondage. Unhampered by the pressures of world stardom, entranced by their opportunities, stimulated by the blossoming of Apple, they will give us new wonders to soothe our pain. The end for now, but there is no end."

THE BEATLES

Disc jockeys reading about "Happy Apple" and the group's "willing and enduring Beatle-bondage" had no idea that the end was closer than anyone could imagine. No doubt they, like the world at large, viewed John, Paul, George and Ringo as "firmly united one for all and all for one as The Beatles." The motto of the Three Musketeers seemed to fit the Fab Four perfectly, and learning that the Beatles were deeply involved recording a new album instilled a sense of comfort that all was as it should be.

The information sheet on the Beatles (shown on the opposite page) focused on the group's new single which was described as "amazing," "quite fantastic" and "incredible." The magnificence of both sides was reflected in the national charts, which based their standings on radio air play and sales. "Hey Jude" entered the Billboard Hot 100 on September 14, 1968, at number ten. After jumping to number three the following week, it passed Jeannie C. Riley's "Harper Valley P.T.A." and the Rascals' "People Got To Be Free" on its way to the top on September 28. "Hey Jude" remained at number one for nine straight weeks during its 19 weeks on the charts. Cash Box also charted the song for 19 weeks, including seven at number one. Record World charted the song for 17 weeks, with four at the top.

"Revolution" also received significant air play. It spent 11 weeks in the Billboard Hot 100, peaking at number 12 for three straight weeks. Cash Box charted the song for 10 weeks, with a peak at 11. When the single made its debut at number 70 in the Record World 100 Top Pops chart on September 7, 1968, it was listed as "Hey Jude." For the next two weeks, when it moved up to number 13 and then to two, the disc was identified as "Hey Jude"/"Revolution." On the September 28 chart, the songs were separated, with "Hey Jude" at one and "Revolution" at two. The B-side dropped to nine the next week, before falling to 53 for its final two of six weeks on the chart.

The October 12 Billboard reported that the single had been certified gold by the RIAA, with sales of over one million units. Two months after its release, "Hey Jude" had sold nearly three million copies. By mid-January, sales reached 3,773,000. Apple's Beatles debut went on to sell between four and five million copies in the U.S. and eight million worldwide.

The Beatles

"Hey Jude" and "Revolution."

It's amazing.

It is really quite fantastic.

It is incredible.

It is the Beatles again, doing it again, doing our minds in again with the magical mystic Beatle mastery of their medium. They are the message, are the medium. They have written and produced two sides for this new single which you know, you know beyond the thinnest wisp

of a shadow of a doubt, will engage the most profound admiration from the public, from the industry, from those in other groups, who strive to match the Beatles achievements.

"Hey Jude" and "Revolution" are the two sides.

"Hey Jude" is lead sung by Paul McCartney and it is a long lovely loving love-song offering hope ("Hey Jude, don't be afraid . . . take a sad song and make it better . . .") and beauty in the words and extraordinary melodic subtleties in the music. "Hey Jude" is the longest song ever recorded by the Beatles (seven minutes and five seconds), and I would say it is the best if it weren't for all those others that have gone before. I would say it was the best if, also, it were not that "Revolution"—main voice John—

were not so breathtakingly vital and insistent. This is the new Beatle peace — with strength message, with the voices forced out of the grooves by a backing as new for Capitol

now as Strawberry Fields was for then.

A theme for today, "Revolution," written by revolutionary visionaries.

The Beatles are without peer.

Their music is magnificent.

It can be said again and again

as they sing and sing it again.

Derek Taylor

The information sheet on the Black Dyke Mills Band urges readers (including radio program directors) to "come on and hear about the best band in the land." The opening text is a play on the lyrics from the tune Alexander's Rag Time Band ("Come on and hear the best band in the land"). The accompanying booklet is titled "The Black Dyke Mills Band and a Beatle." The reader learns that the band is 113 years old and is sponsored by John Foster and Son Ltd. of the Woollen Mills in the village of Queensbury, Yorkshire near Bradford. The band, which has 27 members plus a percussion section, won the National Champion Band of Great Britain award in 1967 for the seventh time since 1945. Derek Taylor's information sheet tells the following story:

"When Paul McCartney was faced with the challenge of producing his theme song for the London TV show 'Thingumybob' he decided to forget studio musicians, and the sophistication of formal studios and took himself up the trunk road which splits England from top to bottom. Up from exciting London to industrial Bradford in the north where, in an ancient city, he recorded The Black Dyke Mills Band in their home town."

The sessions for the single took place on June 30, 1968, with Geoffrey Brand serving as conductor. "Thingumybob" was recorded in Victoria Hall, while "Yellow Submarine" was performed outdoors at the Square of Victoria Hall.

Taylor concludes his prose with a review and a mandate: "The results are strong and amazingly contemporary for within the song there are those strange, unique touches of the Beatle-flair. The 'B' side is Yellow Submarine, one of the great youth marching songs of all time played as a march as it is begged to be played. Be played by them. March to them yourselves across the living room, be young again, and brave."

Although the single was interesting and well produced, most program directors were not brave enough to play a brass band record on their stations. It failed to chart, and, as Apple's first numbered single, is highly collectible.

JOHN FOSTER & SONS LTD.
BLACK DYKE MILLS BAND

The booklet on Mary Hopkin tells the tale of how supermodel Twiggy saw the young Welsh folk singer on the British TV talent show Opportunity Knocks and was so impressed that she told Paul McCartney of her talent. Paul signed her to be part of the launching of his dream organization, Apple. The information sheet boldly predicted that "Mary Hopkin will be #1 in the charts with Those Were The Days." According to Derek Taylor:

"The record is produced by Paul McCartney who is English, sung by Mary Hopkin who is Welsh, written by Gene Raskin who is American. It is for all ages, all tastes, all creeds, sensibilities, for anyone with the capacity to be stirred by music and is there anyone who has not this capacity? It is a long song: it builds, grips, embraces. It will be whistled, hummed, sung, translated, exploited, adopted all over the world. It will be one of the hits of the year."

The song was even more international than that, with Gene Raskin and his wife, Francesca, providing English lyrics to an old Russian song, "Dorogoi Dlinnoyu" ("Дорогой длинною") (translated as "By the long road") in the early 1960s. The original song was written in 1924 by Soviet composer Boris Fomin with words by the poet Konstantin Podrevsky. The song's romantic idealism flows with reminiscences of youth. Raskin and his wife were folk singers, who performed in the clubs in New York's Greenwich Village. The Raskins took their show on the road and played London's Blue Angel on an annual basis, closing with "Those Were The Days." Paul saw the duo perform the song at the club and encouraged other artists, including the Moody Blues, to record the song, but no one heeded his recommendation. When he signed Mary Hopkin to Apple, he realized that the song would be perfect for her.

The song was recorded in July 1968 with Paul and Mary on acoustic guitars, accompanied by studio musicians on balalaika, clarinet, hammered dulcimer, tenor banjo and a children's chorus. Recognizing its international appeal, McCartney had her separately record foreign versions in French, German, Spanish, Italian and Farsi. The song was an international success, topping the charts in the U.K., France, Germany, Spain, Ireland, Canada, Denmark, Finland, Norway, Sweden, Belgium, the Netherlands, Poland, Switzerland and Japan. In America, it reached number one in Cash Box and Record World, but stalled at two in the Billboard Hot 100, unable to pass "Hey Jude."

MARY HOPKIN

The booklet on Jackie Lomax contains five pages of text, likely telling more of his background than most people would care to know. The highlights include his time with the Undertakers (a Liverpool band that went to Germany in July 1962 and later to America) and the Lomax Alliance (a group briefly under the care of Brian Epstein). The information sheet is more to the point: "Jackie Lomax is from Liverpool and it shows." Derek Taylor informs the reader that:

"George Harrison produced and wrote for this first Lomax solo effort on the fresh, new just-ripening APPLE label. It is called Sour Milk Sea – the sea we all find ourselves in from time to time. 'Get out of that Sour Milk Sea, you don't belong there. Come back to where you should be...' A few words of Beatle-warning, Lomax delivered. The backing of the record is astounding – listen to the guitar solo and know that Britain can still play rock 'n' roll."

While the information sheet justifiably raves about the Lomax single, it tells the reader little about the song's history and recording. "Sour Milk Sea" was written by Harrison during the Beatles stay with the Maharishi Mahesh Yogi in Rishikesh, India, in March of 1968. The Beatles recorded a demo of the song in May 1968 at Kinfauns, George Harrison's bungalow in Esher, Surrey. The song was one of over two dozen demos recorded for consideration for the upcoming Beatles album. For reasons unknown, George decided against recording it for the Beatles LP. Instead, he gave it to Lomax for his first Apple single. The song was recorded in late June at Trident Studios with a lineup featuring three of the Beatles. Lomax sings lead and plays rhythm guitar along with Harrison on rhythm guitar, Paul on bass, Ringo on drums, Eric Clapton on lead guitar, Nicky Hopkins on piano and Eddie Clayton on conga drums.

"Sour Milk Sea" is a great rock single that should have been a hit. Unfortunately for Lomax, Harrison and Apple, the song was overshadowed by the Beatles and Mary Hopkin singles and did not chart. The song was reissued in July of 1971 on Apple 1834, this time paired with "(I) Fall Inside Your Eyes." Once again, the song failed to chart.

JACKIE LOMAX

The Apple press kit mailed to U.S. radio stations in August of 1968 is the American equivalent of the elaborately packaged "Our First Four" box, which contained the same debut singles and was distributed to British radio stations and members of the press. While Apple in London hand-delivered copies of the boxes to the Queen and the Prime Minister, Capitol did not send a copy of the U.S. press kit to the White House.

A surviving Capitol Merchandising Project Authorization form dated August 1968 provides details regarding the press kit. The Special Apple Presentation project was budgeted at $8,000 and classified as a "broadcast promotion" expense. Capitol's Los Angeles pressing plant was directed to supply 1,300 copies each of "the initial 4 single record releases on APPLE to be collated into the special mailing kit." The records were scheduled for pick up on August 20 by Commercial Printing, who was instructed to collate the component parts and mail the 1,300 press kits.

Capitol ordered 5,000 white mailing envelopes and 5,000 press kit folders constructed of Kromekote cast-coated stock (the same paper later used for the cover of The White Album). These items would be used for the initial press kit mailings as well as for future press releases. The company also ordered 25,000 sheets of 8½" x 11" white bond paper imprinted with a light green Apple logo. The imprint was done in a 50% screen to allow for overprinting of text. These sheets were used for the press kit's information sheets on each artist. In addition, Capitol ordered 5,000 prints of each of the four black and white glossy photos of the artists. Capitol sent copies of the complete press kits, without the records, to Capitol of Canada who then inserted Canadian pressings of the records.

Complete copies of the press kit are extremely rare. For those lucky enough to possess the package, it is still a thrill to go through the press kit, read its flowery Derek Taylor text, look at the pictures of the beautiful young Mary Hopkin, the cartoon Beatles and Paul with his sheep dog Martha posing with a brass band, and, of course, play the singles that launched Apple Records. One can only imagine the excitement generated by that white folder with the green Apple logo all those years ago.

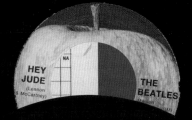

The Beatles on Apple — HEY JUDE (Lennon & McCartney) — THE BEATLES — NA

THOSE WERE THE DAYS (Gene Raskin) — MARY HOPKIN — T.R.O. Organization 5:06

MOTOWN 1135 © 1968 Jobete (BMI) QQQ-484M05 W4KM-5818 — Produced by "THE CLAN" — Arranged by Paul Riser — 2:59 — "LOVE CHILD" (P. Sawyer, R.D. Taylor, F. Wilson, D. Richards) — DIANA ROSS AND THE SUPREMES © 1968 A TRADEMARK OF MOTOWN RECORD CORP. — 87¢

LAURIE RECORDS — Record No. LR 3464 — Roznique Mus. Inc., BMI — ABRAHAM, MARTIN AND JOHN (Dick Holler) — DION — A LAURIE PRODUCTION—PHIL GERNHARD PRODUCTION — ARRANGED BY JOHN ABBOTT — 35 W. 45th ST., NEW YORK

"And here's another clue for you all..."
An American Perspective of *The White Album*

In most American cities, it began shortly after 4:00 PM on Friday, November 15, 1968. That was the time that radio stations could officially begin playing songs from the Beatles latest album. For the next several days, many stations were devoting about half their programming to the latest batch of songs from the group. Those wondering how the Beatles would follow *Sgt. Pepper's Lonely Hearts Club Band* and *Magical Mystery Tour* were teased with clue after clue all weekend long. There was rock 'n' roll, folk songs, a sing-along, an acoustic Western ballad, British blues, raucous rock, soft ballads, an experimental sound collage, a lullaby and more. The psychedelic sounds of the previous two albums were replaced with Beach Boys-style backing vocals, finger-picking guitar, pounding piano, Baroque-influenced harpsichord, country fiddle, harmonium, harmonica, brass, strings and other things. The cast of characters included Prudence, Desmond, Molly, Bungalow Bill, Martha, Rocky Raccoon, Julia, Mother Superior, the King of Marigold and Sexy Sadie. There were Ukraine girls and bent-back tulips, along with a gently-weeping guitar, a savoy truffle and a glass onion. There was a séance in the dark, a helter skelter, a recurring voice going "number nine, number nine," a "bang, bang, shoot, shoot" vocal refrain and a slower version of "Revolution." There were references to other Beatles songs and ob-la-di, ob-la-da. 30 new songs. So much to take in.

The variety and timeliness of the Beatles recordings heard on the radio was reflective of the current music scene, as demonstrated by the top ten songs in the Billboard Hot 100 for the week ending November 23, 1968. There was country (O.C. Smith's "Little Green Apples" at #9 and Glen Campbell's "Wichita Lineman" at #10); R&B (Johnny Taylor's "Who's Making Love" at #8); reggae (Johnny Nash's "Hold Me Tight" at #7); rock (Cream's "White Room" at #6); social consciousness (Dion's "Abraham, Martin And John" at #5 and the Supremes' "Love Child" at #2); psychedelic rock (Steppenwolf's "Magic Carpet Ride" at #4); and nostalgia (Mary Hopkin's "Those Were The Days" at #3). And at the top of the heap was the Beatles "Hey Jude," in its ninth and final week at number one.

The Billboard Top LP's chart for the week also reflected the variety in the music. The top album was *Electric Ladyland* by the Jimi Hendrix Experience, who also held down the sixth spot with *Are You Experienced?* (the group's debut LP). This was followed by *Cheap Thrills* by Big Brother & the Holding Company (with lead singer Janis Joplin), *Feliciano!* by blind Puerto Rican singer and guitarist Jose Feliciano, Steppenwolf's *The Second* (the group's second album) and *Time Peace/The Rascals' Greatest Hits* (anchored by the group's recent number one single "People Got To Be Free"). The top ten was rounded out with *The Crazy World Of Arthur Brown* (with Brown's number two hit single "Fire"), *The Time Has Come* by the Chambers Brothers (with the 11-minute version of the psychedelic rock classic "Time Has Come Today"), the double album *Wheels Of Fire* by Cream, and *Gentle On My Mind* by Glen Campbell.

For the most part, each of those albums featured one primary style of music. But the Beatles new album swept across a head-spinning number of musical genres and lyrical themes spread over four sides of vinyl lasting over an hour and a half.

Anticipation for the Beatles latest offering was high. For the past two and a half months, "Hey Jude" had dominated the charts and received saturation airplay. The disc sold over three million copies in just two months and was still selling 200,000 copies a week with no sign of slowing down. Ultimately, "Hey Jude" remained in the Billboard Hot 100 for 19 weeks, including nine straight at number one. Cash Box also charted the song for 19 weeks, with seven at the top, while Record World reported the song for 17 weeks, with four at number one. The single's dynamic B-side, "Revolution," was a hit in its own right, peaking at number two in Record World, 11 in Cash Box and 12 in Billboard.

Those living in some markets got to hear recordings from the album about a week or so earlier than planned. A few radio stations, including New York's WABC-FM and Detroit's WAXB, obtained a tape containing a dozen early mono mixes from the sessions. The source of the songs was a tape Ringo had given to Peter Sellers. The radio stations played these low fidelity recordings until threatened with legal action by Capitol Records. Other stations jumped the gun a few days by playing songs from the actual album ahead of its designated play time of 4 p.m. on November 15.

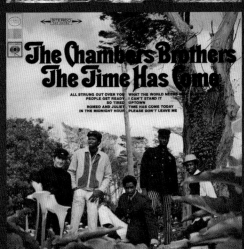

Once the air play began, radio stations were besieged with requests for songs from the new album and information about its upcoming release. According to Tom Donahue, program director at San Francisco's KSAN-FM, "There was such a tremendous number of people calling to ask when it would go on sale that our phones were all but useless." Some FM stations played the entire LP, which ran for over 90 minutes. The album's dominance was such that when San Francisco pop station KFRC prepared its Big 30 survey for November 20, 1968, it symbolically listed all of the album's 30 songs in order, starting with "Back In The U.S.S.R." at number one and "Good Night" at 30. It was most likely the only survey to ever chart "Revolution 9" (in this case at 29).

WORC (Worcester, Massachusetts), which prepared its charts based on listener requests, began tracking songs from the album with its November 23, 1968, survey and continued doing so through late February 1969. Its December 12 chart showed the Beatles dominance: "Ob-La-Di, Ob-La-Da" (#1); "Hey Jude" (#3); "Revolution" (#4); "Back In The U.S.S.R." (#6); "Rocky Raccoon" (#10); "I Will" (#19); "Honey Pie" (#29); and "Good Night" (#33). "Back In The U.S.S.R." would peak at #4, "Rocky Raccoon" at #5 and "I Will" at #12. WORC also charted "Piggies" (#30) and "Martha My Dear" (#50). Had other stations compiled surveys based on requests, they undoubtedly would have shown similar results. All across the country, songs from the Beatles double album were being played as if they were hit singles.

Capitol had gone against conventional music industry wisdom by allowing stations to play songs from the album for a full week ahead of it first reaching stores on November 22. Such practice was thought to inhibit sales. But this time the familiarity did not lead to lost purchases. Instead, the advance air play served to heighten anticipation. Rolling Stone reported that Capitol had advance sales of 1.7 million units. Demand for the album was so great that most stores received less than half of their initial orders. All over America, stores were quickly selling out of their allotments. The Harvard Co-op sold its 1,500 copies on the day the records arrived. The San Francisco Tower Records sold all of its 2,000 copies in one day and then sold out of its 1,500-unit second shipment the next day. The LP's list price of $11.98 ($5.98 was the norm) was not a deterrent. Beatles fans realized that they were getting good value for their money: 30 songs and over 90 minutes of music. It instantly became the group's fasting selling album ever.

KFRC THE BIG 610 PRESENTS THE BIG 30

ISSUE NO. 128 - WEEK ENDING NOVEMBER 20, 1968

THIS WEEK	TITLE ARTIST/LABEL	LAST WEEK
1	BACK IN THE U.S.S.R. Beatles/Apple	--
2	DEAR PRUDENCE Beatles/Apple	--
3	GLASS ONION Beatles/Apple	--
4	OBLADI OBLADA Beatles/Apple	--
5	WILD HONEY PIE Beatles/Apple	--
6	BUNGALOW BILL Beatles/Apple	--
7	WHILE MY GUITAR GENTLY WEEPS Beatles/Apple	--
8	HAPPINESS IS A WARM GUN Beatles/Apple	--
9	MARTHA MY DEAR Beatles/Apple	--
10	I'M SO TIRED Beatles/Apple	--
11	BLACKBIRD Beatles/Apple	--
12	PIGGIES Beatles/Apple	--
13	ROCKY RACOON Beatles/Apple	--
14	DON'T PASS ME BY Beatles/Apple	--
15	WHY DON'T WE DO IT IN THE ROAD Beatles/Apple	--
16	I WILL Beatles/Apple	--
17	JULIA Beatles/Apple	--
18	BIRTHDAY Beatles/Apple	--
19	YER BLUES Beatles/Apple	--
20	MOTHER NATURE'S SON Beatles/Apple	--
21	EVERYBODY'S GOT SOMETHING TO HIDE EXCEPT ME AND MY MONKEY Beatles/Apple	--
22	SEXY SADIE Beatles/Apple	--
23	HELTER SKELTER Beatles/Apple	--
24	LONG LONG LONG Beatles/Apple	--
25	REVOLUTION #1 Beatles/Apple	--
26	HONEY PIE Beatles/Apple	--
27	SAVOY TRUFFLE Beatles/Apple	--
28	CRY BABY CRY Beatles/Apple	--
29	REVOLUTION #9 Beatles/Apple	--
30	GOODNIGHT Beatles/Apple	--

BIG HITBOUNDS

Paul McCartney   Ringo Starr
George Harrison   John Lennon

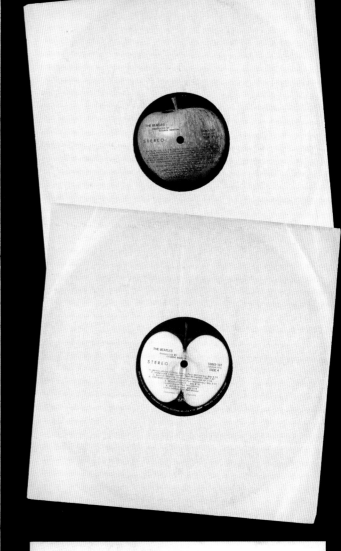

The BEATLES

Back in the U. S. S. R. : Dear Prudence : Glass Onion :
Ob-La-Di, Ob-La-Da : Wild Honey Pie :
The Continuing Story of Bungalow Bill :
While My Guitar Gently Weeps : Happiness is a Warm Gun :
Martha My Dear : I'm so tired : Blackbird : Piggies :
Rocky Raccoon : Don't Pass Me By :
Why don't we do it in the road? : I Will : Julia :
Birthday : Yer Blues : Mother Nature's Son :
Everybody's Got Something to Hide Except Me and My Monkey :
Sexy Sadie : Helter Skelter : Long, Long, Long :
Revolution 1 : Honey Pie : Savoy Truffle : Cry Baby Cry :
Revolution 9 : Good Night :

The album's in-store poster had a simple message for consumers: "IT'S HERE!" As the album's plain white cover would not have made for an eye-catching display, Capitol went in a different direction, merely adding the words in bold red stylized letters to the top of the collage included as an insert to the album. Demand for the album was so great that there was no need to say what "IT" was or to add information about the album or even the group's name.

The album's plain white cover was in stark contrast to what Beatles fans were used to seeing, particularly after the colorful covers of *Sgt. Pepper's Lonely Hearts Club Band* and *Magical Mystery Tour*. But there were subtle touches: "The BEATLES" was embossed slightly below its center and a number was stamped towards the lower right corner as if it were a numbered edition of fine art. "The BEATLES" was both the name of the group and the name of the album. While it was not unusual for an artist's name to serve as the name for an artist's debut album, the Beatles were far from being newcomers. The back cover was also white, with nothing but a small gray "Stereo" in the upper right corner. The record was the first by the group to be issued only in stereo in America, with mono having been all but completely phased out by the time of its release.

The inside of the open gatefold cover was white as well, with the song titles printed in gray in the lower portion of the left panel, along with the album number "SWBO 101" in the lower left corner. The right panel has separate rectangular black and white portraits of each Beatle running left to right in its lower region. These John Kelly photographs were included with the packaging in the form of four 7¾" x 10¾" color prints. The poster insert has a collage of photos on one side and the lyrics to all of the songs on the other. It measured 23" x 34" and was folded to fit inside the sleeve. These extra goodies more than compensated for the simplicity of the pure white cover that would quickly give the album its unofficial but more well-known name, *The White Album*.

The elaborate packaging posed multiple logistical problems for Capitol. To allow for sufficient lead time, the company originally planned to ship the record in early December, but demand made that impractical. According to Capitol's head of marketing, Rocky Catena, "we just couldn't hold off any longer."

IT'S HERE!

Although most of us American Beatles fans had heard several of the songs on the radio prior to buying the album, there was something special about hearing them in order for the first time. And for those of us who had only heard the songs on AM radio, we were now getting to hear them in true stereo. We opened up the poster and turned it over to get to the lyrics. We followed along with the songs as if we were reading fine poetry. And in our minds we were. As was the case with *Sgt. Pepper*, there were no gaps between the songs. Instead, they were cross fades, tight edits and links, the only break coming at the end of each side. It was like a symphony with four complex movements.

The first program begins with the sound of an airplane and quickly boils into a rocker. "Back In The U.S.S.R." has a great rock vocal from Paul, with Beach Boys-style backing vocals and a searing guitar solo. The airplane returns at the end for a cross fade into "Dear Prudence," an elegant song with finger-picked guitar and dreamy backing vocals behind John's lead. "Glass Onion" was another rocker with strange word play and multiple references to other Beatles songs. John asks us to see how the other half live. The song ends with a classical string coda leading straight into the pounding piano intro of "Ob-La-Di, Ob-La-Da." Paul's song has a reggae feel and the group laughing its way through the end. The next track, "Wild Honey Pie," comes across as a brief throw-away link by Paul, leading into a flamenco-style guitar sound that moves into the catchy sing-along chorus of "Bungalow Bill." Its cheerful sound serves as the backdrop to the saga of a man who went tiger hunting with his elephant, gun and mom, only to be admonished by the children: "Hey, Bungalow Bill, what did you kill, Bungalow Bill?" As the song comes to an end, John's "Eh-up" leads into George's "While My Guitar Gently Weeps," a song with introspective lyrics and great guitar work. The first side ends with one of the more complex and interesting tracks on the album, John's "Happiness Is A Warm Gun," which is really three songs in one. From its opening line "She's not a girl who misses much" to its middle section "Mother Superior jumped the gun" to its ending refrain "Bang bang, shoot shoot," it's one of Lennon's finest.

Paul's intricate piano work opens the second program with "Martha My Dear," which is followed by John's "I'm So Tired," complete with one of John's great throw-away lines: "And curse Sir Walter Raleigh, he was such a stupid git." Paul then shows off his acoustic guitar skills with the classical-influenced introduction to "Blackbird." Its lyrics fit comfortably into 1968: "Take these broken wings and learn to fly/All your life, you were only waiting for this moment to arise." Paul's whistling at the end takes us into the harpsichord opening of "Piggies," a bit of whimsical social commentary courtesy of George. The song ends with an extra coda full of pig grunt sound effects. Next up is Paul doing his best Bob Dylan imitation for the Western ballad of "Rocky Raccoon," complete with harmonica, honky-tonk piano and Gideon himself with his Bible. The group then switches styles again with Ringo leading the way through "Don't Pass Me By." The country song features a fiddle solo and lyrics that only Ringo could get away with singing:"I'm sorry that I doubted you, I was so unfair/You were in a car crash and you lost your hair." From the lyric sheet, we see that the song was written by Richard Starkey (the drummer's real name). The song's fiddle hoe-down ending leads into the drum and clapping introduction to a short rocker from Paul titled "Why Don't We Do It In The Road?," whose only other lyric is "No one will be watching us." Paul then effortlessly shifts from raunch rock to one of his sweetest love songs, "I Will." John returns to end the second side with "Julia," accompanying himself with finger-picking acoustic guitar. It is a lovely ballad with lyrics full of poetic imagery such as "ocean-child," "seashell eyes," "windy smile," "sleeping sand" and "silent cloud." It is one of John's most tender and heartfelt moments.

The third program gets off to a rousing start with the pounding riff of "Birthday." The party atmosphere propels another potboiler from Paul. "Yes, we're going to a party party" indeed. The song is immediately followed by the count-in to "Yer Blues." The song is in stark contrast from the joyous rocker that preceded it, with John singing "Yes I'm lonely, want to die." He references the main character of Bob Dylan's "Ballad Of A Thin Man" with the line "I feel so suicidal, just like Dylan's Mr. Jones." The blues send-up is followed by Paul's soft acoustic ballad, "Mother Nature's Son." John then returns, this time with an upbeat rocker full of cow bell and with the longest title of a Beatles song, "Everybody's Got Something To Hide Except Me And My Monkey." John went from singing about wanting to die to "Come on, it's such a joy." Next up is John's piano-driven "Sexy Sadie," who made a fool of everyone. The relatively serene song is followed by the loudest and most chaotic song recorded by the group, "Helter Skelter." It is one of Paul's grittiest vocals, backed by a mountain of drums, guitars and bass. The song fades out and then comes back with a vengeance, with Ringo screaming at its end, "I got blisters on my fingers!" The group then shifts from the LP's loudest track to its softest, "Long, Long, Long." George's song is about lost and regained love, with a middle section that quietly swings as a waltz. The song and third side end with a rattling sound and the thud of Ringo's drums.

The album's fourth and final program begins with a slower and longer version of the Beatles B-side, "Revolution," titled "Revolution 1." Although the recording for the single is more exciting, the slower pace works better to get the song's message across. It has the "shoo-be-do-wop-bow" backing vocals heard on the promotional video for the song, but not on the single. Paul's "Honey Pie" opens with the sound of a scratchy record harking back to the days of shellac 78s and shifting the group to the same vaudeville style heard on "When I'm Sixty-Four" and "Your Mother Should Know." Paul seems to be having fun with this one, ad-libbing "Yeah, like it like that, aah, ooh, I like this kinda hot kinda music, hot kinda music, play it to me, play it to me, Hollywood Blues." Next up is a rocker from George, "Savoy Truffle," whose lyrics float through an assortment of sweets such as creme tangerine, ginger sling, apple tart and coconut fudge. The song references one of the album's other tracks: "We all know Obla-Di, Bla-Da/But can you show me where you are?" John then offers a bit of royal satire mixed with lyrics influenced by nursery rhymes and *Alice In Wonderland*. In "Cry Baby Cry," he sings of King of Marigold, the Duchess of Kirkcaldy, a Queen and a Duke, along with "a séance in the dark, with voices out of nowhere put on specially by the children for a lark." The song ends with Paul singing "Can you take me back where I come from, can you take me back?" in an uncredited link track. The album's next song was unlike anything Beatles fans had heard before, an experimental sound collage titled "Revolution 9." As strange as it sounded on AM radio, it was even weirder in stereo. Upon first listening, the voice going "Number nine, number nine," the female voice saying "If you become naked" and the ending football chants of "Hold that line" and "Block that kick" stood out. Clearly it was a track that you needed to listen to multiple times, unless, of course, you never wanted to hear it again. The chaos of "Revolution 9" is followed by the calm serenity of a lovely lullaby sung by Ringo, "Good Night." The song, the side and the album end with Ringo whispering, "Good night, good night everybody, everybody, everywhere, good night."

It was a stunning 93 and a half minute experience with the Beatles sweeping effortlessly through multiple genres of music. Certain musical passages and sounds jumped out and caught our attention, as did many of the words. It was clear that this was to be an album to listen to over and over again, despite its unusually long playing time. The Beatles, with their new Apple label, had once again given us something special.

The Beatles made its debut in the Billboard Top LP's chart at number 11 on December 14, 1968. The following week it moved up to number two behind Glen Campbell's *Wichita Lineman*, before moving to the top on December 21. The two-album set topped the charts for nine weeks. Overall, *The Beatles* charted for 155 weeks, including 15 straight in the top five. The album also topped the Cash Box and Record World charts for several weeks.

Billboard reviewed the new Beatles LP in its December 7, 1968, issue, calling it "without doubt their most ambitious and impressive to date." The review stated that all the songs were "treated with the first rate performances one has come to expect from the quartet." Billboard also found its completely blank white cover of special interest.

The cover to the December 6, 1968, Time magazine symbolized the race to the moon between the U.S. and the U.S.S.R. with an American astronaut and a Soviet cosmonaut literally running in space towards the moon. In its music section, Time speculated that musicologists of the future might interpret the Beatles latest LP as an example of the group in a "mannerist" vein: "Skill and sophistication abound, but so does a faltering sense of taste and purpose." Time called the album's 30 tracks "a sprawling, motley assemblage of the Beatles' best abilities and worst tendencies." Great praise was given to the songwriting, saluting "Bungalow Bill" (a "cunningly simple ditty that flashes with hints of America's burgeoning violence and shrinking mythology"), "Cry Baby Cry" and "Dear Prudence." However, the magazine found the album too much a virtuoso display and a sweeping panorama of pop genres that "unfolds in parodies, pastiches, take-offs and put-ons." Time complained that "when the foursome meander from style to style without any apparent guiding objective or sense of urgency, they seem to be substituting synthetics for synthesis."

Newsweek was even harsher in its December 9 issue, warning consumers "Caveat Emptor" (buyer beware). After complaining about the plain white jacket, Hubert Saal stated that "the blankness extends into the records within." He wondered that "With 30 arrows of song...how the brilliant quartet missed their marks so often." He thought the group had "put their tongue in their cheek — and apparently got it stuck in the bubble gum." Saal had kind words for "Helter Skelter," "Happiness Is A Warm Gun," "Julia," "Blackbird" and George's "Long, Long, Long" and "Savoy Truffle." He thought the group could have done a fine single album and "maybe even put a picture on the jacket."

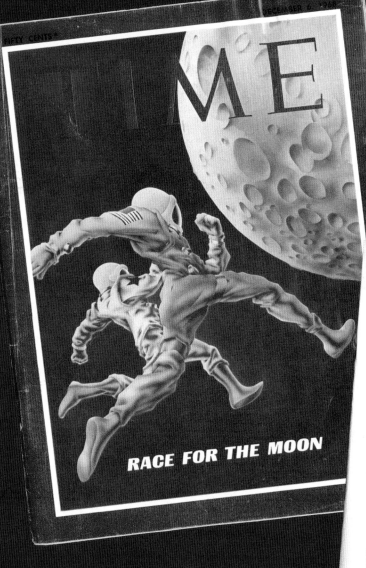

FIFTY CENTS*

DECEMBER 6, 1968

ME

RACE FOR THE MOON

MUSIC

RECORDINGS
The Mannerist Phase

When musicologists of the future start rummaging through the LP artifacts of the '60s, they will be able to discern several distinct phases in the stylistic evolution of the Beatles. *Rubber Soul* (1966) was the last album of their archaic period, blending the best kind of rock naiveté with a mastery of simple forms. *Sgt. Pepper* (1967) represents the Beatles at their classic moment, fusing the pop spirit and an astoundingly eclectic range of sounds into a harrowing but harmonious whole. Their double-disk album called simply *The Beatles*, which has just been released in the U.S.,* may well be interpreted as an example of the group in a mannerist vein. Skill and sophistication abound, but so does a faltering sense of taste and purpose. The album's 30 tracks are a sprawling, motley assemblage of the Beatles' best abilities and worst tendencies.

High among their abilities, of course, is songwriting, and the album provides a handful of superb additions to the canon. *The Continuing Story of Bungalow Bill*, called an "all-American bullet-headed Saxon mother's son," is a cunningly simple ditty that flashes with hints of America's burgeoning violence and shrinking mythology. *Cry Baby Cry* demonstrates anew the Beatles' knack for rendering an Alice-in-Wonderland vision in a melancholy modern vein. *Dear Prudence* superimposes Indian-style drones and swooping tones on childlike lyrics ("Won't you come out to play . . . greet the brand-new day"). It adds up to an invitation to love, to hope, to feel "part of everything."

Pop Panorama. In a way, though, *The Beatles* is too much a virtuoso display of the quartet's versatility. From the ricky-tick *Honey Pie* to the West Indian *Ob-La-Di, Ob-La-Da* to the schmaltzy *Good Night*, a sweeping panorama of pop genres unfolds in parodies, pastiches, takeoffs and put-ons. The boys even spoof themselves. George Harrison's *Savoy Truffle* contains a cross reference to Lennon and McCartney's *Ob-La-Di, Ob-La-Da.* In *Rocky Raccoon*, Paul McCartney imitates successfully and amusingly the nasal delivery of Bob Dylan. The lyric of *Why Don't We Do It in the*

Road?, which lampoons raunch-rock, reads in full:

Why don't we do it in the road?
No one will be watching us
Why don't we do it in the road?

Among other things, the Beatles seem to be signaling the listener that they have pulled back from the electronic adventurousness and thematic unity of *Sgt. Pepper*. Their new album is much more relaxed and modest. Well and good; there is no reason why *Sgt. Pepper* should be a shackling precedent for whatever follows. But when the foursome meander from style to style without any apparent guiding

THE BEATLES COMPOSING
Best abilities and worst tendencies.

objective or sense of urgency, they seem to be substituting synthetics for synthesis. Even their renewed interest in the song styles of the English music hall and rhythm and blues—one of the album's most attractive features—is slightly tainted. In the hollow *Yer Blues* or the sentimental *While My Guitar Gently Weeps*, the longing for roots is too calculated, like the urban sophisticate's nostalgia for the primitive.

A Day in the Life. Apparently, the Beatles themselves realize that their work in the recording studio has become too mannered and grown too far away from their beginnings in Liverpool. Next month they will tape a one-hour TV show for the BBC in concert format, facing a live audience for the first time in more than two years. It may be that the manifest mannerism of *The Beatles* will turn out to be what it now seems—just a day in the life of four of the century's most inventive pop artists.

* Coincidentally with Beatle John Lennon's conviction by a London court for possessing marijuana. Lennon, who said through his lawyer that he had now "cleansed himself" of narcotics, was fined $360.

VIOLINISTS
Cry Now, Play Later

Time for a violin lesson with Ivan Galamian. The place is a memento-cluttered study in his Manhattan apartment, where he does all his teaching. Students call it the torture chamber.

Nobody is allowed here who has not already shown talent and promise. Still, it is hard not to be nervous. Autographed portraits of Kreisler, Szigeti, Milstein—all good friends of Galamian's—glare down from the walls. The air seems to tingle with his awesome reputation in the violin world. Isaac Stern calls him "the most effective violin teacher in the country," and he certainly has the alumni to prove it. Most of the brightest young soloists in the U.S. are Galamian products: Itzhak Perlman, Young Uck Kim, Jaime Laredo, Paul Zukofsky and James Oliver Buswell IV. In addition, Galamian has trained top chamber players like Arnold Steinhardt of the Guarneri Quartet and orchestra concertmasters like David Nadien of the New York Philharmonic.

Ultimate Sin. Tall and deliberate, Galamian, 65, sits there in his white wooden chair, taking everything in with stern, searching eyes. His Russian-accented speech is soft, and the softer it gets the more ominous it can be. When a student commits the ultimate sin—wasting Galamian's time by showing up unprepared—they say he whispers a single word: "Leave." Ivan the Terrible.

The piece for today is Lalo's *Symphonie Espagnole*. Galamian nods and sings along, sometimes snapping his fingers to indicate rhythm. His few comments are deceptively simple. "Intonation," he murmurs, or, "That's it, that's it." When something goes wrong, he raises an eyebrow; the music stops cold. Then he picks up his 1680 Nicola Amati violin and, filling the room with a full, rich tone, shows how the passage should sound. "Mark that," he says.

Oops—awkward bowing there. Galamian is a stickler on that. He teaches all of his students the same technique: the bow parallel to the bridge and the arm extended in a natural sweep. His method is based on mastery of the fundamentals. Paul Zukofsky's first six months of lessons, for instance, were devoted entirely to the A-minor scale.

Galamian's theory is that suffering through exercises liberates a student to go on later and develop his own musical personality. Cry now, play later, is the plan. "Some people say he is all technique and no music," says Itzhak Perlman, "but I say he shows you the way to produce the sound you need. Then he inspires you to have your own ideas." He approaches each student like one of the chess problems he is so good at, and he tailors each solution to individual talents and temperaments. And the students all agree that he is gentle and considerate beneath his severity. "The most dangerous thing in a teacher," he says, "is dogma."

Watch that intonation—and stand up

53

Rolling Stone, which at the time had only been in existence for a little over a year, placed a picture of the group on the cover of its December 21, 1968, issue taken at Paul's house by Don McCullin on July 28, 1968 (Mad Day Out). Inside, it ran an article titled "Beatles' Record-Busting LP May Be All-Time Biggest." The magazine's review of the album, accompanied by seven photos of the group in the studio taken by Paul's new girlfriend and future wife, Linda Eastman, was spread over four pages. It was written by Editor Jann Wenner, with an acknowledgment to David Dalton.

Wenner wasted little time getting to the point, describing the Beatles as "the perfect product and result of everything that rock and roll means and encompasses." As for the album itself, he called it "the best album they have ever released," opining that "only the Beatles are capable of making a better one." Wenner called its impact "overwhelming," noting that one of its ideas was "to contain every part of extant Western music through the all-embracing medium of rock and roll." In contrast to Time magazine, he found the new album to be "a far more deliberate, self-conscious, pretentious, organized and structured, coherent and full, *more perfect* album than *Sgt. Pepper's Lonely Hearts Club Band*." While Time complained of the group meandering from style to style and "substituting synthetics for synthesis," Rolling Stone called the album the "history and synthesis of Western music," which was "what rock and roll is" and "what the Beatles are."

As for the Beatles "deliberately borrowing and accepting any outside influence or idea or emotion," this was viewed as a strength "because their own musical ability and personal/spiritual/artistic identity is so strong that they make it uniquely theirs, and uniquely the Beatles." Furthermore, "They are so good that they not only expand the idiom, but they are also able to penetrate it and take it further." The group is also praised for "their ability to compose music that by itself carries the same message and mood as the lyrics," thus making their lyrics and music perfectly complementary. Another key part of their success is "their ability to make everything they do understandable and acceptable to all listeners." Wenner points out that neither "Paul's near-genius ability with notes nor John's rock and rolling edge of honesty" are absolutely essential for the Beatles. Equally important are the "taste and sense of rightness in their music, to choose the perfect musical setting, the absolutely right instrument."

ROLLING STONE

| ACME | No. 24 | DECEMBER 21, 1968 | UK: 3/6 | 35 CENTS |

Rolling Stones To Tour U.S.A. In April 1969

Ramblin' Notes on the New Beatles Album, With Photos From the Record Sessions

John on Macrobiotics; Yoko Ono on Her Films

Doors' 'Riot' In Phoenix

Plus:
Lou Adler
Richard Brautigan
Edward Kienholz

The review covers all of the album's 30 songs. Although "Back In The U.S.S.R." is called a parody (an imitation of the Beach Boys imitating Chuck Berry), it is fine contemporary rock and roll and a fine performance. "Ob-La-Di, Ob-La-Da" incorporates familiar calypso melodies and beats, but is rock and roll calypso, "Fun music for a fun song about fun." Rather than dismissing "Wild Honey Pie," Wenner calls it a "nice tribute to psychedelic music." "While My Guitar Gently Weeps" is heralded as one of George's very best songs. "Blackbird" is made even more powerful by its irony and its yin-yang of love "so perfectly fitted." "Rocky Raccoon" is both funny and a tour de force, complete with saloon-hall piano and Paul's perfect vocal phrasing, enunciation and slurring. "I Will" is described as a romantic ballad that is entirely original, enjoyable and professional. "Julia," John's tribute to his mother, is the "most emotionally revealing" song on the album. The second disc receives similar praise. As for the weaker songs on the LP, they are only weak when set against some of the superb numbers in the set. On their own, they're "totally groovy."

Wenner ends his review by assuring us that the album "fulfills all our expectations" of a new Beatles record. Along the way he observes that the album is "at once their simplest (plain white cover) and yet most complex effort to date." But his most insightful observation hints at the fracturing of the group: "there is almost no attempt in this new set to be anything but what the Beatles actually are: John, Paul, George and Ringo. Four different people, each with songs and styles and abilities. They are no longer Sgt. Pepper's Lonely Hearts Club Band, and it is possible that they are no longer the Beatles."

The New York Times ran three separate articles on the album, beginning with Mike Jahn's review of November 21, 1968. Jahn called the album "one of their most unusual although not one of their best." He observed that "the Beatles sample from most every phase popular music has gone through in the past 40 years, and imitate many of its heroes," citing traces of Chuck Berry, Bing Crosby, Elvis Presley, Robert Goulet, Bill Haley, Mantovani and the Beach Boys. But most of all, Jahn hears the Beatles of 1965 before the release of *Rubber Soul*. And by that he is not delivering a compliment as he refers to that era as "that long stretch where almost everything done by the Beatles seemed like bleached Memphis," apparently referring to the song "Memphis" by Chuck Berry, who he describes as

B
BE
BEAT
BEATLES
BEATLES
TLE
LES
ES

BY JANN WENNER

The power of rock and roll is a constantly amazing process. Although it is Bob Dylan who is the single most important figure in rock and roll, and although it is the Rolling Stones who are the embodiment of a rock and roll band; it is nonetheless Our Boys, The Beatles, who are the perfect product and result of everything that rock and roll means and encompasses.

Never has this been so plainly evident as on their new two-album set, *The Beatles* (Apple SWBO 101). Whatever else it is or isn't, it is the best album they have ever released, and only the Beatles are capable of making a better one. You are either hip to it, or you ain't.

The impact of it is so overwhelming that one of the ideas of the LP is to contain every part of extant Western music through the all-embracing medium of rock and roll, that such categorical and absolute statements are imperative. Just a slightly closer look shows it to be a far more deliberate, self-conscious, pretentious, organized and structured, coherent and full, more *perfect* album than *Sgt. Pepper's Lonely Hearts Club Band*.

Sgt. Pepper's applied the concept of the symphony to rock and roll, adding an incredible (and soon overruled) dimension to rock and roll. Nothing could

have been more ambitious than the current release: *The Beatles* is the history and synthesis of Western music. And that, of course is what rock and roll is, and that is what the Beatles are.

Rock and roll, the first successful art form of the McLuhan age, is a series of increasing hybrids of musical styles, starting from its basic hybrid of country and western music and black American music (blues, if you will). That merger represents the distantly effected marriage of the music of England and Africa, a yin and yang that could be infinitely extended.

Not only the origin of rock and roll, but also the short history of it can be seen as a series of hybridizations, the constantly changing styles and fads, as rock assimilates every conceivable musical style (folk, blues, soul, Indian, classical, psychedelic, ballad, country) not only a recent process, but one that goes back to the Drifters, Elvis Presley, Little Richard, Buddy Holly, and so on. Rock and roll's longevity is its ability to assimilate the energy and style of all these musical traditions. Rock and roll at once exists and doesn't exist; that is why the term "rock and roll" is the best term we have, as it means nothing and thus everything—and that is quite possibly the musical and mystical secret of the most overwhelming popular music the world has known.

By attempting such a grandiose project with such deliberation and honesty, they have left themselves extremely vulnerable. There is not the dissemblance of being "our boys" from *Hard Day's Night*, nor the disguise of *Sgt. Pepper's Band*; it is on every level an explanation and

an understanding of who and what the Beatles are.

As usual, the personal honesty is met with an attack. (The secret is that innocence is invulnerable, and those who rush too quickly for the kill, are just themselves dead.) On the level of musical ignorance, I read the very first review of this record that appeared; it was in the New York Times. In about 250 words the "critic" dismissed the album as being *neither* as good as the Big Brother *Cheap Thrills* LP nor as the forthcoming Blood, Sweat and Tears album. You come up with only one of two answers about that reviewer: he is either dead or he is evil.

Those who attacked the Beatles for their single "Revolution," should be set down with a good pair of earphones for a listen to Side Four, where the theme of the single is carried out in two different versions, the latter with the most impact. And if the message isn't clear enough, "Revolution No. 9" is followed by "Goodnight."

To say the Beatles are guilty of some kind of revolutionary heresy is absurd; they are being absolutely true to their identity as it has evolved through the last six years. These songs do not deny their own "political" impact or desires, they just indicate the channelling for them.

Rock and roll has indeed become a style and a vehicle for changing the system. But one of the parts of the system to be changed is "politics" and this includes "new Left" politics. There is no verbal recognition required for the beautifully organized music concrete version of "Revolution." A good set of ear-

phones should deliver the message to those we have so far been able to reach. Maybe this album would be a good gift for them, "with love from me to you."

As to the Beatles, it is hard to see what they are going to do next. Like the success of their earlier albums and the success of all others in this field, whether original artists or good imitative ones, the success of it is based on their ability to bring these other traditions to rock and roll (and not vice versa, like the inevitable excesses of "folk-rock," "raga-rock" and "acid-rock") and especially in the case of Dylan, the Stones, the Beatles and to a lesser extent all the other good groups in rock and roll, the ability to maintain their own identity both as rock and roll and as the Beatles, or as Bob Dylan, or as the Rolling Stones, and so on.

Thus, the Beatles can safely afford to be eclectic, deliberately borrowing and accepting any outside influence or idea or emotion, because their own musical ability and personal/spiritual/artistic identity is so strong that they make it uniquely theirs, and uniquely the Beatles. They are so good that they not only expand the idiom, but they are also able to penetrate it and take it further.

"Back in the USSR," this album's first track, is of course, a perfect example of all this: it is not just an imitation (only in parts) of the Beach Boys, but an imitation of the Beach Boys imitating Chuck Berry. This is hardly an original concept or thing to do: just in the past few months we have been deluged with tons of "going back to rock and roll," so much that the idea (first expressed in the pages of ROLLING STONE) is now a tiresome one.

because it is, like all other superficial changes in rock and roll styles, one that soon becomes faddish, over-used and tired-out.

In the past few months we have seen the Turtles doing *The Battle of the Bands* and Frank Zappa and the Mothers with their *Ruben and the Jets*. The Turtles were unable to bring it off (they had to ability to parody, but not the talent to do something new with the old style) and the Mothers were able to operate within a strictly circumscribed area with their usual heavy-handed satirization, a self-limiting process.

Part of the phenomenal talent of the Beatles is their ability to compose music that by itself carries the same message and mood as the lyrics. The lyrics and the music not only say the same thing, but are also perfectly complementary. This comes also with the realization that rock and roll is music, not literature, and that the music is the most important aspect of it.

"Obladi Oblada," where they take one of the familiar calypso melodies and beats, is a perfect example. And it's not just a calypso, but a rock and roll calypso with electric bass and drums. Fine music for a fun song about fun. Who needs answers? Not Molly or Desmond Jones, they're married with a diamond ring and kids and a little "Obladi Oblada." All you need is Obladi Oblada.

"Wild Honey Pie" makes a nice tribute to psychedelic music and allied forms.

"Bungalow Bill," the mode of the Saturday afternoon kiddie shows, is a tribute to a cat the Beatles met in Marrakesh, an American tiger hunter ("the All American bullet headed saxon mother's son"), who was there accompanied by his mother. He was going out hunting, and this song couldn't get the American in better context with his cartoon serial morality of killing.

of course, the Beatles on the subject of the Beatles. Whatever they may feel about people who write about their songs and read things into them, it has undoubtedly affected them, eating away at their foundations and always forcing that introspection and t h a t second thought. And so here is a song for all those trying to figure it out — don't worry, John's telling you right here, while he is rolling another joint.

Harrison's vocal style, in lyrics, has been a slightly self-righteous and preaching approach, which we have here again. One cannot imagine it being a song about a particular person or incident, rather a general set of incidents, a message, like a sermon, impersonally directed to everyone.

And this song speaks at still another level, the very direct one of the title: it is a guitarist's song about his guitar, how and why and what it is that he plays. The music mimics the linear, continuous line of the lead guitarist. It is interesting to note that the song opens with a piano imitating the sound of an electric guitar playing the heavily Spanish lead line well before the guitar picks up the lead. I am willing to bet something substantial that the lead guitarist on this cut is Eric Clapton, yet another involution of the circular logic on which this song so superbly constructed as a musical piece.

The title, "Happiness is A Warm Gun," comes from an advertisement John read in an American rifle magazine. That makes this track the first cousin of "Revolution." The three parts of it, the break into the wonderful 1954 C-Am-F-G style of rock and roll, with appropriate "Bang Bang, choo, choo." What can you say about this song except what is obvious?

"While My Guitar Gently Weeps" is one of George Harrison's very best songs. There are a number of interesting things about it: the similarity in mood to "Bluejay Way" recall California, the simple Baja California beat, the dreamy words of the Los Angeles haze, the organic pace lapping around every room as if in invisible waves.

Part of the success of the Beatles is their ability to make everything they do understandable and acceptable to all listeners. One needn't have an expert acquaintance to dig what they are doing and what they are saying. The other half of letting rock and roll music be receptive of every other form and style of music, is that rock and roll must be perfectly open and accessible to every listener, fulfilling the requirement of what it is—a popular art.

Paul demonstrates throughout the album his incredible talent as one of the most prolific and professional songwriters in the world today. It's embarrassing how good he is, and embarrassing how he can pull off the perfect melody and arrangement in any genre you would care to think of.

Just name it and Paul will do it, like say, for instance, a love song about a dog in the Gilbert and Sullivan style, with a little ragtime, a little baroque thrown in. "Martha, My Dear," about Paul's English sheepdog of the same name, with hairy purrs ("when you find yourself in the thick of it") and all. And of course, it works on the level of the send-up and also as an inherently good song, standing fluffy on its own merits.

"Blackbird" is one of those beautiful Paul McCartney songs in which the yinyang of love is perfectly fitted: the joy and sorrow, always that ironic taste of sadness and melancholy in the lyric and in the minor notes and chords of the melody (remember — "Yesterday," "Eleanor Rigby," "Good Day Sunshine," prominently among many.) The irony makes it so much more powerful.

Not only irony: these songs and Paul McCartney songs in which the yin-

—*Continued on Next Page*

"a black singer and guitarist who set the style for much of the rock music in the late 1950's." Jahn states that the group "takes this old, basic rock sound and sees how many different superstructures are compatible," finding "blues, country, easy listening, folk and 1955-to-1962 rock." Calling it a "light record," he describes the music as "light, clean and crisp." As for the lyrics, they are also light and "Usually they are happy but often they are lacking in substance, rather like potato chips." He singles out "Piggies" and "Good Night," finding the lyrics to the latter "painful to hear." While he admits the album sounds spectacular, for him the fascination quickly fades, becoming "hip Muzak, a soundtrack for head shops, parties and discotheques." Jahn wonders if all that praise heaped upon *Sgt. Pepper* was deserved and rattles off several American artists he prefers, such as Jefferson Airplane, Big Brother and the Holding Company, the Band, the Doors, and Blood, Sweat and Tears.

Jahn's dismissal of the album as being neither as good as the Big Brother LP *Cheap Thrills* nor the new Blood, Sweat and Tears album drew particular ire from Jann Wenner. In his Rolling Stone review of the Beatles disc, Jann ripped Jahn, stating "You come up with only one of two answers about that reviewer: he is either deaf or he is evil."

The comparisons to other recording artists is also present in Nic Cohn's New York Times article from December 15, which touted the superiority of the new Rolling Stones album, *Beggar's Banquet*, over the Beatles latest effort. After praising the Stones LP, Cohn moved on the new Beatles album and blasted away. While observing that "it's been put together with endless care and tenderness," he described the double album set as "boring almost beyond belief." Cohn found more than half the songs being "profound mediocrities," criticizing that: "They're not new, the lyrics are not sharp, they're not even felt. Mostly, they're rehashes of stuff that the Beatles have already done much better elsewhere." The only song that Cohn found himself playing for pleasure was "Happiness Is A Warm Gun," although he did speak favorably about "Bungalow Bill" ("a cheerful homicide, with an instantly hummable melody and some good Lennonesque lyrics"), "Don't Pass Me By" ("clumsy and greatly enjoyable"), "Why Don't We Do It In The Road?", "Revolution" ("excruciatingly smug words but remains a brilliant melody line"), "Helter Skelter" ("solid hard rock") and "I'm So Tired." The rest he found "dross almost all the way." Cohn felt the Beatles were going through a bad patch and that their ego trip was out of control, but that they were too self-critical and too clever to stay like that. He expected that next time, no doubt, they'd make it good again.

Oddly enough, it was Richard Goldstein, the man who infamously trashed *Sgt. Pepper*, who was the album's lone champion in The New York Times with his December 8 review. Perhaps it was the album's abandonment of the meticulous structure of *Sgt. Pepper* for the "less explicit format of random songs" that appealed to Goldstein. While he thought the album lacked direction, he felt "the enormous range of the moods it explores (from hard raunch to soft reflection; from hurdy-gurdy histrionics to deft nostalgia; from put-on to profundity)" was far more effective as vaudeville than was their previous work. Goldstein observed that the Beatles were "capable of parody, profundity and poise," and that "more than anyone else in the pop hegemony, the Beatles involve themselves in the times." He described the group as "inspired groovers," who were equally at home with the *haute monde* (high society) and the underground, making them the "philosopher-kings of pop." They had responded to their diverse audience "by infusing their music with the kind of ambiguity which allows any listener to draw their own conclusions."

Goldstein called the album a major success, finding its mood was "somewhat between nostalgia and innovation." He thought the new collection was melodically and lyrically far more imaginative that either *Sgt. Pepper* or *Magical Mystery Tour*, both of which he felt relied too much on studio magic while neglecting the basics of song composition. He praised the Beatles for daring to be restrained with arrangements solidly built on a bedrock of guitar, bass and drums. Even during the occasional flights of symphonic fancy, he found the songs were sturdy enough to bear the weight of orchestrated variations. Goldstein observed that the Beatles were writing for everyone again, attempting to revive the spontaneous vitality of their earlier songs. He was impressed with the album's burlesque of musical forms, making it "almost a mock-history of pop," but "always tinged with affection." Goldstein recognized that "when the game becomes too exuberant or the burlesque too arcane," the Beatles failed, delivering a few "unqualified bummers." However, he found the album "so vast in its scope, so intimate in its detail, and so skillful in its approach, that even the flaws add to its flavor." [Or as Rolling Stone put it, "You are either hip to it, or you ain't."]

Most Americans were hip to it, with *The Beatles* becoming a fan favorite from the start as evidenced by its strong sales and chart performances. The album, coupled with the "Hey Jude"/"Revolution" single, provided over 114 minutes of incredible music. But those expecting proper recognition from the music industry establishment were left disappointed.

While *Sgt. Pepper* received four Grammy Awards, including album of the year, *The Beatles* found itself in no man's land. Released too late for consideration for a 1968 award at the 11th annual Grammy program, it was overshadowed by the group's own *Abbey Road* album the following year and was not even nominated. *Magical Mystery Tour*, released in late 1967, was nominated for Album of the Year for 1968, but lost out to Glen Campbell's *By The Time I Get To Phoenix*. The Beatles single "Hey Jude" was nominated for Record of the Year and Song of the Year, but did not win either award. The winners that year were Simon and Garfunkel's "Mrs. Robinson" for the top record award and Bobby Russell's "Little Green Apples" (no connection to the Beatles label) for the top song.

The White Album has stood the test of time. Time magazine's prediction that the album would be viewed by future musicologists as an example of the group in a "mannerist vein" did not come to pass. Rather than being seen as "a sprawling, motley assemblage of the Beatles' best abilities and worst tendencies," the album is praised for its variety and great songs and musicianship. For many American Beatles fans, *The White Album* is their favorite Beatles album, which also makes it their favorite album.

Some people, including Beatles producer George Martin, believed that the album would have been better had the group picked its best songs from the sessions and released them on a single disc. While there is some merit to this thinking, such criticism and speculation misses the point. It's the scope and variety of the music that makes the album what it is. In the *Anthology* video, Paul summed it up best: "I think it's a fine little album. And I think the fact that it's got so much on it, is one of the things that's cool about it... It was great. It sold. It's the bloody Beatles *White Album*. Shut up!"

Revolution in the U.K.

The July 1968 issue (No. 60) of The Beatles Book told British fans the good news: The Beatles were back in the studio and would be there through the middle of August. In an article titled "How The Beatles Recorded Their New Single," Frederick James (in reality NEMS PR man Tony Barrow) informed readers that most of the songs they were taping were written by John and Paul while in India from February through April. Barrow explained that the group no longer went into the studio with a set plan to "make a new single." Now they stockpiled new songs, rehearsed them at home, recorded them in the studio and, after six or seven numbers were completed, selected two songs for the single. They then recorded additional songs until they had enough tracks for a full album. During the process, a song could remain unfinished for months if the group could not decide what to add to the recording after they had taped the basic backing track (guitars, bass, drums and sometimes organ or piano) and vocals. The band would move on to other compositions until they came up with ideas of what sounds to add to the unfinished track.

Barrow then told of the recording of Ringo's first solo composition, which had the working title "This Is Some Friendly" (later called "Don't Pass Me By"). It started as a Country & Western song, but the arrangement moved towards rock 'n' roll as the tempo was increased.

The most intriguing bit of the article covered the recording of "Revolution," which was "more than TEN MINUTES LONG in its original form." Barrow speculated that the unfinished track might be issued as the group's longest-ever song, depending on what they decided to add to the existing tape, which consisted of guitars, drums and Paul's organ and piano. He thought the track dragged in the middle, leaving two alternatives: either editing out the middle section to reduce the song by four or five minutes or working with George Martin to come up with extra ideas to add to the center part of the recording. [The Recording Sessions section in this book explains what was eventually done with the track on pages 160-162 and 164-165.]

In contrast to Ringo's song, "Revolution" slowed down from a brisk pace to a slower tempo during its recording. Barrow observed that "Revolution" was not exactly a protest song, but that John's lyrics looked at the world's problems. Overall it was a hopeful song, with a reassuring chorus that everything was going to be all right.

The July 20 Disc and Music Echo announced that "Revolution" was likely to be the next Beatles single, released with other records on the group's Apple label. This included two discs produced by Paul ("Those Were The Days" by Mary Hopkin and "Thingumybob" b/w "Yellow Submarine" by the Black Dyke Mills Band) and the *Wonderwall* soundtrack LP by George. Apple would also issue a Jackie Lomax single produced by George Harrison, "Sour Milk Sea," two weeks later. The magazine reported that the Beatles re-recorded "Revolution" because they were not happy with the first version of the song and that their next album would most likely be released by early October. ["Sour Milk Sea" became part of Apple's First Four and the release of *Wonderwall* was held back. The group's LP was not in stores until late November.]

By the time the all-important first Beatles single on their Apple label was released on August 20, 1968, "Revolution" had been pushed to the B-side by Paul's "Hey Jude." With nearly a half-year had gone by since the Beatles previous disc, "Lady Madonna," anticipation was high. The group's Apple debut lived up to expectations and the August 28 Record Retailer expressed the feelings of Beatles fans through the U.K. and the world: "This is a marathon single, eagerly awaited and well worth the wait." The August 31 New Musical Express ("NME") called "Hey Jude" a "beautiful, compelling song" and "one of the most hauntingly poignant" written by Lennon-McCartney. Although the reviewer would have preferred a shorter song without the 40-piece orchestra, he described its first three minutes as "absolutely sensational, with Paul surpassing himself in his moving and soulful vocal." "Revolution" was "unashamed rock 'n' roll, with John singing vehemently to a backing fuzz guitar, handclaps and a jogging bouncy beat." Its lyrics were thoughtful and highly topical, making the song shimmer with excitement and awareness. The two contrasting songs "prove beyond a shadow of a doubt that the Beatles are still streets ahead of their rivals." In the August 31 Disc and Music Echo, journalist Penny Valentine predicted that people would soon be singing "Hey Jude," calling it brilliant and describing it as a slow, deliberate song that crawled straight into the listener's head.

**the beatles
hey jude · revolution
apple records
R5722**

EMI
THE GREATEST RECORDING ORGANISATION IN THE WORLD

"Hey Jude" entered the Record Retailer singles chart on September 4 at number 21 while the Bee Gees' "I've Gotta Get A Message To You" was topping the charts. The following week it moved up to number one, where it remained for two weeks before being replaced by another Apple single, "Those Were The Days" by Mary Hopkin. "Hey Jude" spent 16 weeks on the charts, including seven in the top five and nine in the top ten. The single made its debut in the September 7 Melody Maker at number one, and held down the top spot for four weeks before being passed by "Those Were The Days." It remained on the charts for 13 weeks, including eight weeks in the top five and nine in the top ten. "Hey Jude" debuted at number 3 in the September 7 NME. The following week it moved up to the top spot where it remained for an additional two weeks before being replaced by "Those Were The Days." The group's debut Apple single was charted by NME for 12 weeks, including eight in the top five. It was also reported at number one by the BBC. By September 4, the single had sold over 300,000 copies. By year's end, sales exceeded 800,000.

In the September 14 Melody Maker, Paul responded to criticisms that "Hey Jude" was too long and a step backwards for the Beatles. He said that step backs were fine, adding that if the group could make a record as good as "Great Balls Of Fire" [Jerry Lee Lewis' 1957 rocker], they would be delighted. It was the "phony intellectuals who want to step forward all the time." Paul pointed out "You can still make good music without going forward." Paul defended the song's long ending, saying that "a lot of people enjoy every second of the end, and there isn't really much repetition in it." As for the group's new album, Paul said that there would be a couple of songs that people would talk about.

In the September 14 NME, Paul said "It's nice to be at No. 1 but it'll be nicer if Mary Hopkin gets there next week." Paul would soon see his protégé topping the charts, with "Those Were The Days" actually out-performing "Hey Jude" in the U.K. Paul thanked everyone for getting Apple off to a great start, stating that "The dreams are coming true, and nobody is more responsible than you." He asked readers to watch out for the Iveys, James Taylor, the *Wonderwall* LP and the new Beatles album. Although all of Apple's first four discs received favorable reviews in NME, neither "Thingumybob" ("ideal material for half-time music at football matches") nor "Sour Milk Sea" ("a raving R&B number...powerfully interpreted by Jackie Lomax") charted. Still, two numbers ones was quite remarkable.

Details regarding the Beatles next LP began surfacing in September. Issue No. 62 of The Beatles Book contained an article on the recording of the "Hey Jude"/"Revolution" single by Mal Evans, who also gave a progress report on the album. Ringo added a bit of piano to "Don't Pass Me By." Paul was working on a "Calypso-type song" (unnamed, but obviously referring to "Ob-La-Di, Ob-La-Da"). According to Evans, the group had completed seven songs for the LP by the end of July.

The September 28 Melody Maker reported that the new Beatles LP would be a double album with 24 tracks. Apple press agent Derek Taylor stated that the material was "very varied, right down the middle of the road." The songs ranged from simple ballads with light guitar to songs with full orchestration. There was also hard rock 'n' roll, light numbers and some standards. According to Taylor, John and Paul had written most of the material, with a couple of numbers by George and one by Ringo, who also sang on a couple of other songs. That week in NME, George confirmed that he'd done a few songs for the next Beatles LP, adding "At least, I think they'll be on it. We haven't worked it all out yet."

Two weeks later, the October 12 NME reported that although the album's title had yet to be decided, a spokesman indicated that it would almost certainly be something simple. "After progressing from their early days to the intricacies of 'Sgt. Pepper,' the Beatles want to be completely straightforward again. The title could be something as utterly simple as 'The Beatles.'" As for the need for two discs, it was emphasized that there would be no "spreading" of the 24 tracks to fill out the records because many of the tracks were longer than normal. Readers learned that the LP included a Chuck Berry-style number named "Back In The U.S.S.R." Although a mid-November release had been planned, the album was now 10 days behind schedule as work was only recently completed on Tuesday, October 8. [Actually, the album would not be finished until ten days later, with the number of songs growing from 24 to 30.] The magazine also announced a December release date for an additional album, *Yellow Submarine*. The October 12 Disc and Music Echo contained similar information, but spoke of a December release for the double LP. Correspondent Judy Sims said she attended a session where the group recorded a John song titled "Happiness Is A Warm Gun."

The October issue (No. 63) of The Beatles Book gave fans a few more bits of information about the new album. The Beatle News section proclaimed that a twin-set of two full-length LP records would be in shops by the middle of November, with the discs housed in a "very special container." There would be 24 tracks, with many of the recordings much longer than average. Ringo sang solo on two songs, including one which was his first composition. George would sing lead on two or three Harrison originals. The rest would be Lennon-McCartney songs. Mal Evans stated that "There's such a great variety of different material that everyone should be happy. Each track is a musical spectacular in its own right." Evans observed that each song took an average of 30 hours to record, although a few were completed in 12-hour all-night sessions. In another section, titled "Mal's Dairy," Evans called the new recordings a worthy follow-up to *Sgt. Pepper* and opined that "Beatles '68 are even better than Beatles '67 — and that's really saying SOMETHING!" He teased readers with bits and pieces about some of the songs without providing the titles. One of Paul's tracks was a "calypso-style song about a bloke who has a barrow in a market place" ["Ob-La-Di, Ob-La-Da"]. Another song, with John on bass, Paul on his Epiphone Casino and George on his new Gibson guitar, started out lasting 24 minutes before the fellows shortened it ["Helter Skelter"]. Evans also wrote about all the work that went into the "Hey Jude" and "Revolution" promotional films. In her October Newsletter, Freda Kelly told fans that Ringo was accompanied by an eight-voice choir and 40-piece orchestra on one of his vocal tracks ["Good Night"] and that Paul played piano and flugelhorn on another ["Dear Prudence"].

Mal provided detailed information from his contemporaneous notes about each of the songs recorded during the sessions in the November issue (No. 64) of The Beatles Book. The tracks are discussed in chronological order based on when recording began for a particular song. Of special interest was his descriptions of two songs not included on the album. "Not Guilty" was written and sung by George, and was the first track that George used Lucy, his red Gibson Les Paul electric guitar given to him by Eric Clapton in early August 1968. "What's The New Mary Jane" was described as "very strange," with outbreaks of raucous laughter and a "controlled sort of Lennon chaos!" Evans also mentioned that the group ran out of time before they could record two other songs, "Polythene Pam" and "Maxwell's Silver Hammer." [The former was rehearsed at George's Esher bungalow; both were later recorded for *Abbey Road*.]

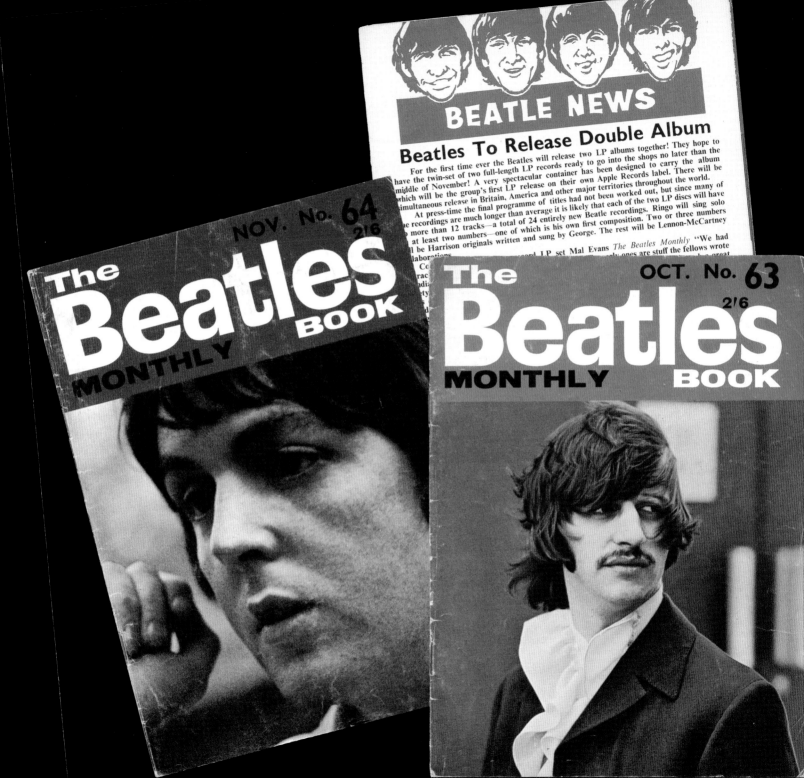

NOV. No. **64** 2'6

The **Beatles** BOOK
MONTHLY

OCT. No. **63** 2'6

The **Beatles** BOOK
MONTHLY

BEATLE NEWS

Beatles To Release Double Album

For the first time ever the Beatles will release two LP albums together! They hope to have the twin-set of two full-length LP records ready to go into the shops no later than the middle of November! A very spectacular container has been designed to carry the album which will be the group's first LP release on their own Apple Records label. There will be simultaneous release in Britain, America and other major territories throughout the world.

At press-time the final programme of titles had not been worked out, but since many of the recordings are much longer than average it is likely that each of the two LP discs will have no more than 12 tracks—a total of 24 entirely new Beatle recordings. Two or three numbers at least two numbers—one of which is his own first composition. The rest will be Lennon-McCartney be Harrison originals written and sung by George. The Beatles Monthly "We had llaborations.

Co   record LP set Mal Evans   ly ones are stuff the fellows wrote
rac   e great
dia
ty
d

Both Melody Maker and Disc and Music Echo contained detailed previews of *The Beatles* in their November 9, 1968 issues. Each of the writers, who apparently attended an EMI listening without benefit of the lyrics and songwriting credits printed on the back of the album poster, provided general comments before describing the 30 songs.

Writing in Melody Maker, Alan Walsh observed that the album in no way resembled *Sgt. Pepper*. The new LP had more variety and a distinct range of moods. It presented rock music laced with McCartney's lyrical charm and flavored with Harrison's guitar gymnastics. In comparing the songwriting of Lennon to that of McCartney, he observed that Paul was gentle, charming and melodic, while John was angry and aggressive. He found the album subtle in a lyrical rather than musical way. Walsh observed that the four members of the band each had their own direction under the umbrella of the Beatles. He disagreed with those who say the Beatles were going backwards. They were merely "not following on the platform erected by *Pepper*." He wrote favorably on most of the tracks, but found "Revolution 9" to be "noisy, boring and meaningless." He mistakenly credited "While My Guitar Gently Weeps" to Paul and John, and "Good Night" (described as a "parody of all the schmaltz in music") to Paul. These mistakes were proof of Walsh's warning at the beginning of his article: "the Beatles music requires a lot of attention, which is why an initial listening is hardly enough to form a considered musical opinion of their new LP."

The cover to the November 9 Disc and Music Echo featured the following banner at the top of its cover page: "Beatles' new album costs 73 shillings. IS IT WORTH IT?" Penny Valentine's review on the back page gave the answer: "73 bobs worth of brilliance." Fans were advised to "Pay up and smile." Valentine's initial reaction to the album told readers all they needed to know: "To hear it leaves you punch-drunk and breathless and wondering exactly what you can say, how you can put into words any constructive criticism of this double venture." She stated that the album proved that the songwriting had gotten better, that the arrangements, orchestrations and thought behind each track had surpassed all previous work and that, on the R&B tracks, "the Beatles are a very good **GROUP.**" In contrast to *Sgt. Pepper,* the new album was the Beatles "pure and simple." Valentine found 27 of the 30 tracks to be brilliant, predicting that at least four would become standard numbers.

DISC
and MUSIC ECHO 1s
NOVEMBER 9, 1968   USA 20c

Beatles' new album costs 73 shillings. IS IT WORTH IT?

See Penny Valentine's review — back page

Barry Ryan is a pop playboy

His second solo single, "Eloise", is racing to the top - in two weeks it's reached number 5.

Today, Barry Ryan - pictured left in his luxury flat in the heart of London - talks about the girls in his life, and the attitude that makes him one of pop's playboys.

Turn to page 9.

Mr. at Mme. O. Strasser
and
Mr. and Mme. D. Noone
announce the marriage of
Mireille Strasser
and
Peter Blair Noone
and request the pleasure of the company of
M. Kay Coleman

at the Church of the Immaculate Conception
Farm Street, London, W.1
on Tuesday, November 5th at 4:30 pm

Reception from 5:30 pm
at Les Ambassadeurs, 5 Hamilton Place, W.1

HERMAN weds his Sunshine Girl: page 5

Melody Maker
1s weekly
NOVEMBER 9, 1968

JOE JUMPS TO TOP SPOT

DYLAN SONG FOLLOW UP

JOE COCKER, soul man from Sheffield, has hit number one!

And Cocker's follow-up to his smash Beatle hit "With A Little Help From My Friends" may be a Bob Dylan song "Tears Of Rage" from the sensational American album "Music From The Big Pink" by Dylan's backing band.

Joe now has his first album, as yet untitled, due for release in January, and the single is expected for simultaneous release.

Dates

He opens in the Who-Arthur Brown tour at Walthamstow, London, tomorrow (Friday), and is heavily booked throughout the month with the Joe...

BEATLES ALBUM REVIEW PAGE 5

DISC ECHO 1s
USA 20c

73 bob is the cost of the Beatles' LP. Pay up and smile

by PENNY VALENTINE

AND SO after a year in the making, "The Beatles"—their hour and a half long, 30 track, 73 bobs worth of brilliance—is ready.

To hear it leaves you punch-drunk and breathless and wondering exactly what you can say, how you can put into words any constructive criticism of this double venture.

And when all the hoo hah has died down. When all the bouquets have stopped flooding in, when yet another crown has been put on the four crown-filled heads, and the superlatives have ceased raving round the world, what does "The Beatles" finally prove?

That the songwriting has got even better? Yes. That the arrangements, orchestrations and actual thought behind each track have surpassed all before? Yes.

But possibly, more than anything else, it proves two things. One is that, as some pointed out most succinctly, on track, that any really R & B based, the Beatles are a very good GROUP. Two, in a way, a continuation of a musical trend already progressing in America, this is the Beatles pure and simple. In cold harsh criticism—and one can't wax poetical endlessly —what comes to light is that of the 30 tracks only two are above average, 27 are brilliant and at least four will become standard pop numbers. Then there is "The Beatles," on sale November 16.

SIDE ONE.
Back in the U.S.S.R.:—

Paul sings lead on a song which the great American society will all its nervous reactions—will hate. An incredible loud, tight determined feel to the whole number is made more, so by endless jet plane noises. "We're flying in," they sing and then comes a glorious Beach Boys wind-up.

Dear Prudence:—

John sings about a man who lives for his girlfriend's smile. For John, this is a very gentle pretty little love song with warm guitar and voices merging in the background. It builds slightly towards the end with piano and brass.

Glass Onion:—

A send-up song dedicated to all the people who think there is deep inner significance to all the Beatles' song lyrics. John does his "Walrus" voice and there are mentions of "Fool On The Hill," "Ob-La-Di, Ob-La-Da," but in fact you will, in fact, realise that the first word is Bloody, which really doesn't have any deep significance as the song is sung with a kind of West Indian jollity and rampages through with a Jamaican band backing that sings, with some band cring backing voices, very good cheery chorus, and someone saying "Thank You" out on the blue at the end.

Honey Pie (part one):—

The real Honey Pie—on side 4 —bears absolutely no relation to this track. Nevertheless it is here and has very hysterical voices with mad Indian sounds in the background.

The Continuing Story of Bungalow Bill:—

Anyone who remembers Saturday morning pictures will warm to this track. John sings the saga of a White. Game Hunter with splendid ferocity. "In case of accidents," it does "He'll always take his mum." A story with a moral. It also mentions Captain Marvel and there's a great deal of worthy applause and whistling at the end.

While My Guitar Gently Weeps:—

The first George Harrison track on the album — there are three more — which has a lot of whining hand guitar work and George singing in a plaintive voice of descending notes. Nice sharp cymbalese in there too.

Happiness Is A Warm Gun:—

There's always a sharp dividing

'THE BEATLES' GETS AWAY FROM 'SERGEANT PEPPER'

line between the songs Lennon writes and the songs McCartney writes — and they are always apparent. This is so typically Lennon, full of astounding connotations, of novelties in way upon you until the whole thing breaks up into a great 1950's pop song send-up.

SIDE 2:

Martha My Dear:—

Paul wrote this about his beloved sheepdog, but in fact it's likely to be done very straight by Paul plays some lovely piano and sings of his dog as though it is the greatest love in his life — which it no doubt is.

I'm So Tired:—

Lennon in a terrible state because of his girlfriend. "Please give me peace of mind," he pleads having cancelled all the daily papers for three weeks. His sad, edgy voice is double tracked and builds to screaming pitch with sharp guitar.

Blackbird:—

The first Beatle track ever to be done unaccompanied. It's just Paul singing, playing guitar and tapping his foot. A very sweet, intensely pretty song with black-bird sound track sounds in the background. Another song which will be taken off the album to be sung by a lot of other people.

Piggies:—

George's second song, a beastly little piece about piggy people, with piggy habits and piggy wives. Harpsichord and cello make into a frantic mock - Elizabethan piece with, naturally a lot of real piggy gruntings and squealings at the end.

Rocky Racoon:—

The saga of Rocky and the girl who did him wrong. Paul starts off in western verse with Dylan harmonica and then turns sweet he unfolds the sad tale. Bar room piano is added to great effect.

Don't Pass Me By:—

The first-ever Ringo Starr composition. Sung by Starky in person with real vigour and a village band backing. It's nice enough but it goes on too long.

Why Don't We Do It In The Road?:—

This is the first of the really hard R & B tracks. Apart from some mind-boggling three lines — which is all the song consists of —and do WHAT in the road of one might wonder? It has a very Canned Heat feeling. Paul, versatile as a chameleon, brings out his hard raving voice for this one.

I Will:—

A pure pop song that will probably be taken and softened up even more by Astrud Gilberto a very gentle number with guitars and light bongos.

Julia:—

John sounding much warmer than usual on a very sweet love song that's destined to be taken, changed slightly, and turned into a standard song by someone like Jack Jones.

SIDE 3

Birthday:—

A real rock-n-roll track with Paul doing his Little Richard bit. Very very hard guitar and an incredible drum break with pounding and stomping.

Yer Blues:—

Big, crashing, home-grown blues number—and if a song by Blind Lemon Jefferson you'd never know it wasn't the authentic stuff. Until, that is, John breaks into a send-up of Elvis Presley's "Heartbreak Hotel," gobbly voice echo chamber, the lot.

Mother Nature's Son:—

A very small, pretty song in the Donovan vein, but so obviously McCartney it hurts. Paul sings with very soft, beautiful guitar, gentle brass and a tremendous warmth.

Everybody's Got Something To Hide Except Me and My Monkey:—

Typical John song which has led the inhabitants of Apple to make a lot of guesses as to whom John's monkey might be! This really shows the Beatles up as a group—with a tremendous rhythm section, Paul on bass and John going literally vocally bonkers.

Sexy Sadie:—

On first hearing, at least, not one of the great tracks of the album. Nice enough, though, and

perhaps one does after a while tend to get super critical. Paul singing. A song that slides into itself with very few breaks.

Helter Skelter:—

If by now your neighbours have not bashed on the walls—this will be the time to finally make them do it! The biggest, heaviest track going consists of John singing about trying to "make" this girl and he's coming down fast, so watch out! Watch out indeed. It's a track of instant aggressiveness that finally gathers momentum into screeching madness. Paul screams out his sentiments: "I've got blisters on my fingers," screeches the poor tormented guitarist at the end—and no wonder.

Long, Long, Long:—

George's third song. It's very pretty and less mysterious than usual for George. An album it's among basically waltzy with very light organ and some crashing drums splitting the waltz rhythm.

Revolution:—

This is in fact, a different track from the original B side of "Hey Jude." Same song is done much slower without all the distortion. It's far more insinuating than before.

Honey Pie:—

And so to the real Honey Pie. The story line, as told by Paul, is about a chap whose girlfriend goes to America and makes it big as a star. Apparently it took Paul years of research to get back that authentic sounding 1920's feeling. It was worth it, you really would never know it was come one of one of those great Hollywood musicals with thousands of girls shoe from above (they they looked like a giant sunflower.

Savoy Truffle:—

Harrison's songwriting has improved. This last of George's offering sounds like it was, inspired by the contents of a chocolate box. Apparently after you've eaten the Savoy Truffle you go mad and the rest of the box, which are described in candy detail, are feeling ill.

Cry Baby Cry:—

Based on the fine old classic "Four And Twenty Blackbirds" (back to school, kids), John sings this strange little song which is hard to suss out. If you feel in the mood you may describe it as either a send-up of high society, a send-up of suburban life—or just a song.

Revolution 9:—

A track the people at Apple consider is going to go down very big on the West Coast"—as, in fact, one of them called it. It will definitely appeal to the same bright, boring merely many minutes of distorted tapes sent like a montage. It will either send you screaming up the wall or will in blind fascination bring to go catch the sounds. In these are pieces from classical orchestras recitals, stray sounds, crowds chanting, and a man endlessly murmur "Nine, nine, nine," 9 reels of John Lennon's almost final contribution to the world. "This is what I have to say to you," he almost seems like saying.

Good Night:—

And so to end this utterly exhausting, stimulating offering comes the final and complete send-up that, it will be has seriously become, when all is said and done, it's very, very pretty. It is sung by Ringo with soppy strings and all the intense balladeers in the country will grab it to sing. In fact, Mantovani will probably record it. Strings all an Ovaltine advert and it's really very sweet.

PAUL who did most of the arranging

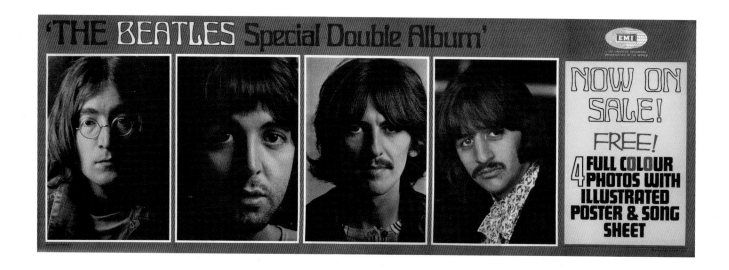

The Beatles special double album went on sale on November 22, 1968, exactly five years after the release of the group's second LP, *With The Beatles*. The logistics of getting the double album into stores was challenging – described by EMI sales director John Fruin as a "nerve shattering experience." According to Fruin, work began during the summer when EMI learned that the next Beatles album would be a two-record set. "We were very keen on this… we were sure the Beatles would be fantastically more successful than any other double-LP." By September, the marketing operation went into high gear, with EMI forecasting sales while wondering if there would be the same demand for a double album. The company concluded that it could "sell half a million in a reasonably short time." The sales force began pre-selling the album a month before its release.

EMI assigned the massive printing job of the sleeves, posters and portraits to Garrod and Lofthouse International Ltd. The process was complicated by the requirement that the sleeves be numbered in sequence, viewed by EMI as a "brilliant marketing device." Because the covers and inserts would not be ready until mid-November, EMI could not wait for them to begin manufacturing the records. The Hayes factory started pressing the discs in early November. As the records came off the pressing machines, they were placed into black inner sleeves (called "bags" in the U.K.) and stored until the covers arrived.

Back in the U.S.S.R.   Dear Prudence   Glass Onion
Ob-La-Di, Ob-La-Da   Wild Honey Pie
The Continuing Story of Bungalow Bill
While My Guitar Gently Weeps   Happiness Is a Warm Gun
Martha My Dear   I'm so tired   Blackbird   Piggies
Rocky Raccoon   Don't Pass Me By
Why don't we do it in the road?   I Will   Julia
Birthday   Yer Blues   Mother Nature's Son
Everybody's Got Something to Hide Except Me and My Monkey
Sexy Sadie   Helter Skelter   Long Long Long
Revolution   Honey Pie   Savoy Truffle   Cry Baby Cry
Revolution 9   Good Night

By the time the covers started arriving at Hayes on November 15, orders were at 200,000 units. The printer was only capable of delivering 20,000 a day. As EMI had no equipment capable of inserting records into double pocket covers, the discs had to be inserted by hand. EMI supplemented its staff by hiring disabled ex-servicemen from four different organizations to help with the tedious task. In order to save time, some albums were shipped with the photos separate for dealers to insert themselves. The albums were packed 20 to a box, weighing over 30 pounds. This made it difficult for Hayes' female employees to move the boxes.

On the day of the album's release, EMI had 12,000 orders for a total of 253,000 albums. Realizing that there was no way to complete the orders, EMI rationed, with each dealer initially getting 40% of its order. Because stereo pressings had outnumbered mono, many dealers received stereo albums even though they had ordered mono. This was done mainly in the South, where stereo had a higher acceptance than in the North. Dealers preferred getting stereo to none at all. EMI was able to clear its backlogged orders by December 10, although it continued pressing the album for anticipated Christmas orders. In order to get the albums quickly to its distribution centers, EMI hired extra trucks and utilized British rail. The truck assigned to Liverpool broke down, thus delaying the availability of the album in the Beatles' hometown.

Writing in the November 22 The Times (of London), William Mann called the release of the new two-disc album from the Beatles the "most important musical event of the year." Mann indicated that most of the album's songs were by "that prodigiously inventive two-headed magic dragon still identified as Lennon/McCartney," though he acknowledged that devotees now attributed their songs to them individually and would confidently continue to do so on the new album. After describing the packaging, including that the words to the songs were printed on the back of the poster, he opined that "the poetic standard varies from inspired (Blackbird) through allusive (Glass Onion) and obscure (Happiness is a Warm Gun) to jokey, trite, and deliberately meaningless," with the Lennon McCartney songs being "as provocative as ever" and calling nine of their compositions "superbly inventive." He placed George Harrison's "Long, Long, Long" in the same class, describing it as "a melting love song in slow waltz tempo."

Mann found the songs "inventive rather than creative," observing that they "retrace charted territory either to mock or to explore further." He found overt references to their earlier songs (brilliant and delightful in "Glass Onion," particularly the recorders for "The Fool On The Hill"), to Bob Dylan ("Yer Blues"), to Chubby Checker and the Beach Boys ("Back In The U.S.S.R.") and to the Ska of Desmond Decker and the Aces ("Ob-La-Di, Ob-La-Da"), as well as "near-quotes" from Indian and Greek poetry. He identified the following musical styles adopted by the songs: Talking Blues, Shouting Blues, Rock 'n' Roll (especially Elvis Presley), the New Vaudeville Band (itself a pastiche of old-style pop), the quasi-improvisatory songs of the Incredible String Band, Nashville Country and Western, Latin America, Calypso, Indian traditional music, musique concrete, flamenco and slushy ballad. "Good Night" had him collapsed in laughter, but he recognized that it was a "well constructed a ballad as any that won Sinatra or Humperdinck a golden disc, though obviously genuine pistachio." Mann acknowledged that there were other styles he hadn't identified, calling them "several fleeting reminiscences had me smiling but stumped for recognition." He described "Revolution 9" as a "Cage-style indeterminate montage of assorted sounds" that he found interesting and narcotic, but too long. Mann heaped praise upon "Helter Skelter" ("exhaustingly marvelous," "a physical but essentially musical thrust into the loins" and "a brilliant feat of invention"), but erroneously attributed the song to John.

While Mann was not convinced that Lennon and McCartney were still pressing forward with their race against other progressive composers, he acknowledged that the genius was all there. He hoped that their next anthology would look forward rather than back, but recognized that the album's songs contained "plenty to be studied, enjoyed, gradually appreciated more fully, in the coming months" and concluded that "No other living composer has achieved so much this year."

Additional critical acclaim from the establishment came in The Sunday Times, with Derek Jewell calling the new Beatles double LP "the best thing in pop since Sgt Pepper." Jewell described the collection of 30 songs as: "[A] world map of contemporary music, drawn with unique flair. Musically, there is beauty, horror, surprise, chaos, order. And that is the world; and that is what The Beatles are about. Created by, creating for, their age."

Journalist and film-maker Tony Palmer raved about the album in The London Observer. His review was reprinted in its entirety on the back cover to the U.K. release of the Beatles *Yellow Submarine* LP. Palmer recognized Lennon and McCartney as "the greatest song writers since Schubert." He observed that "In the Beatles' eyes, as in their songs, you can see the fragile fragmentary mirror of the society which sponsored them, which interprets and makes demands of them, and which punishes them when they do what others reckon to be evil." He hailed them as "heroes for all of us, and better than we deserve." For Palmer, the extra-ordinary quality of the 30 new songs was one of simple happiness: "The lyrics overflow with a sparkling radiance and sense of fun that it is impossible to resist. Almost every track is a send-up of a send-up of a send-up, rollicking, relentless, gentle, magical."

Palmer was impressed that their skill at orchestration had "matured with finite precision," observing that it was used sparingly and thus with deftness. Electronic gimmickry had been suppressed and replaced with musicianship: "References to or quotations from Elvis Presley, Donovan, Little Richard, the Beach Boys, Blind Lemon Jefferson are woven into an aural fabric." And while the Beatles were competent rather than virtuoso instrumentalists, their ensemble playing was "intuitive and astonishing." The way the group bent and twisted rhythms and phrases gave "their harmonic adventures the frenzy of anticipation and unpredictability." Even the voice, particularly that of John, was "just another instrument, wailing, screeching, mocking, weeping." By keeping the music and lyrics simple, "what is left is a prolific out-pouring of melody, music-making of unmistakable clarity and foot-tapping beauty."

Palmer further observed that the Beatles had not lost their edge: "The sarcasm and bitterness that have always given their music its unease and edginess still bubbles out." As examples, he quotes from "Glass Onion" and writes of the harshness of imagery in "Yer Blues" and the grotesque and terrifying track, "Revolution 9": "Cruel, paranoiac, burning, agonised, hopeless, it is given shape by an anonymous bingo voice which just goes on repeating 'Number nine, number nine, number nine'—until you want to scream." In contrast, "McCartney's drifting melancholy overhangs the entire proceedings like a purple veil of shadowy optimism — glistening, inaccessible, loving."

Palmer provided the following glowing summation: "At the end, all you do is stand and applaud. Whatever your taste in popular music, you will find it satisfied here. If you think that pop music is Engelbert Humperdinck, then the Beatles have done it better — without sentimentality, but with passion; if you think that pop is just rock 'n' roll, then the Beatles have done it better — but infinitely more vengefully; if you think that pop is mind-blowing noise, then the Beatles have done it better — on distant shores of the imagination that others have not even sighted."

Although the two-record set's list price of 73 shillings (3 pounds, 13 shillings) was approximately double the price of a single LP, fans were not deterred. With 30 songs, a running time of over one and a half hours and special packaging, the Beatles were once again giving their fans exceptional value for their money.

The Beatles entered the Record Retailer chart on December 4, 1968, at number one, where it remained for seven straight weeks before being replaced for one week by *Best Of The Seekers*. The album then returned to the top on January 29, 1969, for one more week. Although the number of slots on the album chart fluctuated wildly in 1969, The Beatles managed to chart a total of 22 weeks during 1968- 1970, including eight weeks at number one and 13 weeks in the top ten. It was also listed as a "mover" during weeks when the album chart was reduced to a mere 15 positions. *The Beatles* was the first double-LP set to top the U.K. charts.

The album entered the Melody Maker chart at number three on November 30, 1968. The following week, it moved into the top spot, where it remained for ten straight weeks. The LP charted for 23 weeks, including 14 in the top five and 17 in the top ten. *The Beatles* debuted at number one in the November 30, 1968, NME. That same week the magazine listed the album at number 20 in its singles chart, making it the first double-LP to appear in the singles chart. *The Beatles* held down the top spot in the NME album charts for eight weeks. For those wondering and doubting if the Beatles could come up with a worthy follow-up to *Sgt. Pepper*, John had given us the prognosis in "Revolution," the very first track recorded for the album: "Don't you know its gonna be all right."

Le Temps Des Fleurs

by Piers Hemmingsen

On June 22, 1968, representatives from Capitol Records (Canada) Limited, including A&R Director Paul White, attended the annual sales meeting of Capitol Records held at the Beverly Hills Hilton. Much to the surprise and delight of the attendees, Paul McCartney addressed the conference and announced the formation of Apple and its relationship with Capitol.

Two months later, on August 26, the Apple label was launched in Canada at a party held in Toronto's STOP 33 disco on the 33rd and top floor of the posh Sutton Place Hotel. The September 9 issue of RPM Weekly reported: "Apple product, worthy of special handling, was presented to a host of radio, press and key dealer representatives...After a short explanation of the whys and wherefores of Apple, the new Beatles' label, the four initial singles released were played for those in attendance." Those attending were given a beautiful press kit full of information on the Apple artists, along with photos of the four artists and copies of the first four singles. The press kit was the same as the U.S. press kit, but with Canadian pressings of the singles. RPM Weekly found the Apple record labels to be of exceptional interest, with a "beautifully coloured whole green apple" on the plug side and a "halved apple" on the flip side.

All four of the Canadian singles have the text appearing vertically on the B-sides. These discs must be rotated with the apple stem at three o'clock to have the label copy appear horizontally. In contrast to the black sleeves housing the U.S. and U.K. Apple singles, the Canadian discs were packaged in white sleeves with "Apple" in light green script letters. The Beatles singles also have "The Beatles on" in black script letters before the word "Apple." The Black Dyke Mills Band disc flips the tracks, with "Yellow Submarine" on the full green apple rather than "Thingumybob," which served as the A-side in the U.S. and U.K.

HEY
JUDE
(Lennon--
McCartney)
Produced by
George
Martin

THE
BEATLES
Maclen
Music, Inc.
BMI-7:11
2276
(45-X46434)
Recorded
in
England

REVOLUTION
(Lennon & McCartney)
Produced by: George Martin
Recorded in England

2276
(45-X46435)

THE BEATLES
Maclen Music, Inc. BMI
3:22

YELLOW
SUBMA–
RINE
(J. Lennon--
P. McCartney)
Produced by
PAUL
McCARTNEY

JOHN
FOSTER
& SONS
LTD.
BLACK
DYKE
MILLS
BAND

Maclen
Music, Inc
BMI - 2:56

1800
(45-X46414)
Recorded in
England

THOSE
WERE
THE DAYS
(Gene Raskin)
Produced by:
PAUL
McCARTNEY

MARY
HOPKIN
T.R.O.
BMI-5:06
1801
(45-X46416)
Recorded in
England

SOUR
MILK
SEA
(George
Harrison)
Produced by:
GEORGE
HARRISON

JACKIE
LOMAX
Python
Music
Publishing
BMI -3:54
1802
(45-X46418)
Recorded in
England

THINGUMYBOB
(J. Lennon - P. McCartney)
Produced by: PAUL McCARTNEY
Recorded in England

1800
(45-X46415)

JOHN FOSTER & SONS LTD.
BLACK DYKE MILLS BAND
Maclen Music, Inc.
BMI - 1:51

TURN, TURN, TURN
(Pete Seeger)
Produced by: PAUL McCARTNEY
Recorded in England

1801
(45-X46417)

MARY HOPKIN
Melody Trails, Inc.
BMI-2:48

THE EAGLE
LAUGHS AT YOU
(George Harrison)
Produced by : GEORGE HARRISON
Recorded in England

1802
(45-X46419)

JACKIE LOMAX
Python Music Publishing
BMI-2:27

Stan Klees reviewed all four of the initial Apple singles for the September 9 Issue of RPM Weekly in an article titled "A Canadian Record Producer Looks At APPLE." Klees raved about the Beatles Apple product, calling it ahead of its time while expressing concern that critics and broadcasters might pass by all its splendor due to a lack of understanding. He praised the Beatles for being inventive, imaginative and progressive beyond belief, with each of the eight songs being distinctively different and fantastically appealing. "Those Were The Days" captured the feeling of nostalgia of the forties and fifties and introduced the sixties to "a very up-to-date 'gypsy folk sound.'" He heralded Paul's attempt to bring back the sound of brass bands with "Thingumybob," commenting that there was no age limit with such music while wondering if a music director would be brave enough to chart the single. He found both sides of the Lomax single equally impressive, wishing he had produced them. As for "Hey Jude," he found it "everything the Beatles are TURNING OUT TO BE." While stating that it wasn't the best they had ever done, he admitted that would be hard. He observed that the group wasn't trying to be commercial, but rather was trying to tell us something. They weren't doing it with words or music, but were using "an overall effect that is trying to bring the music of today into a more legit vein." He assured us that the message was there, cautioning us that it was "up to the people who manipulate the tastes of the music buyer to discover what the Beatles are saying." Klees concluded by saying there wasn't "a bad one in the barrel" and that in their first four, Apple was "ripe with product that should be picked."

As expected, "Hey Jude" was the Apple single that garnered the most attention. It debuted at number 61 on the September 9, 1968, RPM Weekly chart. Three weeks later, on September 30, the song reached the top. "Hey Jude" charted for 16 weeks, including three weeks at number one and five weeks in the second spot. The disc went on to sell over 300,000 units, making it the biggest selling Beatles single in Canada, surpassing the previous top-seller, "All My Loving." Mary Hopkin's "Those Were The Days" also performed well, charting for ten weeks, with two at the top and five in the top five. While Jackie Lomax's "Sour Milk Sea" failed to make a splash in either the U.S. or the U.K., the song charted for eight weeks in Canada, sneaking into the top thirty at number 29. The only Apple product that wasn't picked from the tree in Canada was "Thingumybob." But with two number ones and a top thirty hit out of its first four releases, the company's Canadian debut was impressive no matter how you slice the apple.

CAPITOL INTROS APPLE

Toronto: Apple product, worthy of extra special handling, was presented to a host of radio, press and key dealer representatives at an August 26 reception at the Sutton Place Hotel, by Capitol Records (Canada) Ltd.

G. Edward Leetham, president of Capitol (Canada) hosted the reception with an assist from Taylor Campbell, vice president of marketing; Paul White, A&R director; and Gord Edwards, national promotion director.

Gord Edwards conducted the presentation along with his Ontario promotion manager Bill Bannon. After a short explanation of the whys and wherefores of Apple, the four initial singles released were played for those in attendance. These were: "Thingumybob" by John Foster & Sons Ltd. Black Dyke Mills Band (1800); "Those Were The Days" by Mary Hopkin (1801); "Sour Milk Tea" by Jackie Lomax (1802) ; and "Hey Jude" by the Beatles. (See "Special Report On Apple" by

record producer Stan Klees opposite page).

Also presented to the gathering was a beautifully packaged press kit containing pertinent information on Apple and its artists, along with photos and copies of the four new singles. Of exceptional interest was the new label. The plug side is shown on a beautifully coloured whole green apple with the flip on a halved apple.

A CANADIAN RECORD PRODUCER LOOKS AT

APPLE

by Stan Klees

RPM has commissioned noted Canadian record producer Stan Klees to listen to and comment on the initial release from the Beatles' record label, Apple. In the following article, Mr. Klees looks deeper into the product than the "sound". We feel the industry would appreciate a knowledgeable view of the product from this much discussed new label. - Ed:

The Beatles (it seems) have taken the rule book, crumpled it, stomped on it and ceremonially BURNED it. They might even be considering sprinkling the ashes all over the Excited States of America. I can analyse Apple with one sentence. The Beatles Apple product is AHEAD OF IT'S TIME and the critics and the broadcasters may pass all this splendor by, because of a lack of understanding. There is not one bad side in the barrel.

The whole concept of Apple is a tribute to the Beatles. The Label (which shows a whole apple on one side of the record, and a cross-section of a cut apple of the back) shows the inventiveness that the Beatles have come up with. The foreign trade may not be able to ignore the Beatles sides themselves, but there will be a great deal of very hot air criticism thrown in the way of all the product except "Hey Jude" which (as we all well know) can't possibly be held back). "Hey Jude" which isn't the best in the batch of Apple releases will probably get the most exposure because it is by the most famous group in the world. Meanwhile, there is a wealth of fantastic product that should get airplay and lots of it. I predict IT WON'T. The Beatles are possibly the best A&R men in the world. They don't make mistakes and they probably had more talent and fresh material to chose from than any other group of record people in history. They have spent years equipping themselves to judge. In this case they seem to have based their choice on their true belief and overlooked those who was commercial enough to pass in the ears of the average "over the hill" music director and critic. You see, we don't yet value the opinion of the true buyer. We have actually created the communication gap that we are so excited about discussing while we get deeper and deeper into it.

The Beatles obviously don't suffer from old age. They are younger today than they have ever been in their judgement of music. They are progressive beyond belief. They are

inventive and imaginative and even though they have produced all the sides in the initial release, each attempt is distinctively different and fantastically appealing.

I would guess that every producer in the United States and possibly the world is donning ultra-sensitive headsets to listen to and analyse every movement of every fader on every track. They will be taking notes of what the Beatles have done and in the months and years to come, the sound of Apple might well become the new sound of the industry.

When it comes to "Those Were The Days" by Mary Hopkin. Listen to the A side as an A side. Resist programming the B side "Turn Turn Turn" which really shows the talent and ability of Miss Hopkin (and McCartney as a producer). The A side is a side that has to be listened to by someone who has had a great amount of experience in the music business to know that the Beatles captured the feeling of nostalgia of the 1940s, 50s and introduced the 60s to what you might call (if I may) a very up-to-date "gypsy folk sound". As their press release says, "It will be whistled, hummed, sung, translated, exploited, adapted all over the world".

Girl singers have a great deal of trouble making it. Mary Hopkin should overcome that. She should!

McCartney's attempt to bring back into focus the sound of brass bands should be heralded. "Thingumybob" by the Black Dyke Mills Brass Band is performed by a legit brass band that has been known for years in England. Before I discovered that they were a true studio men. What programmer could resist the change of pace that this instrumental would give to programming, and what programmer could resist the vast listener market that this record would attract. There is no age limit when it comes to music like this. The Beatles probably realize they are the privileged ones who could bring this music to the ears of the world. Where is there the brave music director that will put this

record into No. 28 spot on his chart. Prepare the girl on the switchboard. It will light up with enquiries.

The Jackie Lomax release of "Sour Milk Sea" and "The Eagle Laughs At Me" turns out to be the "tuffie". Both sides are equally impressing. If I were programming it, I would play both sides. Why the Beatles didn't hold one of the sides for his next release confuses me. The release from Apple calls the sides "rock". I don't agree. The sides excede even what we are calling progressive rock. If I may say this, these are two sides I wish I had produced, If personal preference is valid, I would put this record into my own very small but select collection and await the first LP by Lomax. Produced by Harrison, these two sides inspired me to wish I could take the time to study meditation. Possibly this has something to do with Harrison's ability to go beyond what is now and look into what should be. Why not?

Finally, and briefly, "Hey Jude". The side is 7:11 minutes long and is everything the Beatles are TURNING OUT TO BE. It isn't the best side they have ever done, but that would be hard to do. It is the best of the new sound of the Beatles, and everything they do lately can't be compared to their early work. They aren't trying to be commercial. They are trying to tell us something. They aren't using words to tell us, and they aren't using the music. They are using an overall effect that is trying to bring the music of today into a more legit vein. The message is there. It is up to the people who manipulate the tastes of the music buyer to discover what the Beatles are saying.

There isn't a bad one in the barrel. You can play any of them if you wish. In their first release of four records Apple is ripe with product that should be picked. If this is the beginning, I can't wait for more.

What a pity the Beatles aren't American. On the other hand possibly it is one of their most important assets.

Capitol of Canada released a French lyric version of "Those Were The Days" in the French language market of Quebec. Anticipating the song's international appeal, Paul had Mary Hopkin record the song in multiple languages. The French lyric version, "Le Temps Des Fleurs" (translated "The Time Of The Flowers"), with words by Eddy Marnay, was issued in late November 1968. The single, designated Apple 2, was charted by Quebec City radio station CHRC from December 7, 1968, through April 5, 1969, with a peak at number one on February 8, 1969. The regional Quebec chart shows the song at number one, listing five different versions of the song, including Hopkin's single.

The Beatles first Apple LP was released in Canada on November 27, 1968, less than a week after the double album appeared in U.S. stores. Because Capitol of Canada did not import sufficient U.S. manufactured covers to meet initial demand, it arranged for Ever-Reddy to produce additional jackets. As time was of the essence, these Canadian covers are not numbered. The portraits and posters were printed in Canada and inserted into both cover versions. Although the album's list price was $12.98, price wars in major Canadian cities resulted in sales prices of $8.98.

The December 9 RPM Weekly contained the following mini-review: "Advance publicity has made for ready market.... Excellent material." Two weeks later, Stan Klees reviewed the album track by track in a two-page article. He called the album "a highpoint in the progress of the Beatles." To Klees, the album marked more than the group's return to rock, noting that "The Beatles have dipped into every bag they could lay their hands on to show that they are essentially aware of music as it is known in the late 60s." He speculated that if there was a message it might be "this is entertainment in the late sixties which encompasses everything we do, know and enjoy passing on." The album topped the RPM Weekly charts for multiple weeks and sold over 200,000 units in the first six months of its release.

As a high school student with a limited budget, I could not afford to buy the double album when it first hit the stores. But, thanks to Mother Nature, I was able to listen to the new LP repeatedly over a two-day period. On December 8 and 9, 1968, my school in Hull, Quebec was closed due to an electrical fault during a bitter cold spell. With no homework assigned and such cold weather outside, my parents dispatched me to the house of my neighbor, Linda Thompson. She was a year older than me and perhaps a wiser and more mature Beatles fan at the time.

1er FÉVRIER 1969

45 r.p.m.

SUCCÈS DU JOUR

★ DEMANDE F

LE TEMPS DES FLEURS

THOSE WERE THE DAYS

MARY HOPKIN

LE TEMPS DES FLEURS (THOSE WERE THE DAYS) (G. Raskin - E. Marnay)

MARY HOPKIN
T.R.O. Organization
5:05
Apple 2
Apple 2A

Produced by Paul McCartney
Arr.: Richard Hewson

Apple

Upon my arrival that Monday morning, Linda quickly asked me if I would like to listen to her brand new copy of the new Beatles album. As her younger schoolmate and a fellow Beatles fan, I spent a good part of two days listening to the album with Linda on her parent's new console stereo hi-fi system. It was a very large piece of Mediterranean-styled wooden furniture with a high-end turntable and combined amplifier/AM-FM tuner inside under a hinged lid and a large speaker mounted behind wooden and cloth grilles at each end of the unit. It was a very cool console system in the fall of 1968, and I was amazed at the heavy bass sound that was coming out of the speakers! Wow! The 1961 vintage Pye stereophonic "black box" at my house was vastly eclipsed by this new monster! It was her album, so we listened over and over to Linda's favourite tracks — "Back In The U.S.S.R.," "Dear Prudence," "Bungalow Bill," "Rocky Raccoon" and "Sexy Sadie" — while we looked intently at the large poster and individual photo-portraits that came with the set. The hi-fi was in the living room, but we sat in the den which was directly opposite as we were not allowed to lounge and listen to music in the formal living room! We just turned up the volume so we could hear everything — especially to hear the Beach Boys' harmonies and bass lines on "Back In The U.S.S.R."! Who needed to buy the LP when I could go next door and hear it on a far newer and superior stereo system!

We listened to the new Beatles album many times as we read comics, LIFE and National Geographic magazines, and looked through her stamp albums, while the sub-zero weather outside made us happy we were indoors. To my young ears, the new Beatles two-album set was initially a large collection of unrelated songs. I had difficulty putting these songs in a logical sequence as I had been able to do with my previous Beatles albums. Perhaps it was because we were listening to the songs she liked. For me, this new LP was a long way from *Help!* and initially seemed to be a collection of unfinished and unpolished tracks by the individual Beatles. However, I found "Revolution 9" to be a particularly interesting sound montage, as opposed to the tuneful Beatles songs I was used to hearing from one of my own Beatles records. A new Beatles album was always treated as an exciting event in those days. Just a few short years later, Linda died tragically at far too young an age. But for those two frozen days in December 1968, Linda was the bigger Beatles fan, and was kind enough to share her new *White Album* with me. Looking back, it was indeed the time of the flowers (le temps des fleurs).

Our First Four:

Jackie Lomax

Jackie is 24 and comes from Wallasey which lies on the river Mersey.

He worked as a lorry driver and a wages clerk among other things.

In 1962 he formed a rock n' roll group called the Undertakers. In 1966 Jackie went with them to America.

Now he's with Apple and has made his first single with us. It's called Sour Milk Sea. Written and produced by George Harrison.

Jackie himself wrote the "B" side – The Eagle Laughs at You. Both have a tough hard beat. Rock n'roll 1968.

Hear them now.

Jackie Lomax: Sour Milk Sea (b/w The Eagle Laughs At You)
An Apple Single. Number 1802

Mary Hopkin

Mary is 18 and comes from Wales. Pontardawe in fact. She's been singing since she was four.

Mary took singing lessons on Saturday and her mother hoped that this would lead to studies at the Cardiff College of Music.

It didn't.

It led via Opportunity Knocks and appearances on Welsh television, to Twiggy hearing her. Twiggy told Paul McCartney and Paul McCartney asked her to come up to London.

Her voice was as beautiful as Twiggy had said.

Apple records signed her up.

Now you can hear and buy her first single – "Those were the days" produced by Paul McCartney. It's pure and beautiful.

Like Mary.

Mary Hopkin: Those Were The Days (b/w Turn, Turn, Turn)
An Apple Single. Number 1801

The Black Dyke Mills Brass Band

When Paul McCartney wrote "Thingumybob" for a television series of the same name, he said he wanted to get a true brass band sound.

So what did he do. He used the best band in the land – The Black Dyke Mills Brass Band.

They won the title in October last year. Conducted by Geoffrey Brand they've held this title 7 times since 1945.

Back to "Thingumybob". On the "B" side there's "Yellow Submarine" like you've never heard it played before.

The sound is beautiful and brassy.

Just what Paul wanted.

You'll want it too, once you've heard it.

The Black Dyke Mills Brass Band: Thingumybob (b/w Yellow Submarine)
An Apple Single. Number 1800

John, Paul, George and Ringo.

Their latest . . . A seven minute long single called "Hey Jude!" On the flip side "Revolution".

Enough said.

The Beatles: Hey Jude (b/w Revolution)
An Apple Single. Number 2276

Apple Records.

1968: You Say You Want A Revolution

by Al Sussman

For those of us who experienced it, the nearly-all-encompassing melodrama that was 1968 was a year unlike any in our lifetimes, a year when, as some pundits termed it, the world had a "collective nervous breakdown." It was a year dominated by the war in Vietnam, which reached its peak in 1968, and it was the reverberations from the war that were largely responsible for so much else that happened over the course of the year. As well, though, there was the journey through the year by the most popular and influential pop music act in the world.

The Beatles were coming off a turning-point year in 1967. They had the nearly-indisputable triumph of *Sgt. Pepper*, but also the loss of their manager, Brian Epstein. They decided they would manage their own business affairs through a new company called Apple. Although their *Magical Mystery Tour* EP in the U.K. and album in America topped the charts for several weeks, the TV film of the same name garnered the group their first truly bad reviews. As 1968 began, their latest single, "Hello Goodbye," was No. 1 in the U.K., U.S. and other markets.

The day after Apple opened its Wigmore Street offices in London, a crisis erupted when the USS Pueblo, a U.S. Navy intelligence vessel, was intercepted by North Korean forces on January 23, 1968. The ship's crew was held captive for 11 months, ratcheting up tensions going back to the Korean War and which would continue to simmer into the 21st century. One week after the capture of the Pueblo, on the Vietnamese lunar new year of Tet, North Vietnamese forces launched one of the largest offenses of the war. Even though the Tet Offensive initially caught U.S. and South Vietnamese forces by surprise, they quickly regrouped and beat back the invading forces, but at a very heavy cost. With upwards of 500 U.S. soldiers dying each week at this stage of the war and with Gen. William Westmoreland calling for as many as 200,000 more troops, it became obvious that there was no "light at the end of the tunnel," as Secretary of Defense Robert McNamara had inferred a few months earlier, and the war would continue indefinitely.

Newsweek

FEBRUARY 5, 1968 50c

SEIZURE AT SEA

Pueblo Prisoners in North Korea

Newsweek

JANUARY 1, 1968 50c

HOW GOES THE WAR?

A nice respite from all this grim news could be found via television and the movies. On January 22, Rowan & Martin's Laugh-In, a revolutionary series that brought hip '60s sensibilities to prime-time with rapid-fire jokes and video cuts, risqué visuals and one-liners that became catchphrases ("You bet your sweet bippy!"). At the cinema, one of the most popular films was *The Graduate*, which had been released in late December. This was the film that made Dustin Hoffman a star and gave a whole new meaning to the word "plastics." Director Mike Nichols made brilliant use of the music of Simon & Garfunkel, especially with Hoffman's walk through an airport under the opening credits with "The Sound Of Silence." Indeed, S&G would garner a Top 15 single that spring with the year-and-a-half-old "Scarborough Fair (Canticle)," which was used prominently in *The Graduate*, and then a No. 1 single with "Mrs. Robinson," which had appeared in an early form in the film. Moviegoers could also see Ringo as a lecherous gardener in *Candy* and take in Mel Brooks' *The Producers*, a mad-cap comedy with the epic production number "Springtime For Hitler."

The Beatles returned to Abbey Road in early February for their first recording sessions since the fall of 1967. With a small time window to record the first Beatles single of the year before they would journey to India for a season of studying transcendental meditation with Maharishi Mahesh Yogi, the group knocked out four songs. Two, "Lady Madonna" and "Hey Bulldog," were old fashioned rockers that reflected the rock 'n' roll revival then just beginning to take hold in England. The others, "Across The Universe" and Harrison's "The Inner Light," were more inward-looking and philosophical, especially given that the lyrics for "The Inner Light" were a rendering of a poem from the Taoist *Tao Te Ching*. Paul's "Lady Madonna" was selected for the group's next single. Although Lennon's "Across The Universe" could have been a sequel to Summer of Love anthem "All You Need Is Love," he didn't like the recording and recommended that "The Inner Light" serve as the B-side to the single. "Hey Bulldog" was designated for the *Yellow Submarine* cartoon film, while "Across The Universe" would remain on the shelf until its release in December 1969 as part of a charity album and a half-year later on the *Let It Be* LP in a version re-produced by Phil Spector.

By February 20, all four Beatles and their wives and Paul's then-fiancé Jane Asher were in Rishikesh, India for a meditation course with the Maharishi. Ringo left after just two weeks because the cuisine played havoc with his food allergies. Shortly after his return to London, the "Lady Madonna" single was released and reached No. 1 in the

U.K., but uncharacteristically stalled at No. 4 in the Billboard Hot 100. Paul stayed in India for a little over a month. Lennon, who was always searching for "the answer" as a way of dealing with the emotional pain he had carried from childhood, had long meditation sessions but soon became disenchanted with the Maharishi. Harrison took the course more seriously than the others. He and wife Pattie reluctantly returned to London with the Lennons in mid April after rumors of inappropriate behavior by the Maharishi spread around the camp. As George later put it, "There were a lot of flakes there; the whole place was full of flaky people. Some of them were us." On the positive side, their stay in Rishikesh gave Lennon, McCartney and Harrison the chance to do a lot of songwriting. They left India with a bumper crop of new songs for the group's next album.

In the wake of the Tet Offensive, CBS Evening News anchorman Walter Cronkite journeyed to Vietnam in February and came back convinced that the war was not winnable. At the conclusion of a CBS News Report From Vietnam on February 27, Cronkite gave a rare on-air commentary in which he concluded that "the only rational way out then will be to negotiate, not as victors, but as an honorable people who lived up to their pledge to defend democracy, and did the best they could." President Johnson's reaction reportedly was, "If I've lost Cronkite, I've lost Middle America." On March 12, Democratic voters in New Hampshire nearly gave LBJ a vote of no confidence as Minnesota Sen. Eugene McCarthy, who had challenged Johnson principally over opposition to the war, received 42% of the vote in the first primary of the election campaign. Four days later, New York Sen. Robert Kennedy finally entered the race after months of vacillating and, two Sundays later, Johnson, at the end of a speech in which he announced a partial bombing halt in Vietnam, stunned the nation by announcing that he would not seek a second full term as president.

April brought chaos and the U.S. premieres of two films seemingly made for a complicated moment in time. Stanley Kubrick's *2001: A Space Odyssey* was a science fiction film unlike any other made to that point. Steven Spielberg called it the "big bang" for filmmakers of his generation, while others of his generation found it best viewed under certain outside stimuli. *Planet Of The Apes* shared the plot device of an astronaut crew with *2001,* but this crew, headed by Charlton Heston, crash-lands on a strange planet ruled by an intelligent breed of apes. While *2001* set new standards in special effects in film, *Planet Of The Apes* was a trailblazer in character prosthetics and costumes.

On April 4, the civil rights movement's "apostle of non-violence," Rev. Dr. Martin Luther King, Jr., in Memphis in support of a sanitation workers' strike, was shot and killed as he stood on the balcony of the Lorraine Motel. His assassination immediately set off rioting in many major U.S. cities, especially in Washington, D.C., where National Guard troops were called to guard the U.S. Capitol and other government buildings. Protests over racial inequality and the war had been breaking out on college campuses even before Dr. King's murder, and not just in the United States. Canada, Japan and England had already seen major protests over the war. On April 23, months of tensions between Columbia University and radical students protesting racial discrimination tied to the construction of a new gymnasium in Harlem's Morningside Park boiled over as the radicals took over the university's Hamilton Hall and Low Library and remained there until the early morning hours of April 30, when New York City police stormed the buildings. Some 700 protesters were injured in clearing the occupied buildings. Just two days after the violent end to the Columbia University occupation, months of wide-ranging protests in Paris escalated when the administration of the Nanterre campus of the University of Paris shut down the university. That began nearly a month of strikes by students and then workers, violent confrontations between police and students on the Sorbonne and Rive Gauche, and huge demonstrations in the streets of Paris. By the end of May, this new French Revolution nearly toppled President Charles De Gaulle's government, forcing him to call for new national elections.

It was in this tinderbox atmosphere that John and Paul arrived in New York for the public introduction to Apple with a May 14 media blitz: a press conference at the Americana Hotel; interviews with various magazines and newspapers; and a bizarre appearance on The Tonight Show. Newsweek ran an article on Apple in its Business section in the same May 27, 1968 issue that featured the French riots on its cover. It quoted Lennon as saying that the aim of Apple wasn't "a stack of gold teeth in the bank," but to "see if we can get artistic freedom in a business structure."

After rehearsing their newly-written songs at George's Esher bungalow in late May, the Beatles reconvened on May 30 at Abbey Road to begin work on their first full album since *Sgt. Pepper*. The first song they tackled was, appropriately, Lennon's "Revolution," which took on the civil unrest that was spreading around the world. (This recording would be renamed "Revolution 1," distinguishing it from the faster version later recorded for single release.)

LIFE

WEEK OF SHOCK

▶ **Vietnam: Burst of Hope**

▶ **Convulsion in U.S. Politics**

▶ **EXCLUSIVE PICTURES**
The Murder in Memphis

Swarming instantly into the motel area, police—aided by King's colleagues (above)—try to pin down where the shot had come from. Responding to a police call, an ambulance utes (left). As stretcher along King lay mort and with awk it down the s possible (right) he reached St the civil right nounced dead

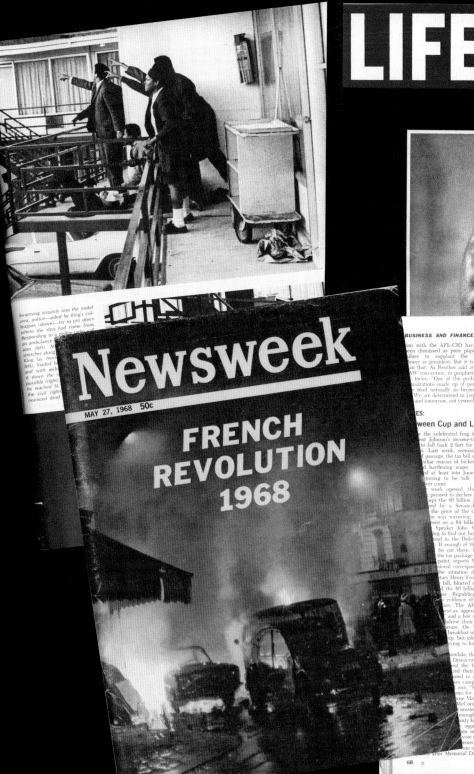

Newsweek

MAY 27, 1968 50c

FRENCH REVOLUTION 1968

BUSINESS AND FINANCE

tion with the AFL-CIO has sometimes een dismissed as pure pique over his ent Johnson's failure to supplant the 73-year-old eany as president. But it is far deeper an that. As Reuther said at the recent AW convention, in prophetically obitu- tones: "One of the problems about anizations made up of people is that tend naturally to become obsolete We are determined to [represent] to- and tomorrow, not yesterday."

ES:

ween Cup and Lip

e the celebrated frog in the well, Johnson's income-tax proposal to fall back 2 feet for every yard s. Last week, seemingly on the f passage, the tax bill slid back in- miliar morass of bickering, confu- d hardening anger. Action was to a new free-market record of $41.75 tend naturally be talk that action ver come.

week opened, the President pressed to declare whether he ept the $6 billion in spending ed by a Senate-House con- the price of the tax increase. n was wavering; he was in- sist on a $4 billion limit, be ng to find out how much fat und in the Defense Depart- If enough of the added $2 be cut there, he said, he the tax package.

point, reports NEWSWEEK's ssional correspondent, Sam- the situation deteriorated. tary Henry Fowler, testify- bill, blurted out that he, d the $6 billion spending se Republicans leaped s evidence of disarray in on. The AFL-CIO de- eat-ax approach to cut- and a few more liberal drew their shaky sup- asure. On Wednesday, breakfast with his Con- ip, but told them only rying to keep an open

nwhile, the lines were Democrats who had out the huge spend- red their opposition. osed to do with the rs camped right on one. "Spit in their ptes for the package McCormack that if muster a majority, enough GOP votes ody knew for sure opposition was; en reported that vote count. erned no choice ote on the bill at after Memorial Day. The dis-

putants were in solid agreement that the longer the bill was delayed, the greater the danger of a sudden erosion of confidence around the world and another huge monetary crisis. Only the President, Congressional leaders agreed, could break the logjam by endorsing the package; but he was saying nothing.

Meanwhile, the monetary crisis, quiescent since the establishment of a two-tier gold market last March, simmered a bit more feverishly. Announcement of the nation's first-quarter balance-of-payments deficit confirmed early reports that it had fallen to $600 million, one-third the rate of the preceding quarter. But on close scrutiny, a good many of the favorable factors turned out to be nonrecurring, and the old reliable trade trade surplus was eroding dangerously. International bankers pronounced the news disappointing. The price of gold, in active trading, rose to a new free-market record of $41.75 an ounce. And a Zurich banker said, "There's a bad mood in the market."

McCartney and Lennon: No more gold teeth

ENTERPRISE:

Beatles, Inc.

Two of England's famous Beatles, John Lennon and Paul McCartney, propped their feet on a coffee table in New York's St. Regis Hotel last week, sipped beer, flicked ashes on the rug and explained why they were so relaxed.

"We're in the happy position of not needing any more money," said Mc-Cartney airily.

"Yeah," said Lennon, "everything we make now goes right to the tax man."

With that they announced that they and their shaggy-haired partners, George Harrison and Ringo Starr, have sunk a hunk of their fortune into a new multimillion-dollar entertainment, electronics and merchandising enterprise called Apple Corps, Ltd. ("It's a pun," said McCartney helpfully.)

The company has a string of projects

already in the works, including a recording studio under construction, four feature films, two mod clothing stores and some eighteen patented inventions by a young electronics expert the Beatles have nicknamed Magic Alex. "The things he produces are fantastic," Lennon told NEWSWEEK's John Lynagh. "I wish I could tell you about them, but we've learned in this happy business world that spies in brown raincoats and sunglasses go around and you can't say anything about a product until it's out."

Apple will also handle all Beatle enterprises except records (they're still under contract to Capitol) and will discover and develop new talent. "We want to give young people a chance to get started," said Paul McCartney, "without going on their knees to the boss of some giant company."

Managing director of the firm's diverse activities is Neil Aspinall, a 26-year-old childhood friend of the Beatles. Aspinall, who studied accounting while he was serving as road manager for their concerts, says it will take at least a year for the company to get on its feet, but when it does, "I'm sure it'll make millions."

New Talents: The Beatles appear less concerned with profits than with the idea behind the project. "The aim of this company," said Lennon, "isn't a stack of gold teeth in the bank. We've done that bit. It's more of a trick to see if we can get artistic freedom in a business structure and to see if we can create things and sell them without charging three times our cost."

To accomplish their aim, the Beatles and their six-man board of directors will open their doors to aspiring new talents and allow them to work with a minimum of corporate confinements. But they will maintain their complete ownership of any finished product.

"We've got experienced people around to handle the business," said McCartney, "but we'll have the final say. It should work. It's our game getting things across to the public."

Apple Corps has been set up in nine countries. Its permanent administrative staff of 36 will soon be moving into their new London headquarters—a recently purchased $1.5 million, four-story office building. And if the company is successful, say its managers, it "might even sell shares to the public."

Though they've been spending a little time in the office lately, the Beatles have no intention of being buttoned down in the white-collar world. "This is a business," said McCartney. "But we want to have fun doing it." In that spirit, they hired a Chinese junk and held their first U.S. board meeting while sailing around the Statue of Liberty.

The full ten-minute plus track recorded in the first couple of sessions included input from a new presence at a Beatles recording session, Lennon's new girlfriend, avant-garde artist Yoko Ono. This immediately was looked at as an intrusion into the boys' club that was the norm for Beatles sessions. But, in retrospect, this was just another example of how, in the year since *Sgt. Pepper*, the Beatles had ceased being the tightly-knit unit they had been during the touring years.

While the Beatles were at Abbey Road recording "Revolution," Max Frost and the Troops were running *Wild In The Streets*. American International Pictures, home of cheap quickie flicks, released this film, which starred Christopher Jones as a 22-year-old rock superstar who somehow is elected President of the United States and has anyone over 34 institutionalized. Better than the ludicrous plot was the soundtrack, written by Brill Building mainstays Barry Mann and Cynthia Weil, including Frost and band's showcase song, "The Shape Of Things To Come."

In early June, John's vision for "Revolution" changed. After adding vocals, sound effects and conversation between he and Yoko to the second half of the song, John decided to take the latter part of the recording and turn it into a chaotic audio veritè titled "Revolution 9." On the evening of June 6, John assembled 12 takes of sound effects for the track. A few hours after this was done, tragedy struck again in America with the assassination of Bobby Kennedy after he had won the California presidential primary. This body blow to the American psyche seemed to confirm the feeling that the country was spinning out of control while people in other countries simply shook their heads.

John continued work on both parts of "Revolution" during sessions held through June 25. Paul, who did not participate in "Revolution 9," recorded "Blackbird" as a solo effort on acoustic guitar on June 11. Paul would later say that "Blackbird" was written with the civil rights movement in mind. After recording songs such as the exuberant rocker "Everybody's Got Something To Hide Except Me And My Monkey," an early take of the lullaby "Good Night" and the calypso-flavored "Ob-La-Di, Ob-La-Da," the group recorded a fast version of "Revolution" with distorted guitars and highly-compressed drums. John had wanted "Revolution" issued as a single, but Paul and George were concerned that the slow tempo song was not commercial enough for single release. As a compromise, they recorded a new version.

On July 15, Apple moved into its new headquarters at 3 Savile Row. Two nights later, the Beatles took a break from recording "Cry Baby Cry" to attend the London premiere of the animated film *Yellow Submarine*, triggering scenes reminiscent of the heyday of Beatlemania with a paralyzed Piccadilly Circus. Even though John & Yoko had become a very public couple a month before, their arrival together was still a big deal, as was McCartney's arrival alone. Three days later, Jane Asher announced on BBC-TV that her engagement to Paul was off and she has virtually never discussed him since.

While *Yellow Submarine* would not be shown in U.S. theaters until mid-November, Americans could see films such as Jack Lemmon and Walter Matthau's original cinema version of the Neil Simon play *The Odd Couple* and the Roman Polanski-directed *Rosemary's Baby*, which starred the Beatles recent TM-mate, Mia Farrow, and was largely filmed in Lennon's future home, the Dakota, at 72nd Street and Central Park West in Manhattan.

From mid-July through mid-August, the Beatles recorded "Sexy Sadie" (John's broadside at the Maharishi), "Good Night" (John's tender lullaby sung by Ringo), "Not Guilty" (a George song that didn't make the cut), Paul's "Mother Nature's Son" and "Rocky Raccoon," John's "Yer Blues" and "What's The New Mary Jane" (the latter being a strange John and George recording that was not included on the LP), early takes of George's "While My Guitar Gently Weeps" and the song that would bump "Revolution" to the B-side of the group's first Apple single, "Hey Jude." That disc would be released late in August, at a moment when it could not have been more appropriate.

The non-stop melodrama of 1968 continued apace through the summer, with racial disturbances in Cleveland and Gary, Indiana in July and Miami in early August as a backstory to the Republican National Convention. Despite challenges from New York Gov. Nelson Rockefeller and California Gov. Ronald Reagan, the convention climaxed with Richard Nixon, seemingly finished after losing the presidential election in 1960 and the California gubernatorial election in '62, winning the Republican nomination. And Nixon shored up his "law and order" bona fides by choosing Maryland Gov. Spiro T. Agnew as his vice-presidential nominee and designated political hit man, even as Agnew was receiving $1,500 monthly under-the-table payments in Maryland that would eventually end his political career.

On August 20-21, as the "Hey Jude"/"Revolution" single was being serviced to radio stations in the U.S., hundreds of thousands of Soviet and Warsaw Pact troops rolled into Czechoslovakia to crush the "Prague Spring" reforms put in by Czech First Secretary Alexander Dubçek, the most blatant attempt at liberalizing a Communist country until the wave of reforms and revolts in the fall of 1989 that spelled the end of Communism in eastern Europe.

The Soviet invasion of Czechoslovakia, their biggest military operation since World War II, came as contentious platform committee hearings were going on as a prelude to the Democratic National Convention in Chicago. With Robert Kennedy dead and Eugene McCarthy carrying only a handful of committed delegates, Democratic Party leaders, overseen by President Johnson, were prepared to push Vice-President Hubert Humphrey to the presidential nomination. At the same time, thousands of anti-war demonstrators were headed for an inevitable collision with Chicago Mayor Richard J. Daley and his police force.

The result was, as Walter Cronkite put it in the end-of-decade audio documentary *I Can Hear It Now: The Sixties*, "a meeting of two theaters of the absurd." Inside the International Amphitheatre, Daley's security forces manhandled TV network floor reporters and chaos reigned as the party bosses dismissed attempts at putting an anti-war plank into the party platform. And the atmosphere became even uglier when the delegates saw what was happening outside. In Grant Park and along Michigan Avenue, demonstrators cursed and coerced the police, who responded with what was later officially termed "a police riot," clubbing and dragging demonstrators into paddy wagons in a scene hard to imagine was happening in a major American city. In the hall, there were calls for the convention to be halted and moved to another city as Daley lashed out at anyone criticizing his handling of the chaotic situation. Finally, on the convention's final night, as Daley filled the gallery with flunkies demonstrating their support for the mayor, Humphrey accepted what appeared to be a hollow nomination. During the week, American television showed protesters in Chicago shouting, "The whole is world watching!," while the radio played: "Hey Jude, don't make it bad/Take a sad song and make it better;" "You say you want a revolution/Well, you know, we all want to change the world" and "You say you got a real solution/Well, you know, we'd all love to see the plan."

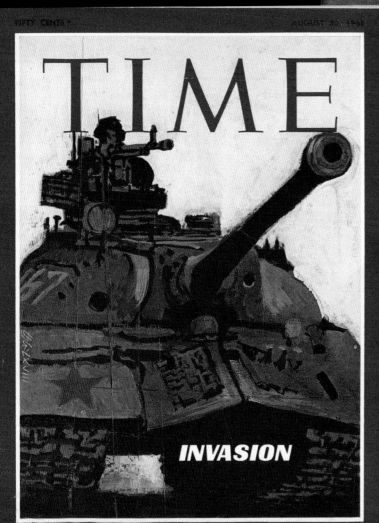

FIFTY CENTS

AUGUST 30, 1968

TIME

INVASION

Conrad Hilton

SEPTEMBER 9, 1968   50c

Newsweek

BATTLE OF CHICAGO

On August 22, Ringo came up with a real solution of his own for the boredom and increasing tensions of the sessions for the next Beatles album. He walked out, took the family to Sardinia (where he wrote "Octopus's Garden") and didn't return until September 3. During Ringo's absence, the Beatles recorded "Back In The U.S.S.R.," ironically as Soviet tanks rolled through the streets of Czechoslovakia, and "Dear Prudence," both with Paul on drums.

When the group returned to Abbey Road on September 3, Ringo found his drum kit covered with welcome back flowers. While the group was once again at full strength, there was a notable person missing from the studio's control room, George Martin, who took a vacation for the entire month. The Beatles and engineer Ken Scott worked without a producer for two sessions until Chris Thomas filled in for Martin during his absence. The September 3 session was also notable for it being the first at Abbey Road with an eight-track recorder. The group began work on a remake of "While My Guitar Gently Weeps," taking the next day off for the taping of the promo videos for "Hey Jude" and "Revolution." George's song was completed over the following two days. The recording of this outstanding Harrisong was made even more special when George's friend Eric Clapton came by to lay down what would become one of rock's iconic lead guitar solos. During the rest of the month, the Beatles recorded a remake of "Helter Skelter," "Glass Onion," "I Will," "Birthday," "Piggies" and "Happiness Is A Warm Gun." The title to the last song served as a dark and fitting commentary on America's fascination with guns, brought to the forefront earlier in the year with the assassinations of Dr. King and Bobby Kennedy. The doo-wop-flavored final section of the song, with its "bang, bang, shoot, shoot" refrain, provided a bit of Goon-like satirical humor to one of the album's most fascinating songs.

With George Martin back at the helm on October 1, the group knocked out a trio of songs at Trident Studios: "Honey Pie," "Savoy Truffle" and "Martha My Dear." Upon returning to Abbey Road on October 7, the group recorded the final tracks for the album, starting with George's "Long, Long, Long" and John's "I'm So Tired" and "The Continuing Story Of Bungalow Bill," with the latter song taking another shot at Americans and their guns. The sessions concluded with two recordings worlds apart in tone and sentiment, Paul's raunchy rocker "Why Don't We Do It In The Road?" and John's lovely finger picking-style acoustic guitar tribute to his mother, "Julia." The final mixing and banding session took place on October 16 and 17, without George, who was in Los Angeles to produce tracks for Jackie Lomax's LP.

The day after work on *The White Album* was completed, John & Yoko were busted at a London apartment that belonged to Ringo for possession of 219 grams of cannabis resin (as it turned out, planted by a corrupt London cop). On November 28, in an effort to keep Yoko from being deported, Lennon pleaded guilty to the charge and paid a fine and court costs. This would come back to haunt him in 1972, when the Nixon administration used the pot bust as a pretext to try to deport Lennon from America as an undesirable alien.

During the Beatles self-imposed seclusion at Abbey Road, turmoil and calls for change were still among the dominant stories around the world. On September 7, 150 female demonstrators arrived in Atlantic City to protest what they felt was the demeaning and exploitative Miss America pageant. In early October, the Northern Ireland Civil Rights Association held a march in Derry to protest various forms of discrimination and campaign for civil rights in Northern Ireland. Despite being banned by the Northern Ireland Home Affairs Minister, some 400 protesters marched and had a confrontation with members of the Royal Ulster Constabulary that was the first major step toward The Troubles, the civil unrest that would roil Northern Ireland for the next three decades. On October 14, the Summer Olympics got underway in Mexico City. Two days later, Tommie Smith, won the gold medal in the men's 200 meter race, with John Carlos winning the bronze. Smith and Carlos were both black and, for the medal presentation, they made a number of visual statements of solidarity with the black community and poor people, most notably a black power salute during the playing of *The Star Spangled Banner*. International Olympic Committee President Avery Brundage, wanting to keep the Olympics free from politics (though later revealed to be a closeted racist and anti-Semite), suspended and then expelled Smith and Carlos and banned them from the Olympic Village.

And, of course, there was the presidential election campaign. Following the chaos at the Democratic Convention in Chicago, demonstrators dominated campaign appearances by Democratic nominee Humphrey and the third party insurgent, the segregationist governor of Alabama, George Wallace. Meanwhile, Republican nominee Nixon seemed to be the beneficiary of all this chaos and had sprinted out to a lead. In October, though, Democratic voters who were planning on sitting out the election as a protest against Humphrey and, by extension, LBJ, realized that the consequence of not voting would be making Nixon president so Humphrey's poll numbers began to rebound, especially after he announced that he would suspend the bombing of North Vietnam if he was elected and, on October 31, Johnson's very belated announcement of a complete bombing halt as of the next day. In the meantime, Nixon, no stranger to political chicanery, had subverted those efforts by having his emissaries convince South Vietnam President Thieu to stay away from the burgeoning peace talks in Paris on Nixon's promise of a better deal for the South Vietnamese if he was elected. Johnson and Humphrey were informed of Nixon's gambit, but didn't go public with the information, a bizarre strategy that proved fatal to Humphrey's hopes of winning. In an election nearly as close as the one Nixon lost in 1960, he didn't reach the needed electoral college total until the morning after the November 5 election, when the votes from Illinois, which sank Nixon's chances in 1960, put him over the top and sealed a remarkable, if somewhat tainted, political comeback.

No one could have been blamed those who decided to retreat to the local movie theater for some escapist entertainment that fall and there was plenty of it. Mid-September brought the film version of the musical vehicle that made Barbra Streisand a star on Broadway, *Funny Girl*. This was Streisand's first feature film and her performance was judged good enough that she tied with Katherine Hepburn for the Best Actress Oscar the following spring. A couple of weeks later came the directorial debut of George A. Romero with the zombie cult classic horror film *Night Of The Living Dead*. Two more weeks brought the action hit of the fall, *Bullitt*, starring Steve McQueen and featuring one of the greatest car chase scenes in film history. And, with the Pueblo and its crew still in North Korean hands, October 23 saw the debut of the Cold War suspense film *Ice Station Zebra*, starring Rock Hudson, Jim Brown, Ernest Borgnine, and, taking time off from filming his iconic TV series The Prisoner, Patrick McGoohan, in an adaptation of Alistair MacLean's novel of a U.S. nuclear submarine's mission to rescue the crew of an arctic weather station.

Not all the news of that fall was tumultuous or controversial. On October 11, more than a year and a half after the January 27, 1967, fire that killed three American astronauts and temporarily crippled the Apollo moon program, Apollo 7 lifted off with a crew of Mercury/Gemini program veteran Wally Schirra and rookies Donn Eisele and Walt Cunningham. The 11-day mission was highlighted by the first live TV transmission from an orbiting spacecraft. It successfully tested the Apollo space capsule, setting the stage for a more spectacular flight two months later.

In mid-November, Beatles fans in the United States began hearing from the Beatles again while *Hey Jude* was still topping the charts. The group's feature length cartoon, *Yellow Submarine*, debuted in American theaters on Wednesday, November 13. The film featured three new Beatles songs: Paul's "All Together Now" and George's "Only A Northern Song" and "It's All Too Much" (in a truncated edit). By the time of the American screening, "Hey Bulldog" had been dropped from film. That Friday, radio stations began playing songs from the group's new double LP, which was simply titled *The Beatles* but soon be known as *The White Album* due to its plain white cover. On Sunday night, George Harrison joined the Smothers Brothers for the opening of their weekly comedy show. The show was taped in a special theater-in-the-round setting and featured musical guests Donovan (who was with the Beatles in Rishikesh), Dion (who performed his tribute to fallen heroes, "Abraham, Martin And John") and Jennifer Warnes. One of the comedy sketches was intertwined with "Those Were The Days," whose recording by Apple artist Mary Hopkin was number two in the Billboard Hot 100 behind the Beatles "Hey Jude." The following Friday, November 22, the new Beatles album went on sale, kicking off marathon listening sessions for Beatles fans that were truly a labor of love.

Eleven nights after the release of *The White Album*, NBC-TV presented the first special by the man who was chiefly responsible for the existence of the Beatles, Elvis Presley. Under the sway of his manager, "Colonel" Tom Parker, the King of Rock 'N' Roll had spent much of the sixties making increasingly bad movies with mediocre-to-just-plain-awful songs. Elvis seemed to get his musical mojo back in late 1967 and, that October, Parker signed a deal with NBC for a one-hour special that he envisioned as an hour of Elvis singing Christmas songs. But producer Bob Finkel and especially director Steve Binder had other ideas. The special was taped at the NBC studios in Burbank in the second half of June but, in an era long before the Internet and social media, virtually nothing was known about the show until the soundtrack album was released four days before the telecast. What the large audience (a 42 share of the available audience) saw on Tuesday night, December 3, was no less than the resurrection of a rock 'n' roll legend. The core of the show had Elvis, freshly tanned and dressed in a leather suit, sitting with the surviving members of his fifties band, guitarist Scotty Moore and drummer D.J. Fontana, and a couple of his Memphis Mafia in a jam session and then performing solo for the studio audience, his first performance before an audience since 1961. At first tentative, one could see the confidence and his on-stage magnetism return as he performed a medley of his early hits. The show ended with Elvis, dressed in a white suit, singing "If I Can Dream," a gospel-flavored piece of social commentary written by Billy Goldenberg and W. Earl Brown that was already on its way to becoming The King's first Top 15 hit in better than two years. Given how the year had played out, it was the perfect end to a bravura performance by one of the symbols of a seemingly better, less complicated time and it provided Elvis with the popular momentum to begin a new chapter in his career.

Then, on December 21, Apollo 8 was launched from Cape Kennedy atop a mighty Saturn V rocket with a crew of Gemini program veterans Frank Borman and Jim Lovell and space rookie Bill Anders. This was the mission that would attempt to become the first manned spacecraft to orbit the moon. Two days into the mission, while the spacecraft was on its journey toward lunar orbit, the 11-month ordeal of the Pueblo ended with the release of the ship's crew, though North Korea held on to the ship. The next day, Christmas Eve, Apollo 8 became the first vehicle carrying humans to accomplish what was officially called lunar orbital insertion. As they traveled in lunar orbit, Lovell described for Mission Control crucial detail of the lunar surface while Anders took hundreds of photos of the moon and the first-ever photos of earth taken by a human from lunar orbit, including the iconic Earthrise. Then, on the ninth orbit of the moon, late on Christmas Eve, the crew turned on the spacecraft's television equipment and showed live pictures of the lunar surface while each member of the crew gave his impressions of what he had seen. They ended the transmission with a message — the story of creation from the book of Genesis, read in turn by each member of the crew, with mission commander Borman capping it off with, "And from the crew of Apollo 8, we close with good night, good luck, a Merry Christmas, and God bless all of you-all of you on the Good Earth."

Apollo 8 left lunar orbit early on Christmas morning and began the journey home, having done important advance work in the effort to achieve President Kennedy's goal from 1961 of "landing a man on the moon and returning him safely to earth." The capsule landed in the North Pacific on the afternoon of December 27. Time magazine named the Apollo 8 crew its Men of the Year for 1968 and Borman soon received a telegram that read, "Thank you Apollo 8. You saved 1968." Or, as Paul said, "Take a sad song and make it better."

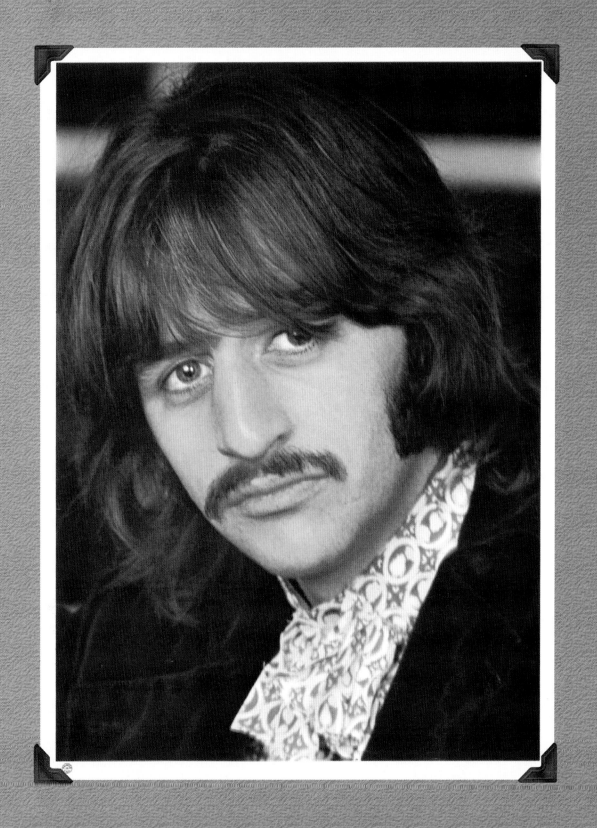

FAN RECOLLECTIONS

I remember it like it was yesterday: I had just turned 10 years old when *The White Album* was released, and my parents bought it for me as a Chanukah present from a local record shop where we lived in Chicago. This was an especially significant event, as it was the first Beatle album that I got upon release, and I played it over and over on my mono record player (the kind that was in what looked like a grey-colored brief case). The poster and individual pics were of course immediately thumb-tacked to my bedroom wall. I still have my original copy of the album, including my own "enhancements" to the plain white cover: 4 Day-Glo stickers from a local head-shop, including one that says "snoopy has fleas." Keep in mind I was only 10! My buddies in the neighborhood and I were all big Beatle fans, and *The White Album*, along with the "Hey Jude" single that preceded it, were constantly played and talked about. I have to admit that back in that era I was a little spooked by "Revolution 9," having no idea what it was about (and not really sure that I do today). Fortunately, there were plenty of other songs on the double album that I really liked, and still listen to 50 years later.

Harvey Greenberg (● **1007857**)

I turned 13 on November 23 and up untill then this was the best birthday present I ever had. My father drove me to Sam Goody's and bought me *The White Album* for my birthday! Fifty years and several well-worn copies later, it's still my favorite.

Ted Amoruso

I remember my first copy of *The Beatles* like it was yesterday. I was waiting at my local record store when they received their shipment that day. I helped them open the boxes and everyone thought that there was a problem: a new album with no cover! Only upon closer inspection did we see the raised print and number along the bottom of the LP. Of course, I wore that copy out playing it over and over and over. I even played it backwards to explore the "Paul is dead" clues which didn't help preserve the grooves or my turntable!

Stephen M. Spence

In late Fall, back in 1968, I was a 14-year-old 8th grader in a small town in upstate New York. My older brother and I were huge Beatle fans since day one (February 9, 1964). We each bought every album when they came out. When we heard that the new album was going to be a double LP, we couldn't wait to hear it. The day it was released my brother and his friend took me and one of my friends (all of us Beatle fans) to the shopping center so that we could all buy a copy. I remember coming home and my friend and I in one room, and my brother and his friend in his room, began listening to this masterpiece. We were all so excited. We each kept sticking our heads in each other's room saying, "WOW, did you hear that?!!". That's why in my 1973 High School Graduation Yearbook my fondest memory is listed as "when they released the Beatles' *White Album*."

Robert G. Robbins

I cherish memories of buying *The White Album*. I was fifteen in 1968, and a huge music fan. Although I was hearing some of the cuts playing in a local record store, and loving them, I had to wait until I received Christmas money from my aunt to be able to buy the album. On a very cold day after Christmas, I caught a bus downtown (Baltimore), bought the record and rushed right back home. I played both discs immediately. I had to take a break for dinner, but of course continued to listen for the rest of the night and for the next week (it being Christmas break!). I was amazed at the variety in the songs. I also loved the printed lyrics on the poster! I still tell this story fifty years later.

Alfred Eckels (**A2058143**)

September 1968: I am 13, before the start of the school year, a big surprise awaits me at my favorite record store. A new Beatles 45, with no more Capitol label and a song that does not seem to finish. I even thought that my record was broken. Friday, November 22, after school, I went to my record store to buy the new Beatles album. Shocking: while showing me a white cover with the name of The BEATLES embossed, my nice record dealer kept the only copy he received.

So the next morning, I went downtown to Montreal at Eaton to get my hands on an album that would become my album fetish, *The Beatles*. Happening: my older brother and several friends showed up to listen to it. I already had my favorite side (2). All agreed that the Beatles had become unsurpassed.

On the following Friday, at school, during the free period of drawing, I was allowed to bring my LP and, after listening to Side 1 and in front of a class in ecstasy, the teacher claimed that the Beatles would be a thing of the past well before the year 2000!

Normand Tremblay (**A2212170**)

I bought *The Beatles* on the day of release. A great 2-disc set. I disagree that it should of been released as a single LP. "Revolution 9" was an ear opener. My number on the album is A1497152.

Ed Fagan (**A1497152**)

I did not get to hear *The White Album* upon its release – and not only because I just turned two. I may as well have turned 12 or 22 – growing up in Kiev, Ukraine (very much the part of USSR in 1968) did not lend one an opportunity to listen to the Western music upon its release. Placed well behind the Iron Curtain, even the adult listeners and collectors had to wait for the "black market" or "special connections" to deliver the goods. So, I must have been around 13, trudging around with my reel-to-reel player half-way across the city of Kiev to my cousin Alexey's apartment to record those most precious LPs from his (mostly, jazz) collection – those released by the four Liverpool lads. *The White Album* was the only one to have required two reels to copy, but it was well worth it – I knew it straight away. From the opening noise of "Back In U.S.S.R." to the soothing waves of "Good Night," it was a complete journey around the world of music – and no foreign visas needed! It sounded magical and vital all at once – and, thankfully, still does. Into the bargain, I was also introduced to the common Soviet myth that the song "Back in the U.S.S.R." was written by Paul after a special, one-time only, secret concert that was, indeed, performed by the Beatles in the U.S.S.R. just prior to recording this album. Now, I have never been able to find the evidence of such concert being held, but as far as that 13-year old was concerned back then, it did not matter – the greatest music ever made was coming through my speakers in my tiny bedroom and I was willing to believe anything, transported far inside the "Glass Onion."

Alex Pritsker

When I got *The White Album* in 1974 for my 13th birthday, I remember it being quite the package. I had most of the other Beatles albums by then, but this was a new experience. It was the most mature album I had ever heard. It was long and sprawling; song titles with girls names, animal names, places. Just the imagery from the song titles was compelling. It was a lot to take in. John's songs resonated with me the most, although I was really more of a Paul fan.

I remember that after listening to the album once through, my mind was kinda numb. I liked much of it, but it just so different from their other albums. For a while I thought of the album as a compilation of nearly solo songs, which still rings somewhat true, but I also see it as a whole whose sum is greater than its parts.

Garry Roddy

The White Album is my favorite Beatles album, but it wasn't always. I became a Beatles fan in 1977 at age 10, and started slowly picking up their albums. I knew of *The White Album*, but as it was a double album, it cost more than their other albums, so I avoided it until I had saved enough money buy it. I played the LP in one sitting and was as amazed as I was with their other late era albums, but I noticed one difference that was similar to *Let It Be*. It wasn't completely polished, which actually charmed me.

I didn't know if I liked it at first, but eventually it grew on me, even "Revolution 9." I find the album to be like a battle with the rocker-type songs on Sides One and Three, and the ballad-type songs on Sides Two and Four. It's like a three-act play culminating with "Revolution 9," and then there is peace… and "Good Night." I feel that it was the final time that the Beatles were really pushing the limits of what they could do.

Mark Arnold, Author

I will never forget the circumstances under which I first heard *The White Album*. While I am sure everyone has their own story, my experience was quite unique. I didn't give it a listen in a normal fashion – like sitting down and hearing the Beatles latest LP uninterrupted from start to finish, either alone or with some friends. Instead, I was sitting in the control room of Sound Recorders, a small studio on Yuca Street located about a block from the Capitol Tower, with George Harrison. There I was, alone with just him and an engineer in a very special environment. How cool was that? Even for me, this was an unusual way to hear a new Beatles album. While having my listening experience interrupted by the comments of George and the actions of the engineer, the good news is I was getting a first-hand listening from the actual master tapes as they were being refined.

George had flown in to LA from London for a variety of reasons, one of which was to produce Jackie Lomax's *Is This What You Want?* debut LP. While at the Tower, he heard Capitol's mastering of the new Beatles album and was deeply disappointed by its sound, complaining that the volume range had been compressed by cutting back the high peaks and bringing up the low passages. He insisted that all of the masters previously cut at the Tower be scrapped and that he be allowed to supervise the remastering of the album himself.

Sensing George's apparent distress while sitting there in the studio with him was distracting and I know that affected my initial response. As the mastering progressed, it took me a while to really comprehend what I was listening to, because for me personally, it didn't seem to have that unique concept feel of a Beatles album. I had become used to a thread that always tied the songs, the sound and the band together. I really liked some of the songs, but others not so much and even a few I didn't care for at all. I know the latter is blasphemy

to many fans and followers who believe it is one their greatest albums, if not their greatest. To complicate things further for me was the fact that "Hey Jude" was recorded within the same time frame as the ones on the album, which caused my expectations to be very high.

Later on, when George and I were alone at his rental house in LA, George confided in me about how demanding the making of that album had been and that he just wanted to get it over with. He felt he needed to take charge of the project by re-mastering it and wrapping the whole thing up and putting it behind him.

I did have a different perspective on the album. Maybe I am entirely on my own in this, but I believe what made it confusing to me was because I was with them in London for a few days in August while we were putting together the first Apple release schedule. Other than the uncomfortable presence of Yoko in our meetings and activities, they seemed so together and united in purpose. But when I heard the new songs, it was like a defiant combination of solo efforts. It felt like sonic whip-lash going from song to song, especially in the way they were blended into each other.

Writing about *The White Album* is complicated for me because its material and presentation represented their lives during a specifically chaotic time. Instead of a cohesive album, it felt like a jumbled movie sound track jumping from scene to scene. In a way it was "in your face" backing music to all the drama going on at the time both in the UK and the US.

At times there was tension between the suits at Capitol and the dreamers at Apple, but the Tower had to accommodate the Beatles innovative ideas as they accounted for 50% of Capitol's gross income. While the world was singing "Come Together," we were chanting keep it together with the lads from Liverpool!

Ken Mansfield, former US Manager Apple Records

Back in the pre-internet days, it was very difficult to get information about pop culture other than what the TV handed out. So when my junior high school friends and I saw *The Beatles* with a plain white cover costing twice as much as any other Beatles album, we didn't know what to expect. Unfortunately, none of us could afford it.

Then one morning my friend Steve came to me all excited. He had bought the album! He proudly copied down all the song titles for me and I eagerly read them.

"Happiness is a Warm Gun"? "The Continuing Story of Bungalow Bill"? "While My Guitar Gently Weeps"? "Piggies"? "Glass Onion"? "Back in the USSR"? "Why Don't We Do it in the Road?"????

I threw the paper back at him. I wasn't going to put up with this silly trick with his made-up Beatles songs. Hey, I was young.

Michael A. Ventrella

I first encountered *The White Album* in late '77 or early '78 when I was 10 and my father bought a car with a tape deck. My stepmother bought it on cassette and we listened to it on drives around Los Angeles. I was already familiar with *Abbey Road* (favorite track at 10: "Octopus's Garden") and gravitated towards the more whimsical tracks like "Rocky Raccoon" and "Why Don't We Do It In The Road." I probably would have played side two on continuous repeat, given the choice. Dad would turn down "Revolution 9," so that conversation could continue, but he never turned it off. Ten years later, I was sharing an apartment with a serious Beatles freak and we bought copies of the CD on the first day of its release. I recall my booklet had a number in the low 3-digits and Mark's was much higher. I was a prick about this stuff and didn't trade with him.

Joe Silber

My one and only memory of The Beatles *White Album* first arriving in my record store: I was 10 years old and I can remember this moment as if it were yesterday as it's been burned into my long term memory... I loved The Beatles music and was forever listening to the radio for any new songs. I frequented LaVerdiere's Drug Store in Gardner, Maine, which had a large music department. I was there on a Saturday with my Dad and left alone to visit my favorite departments: the toy dept and the record department! I remember seeing dozens of *The White Album* taking up two full record bins. I carefully looked at each one, which carried a $9.98 cardboard tag stapled to the top left side of the covers with me wondering how I could ever come up with that much money! Each sealed *White Album* had a large sticker on the front listing every song on the new album! I remember reading through every song title. I thumbed through every copy in both bins wishing I had the money to buy this record and wondering what magic lies waiting to be heard on this new Beatles album that was void of all photos of my favorite four. Where are The Beatles I wondered?! Little did I know then that I was to wait nearly a full year before getting a copy of this wonderful album!

Joe Hilton

I rode my bike over to the Two Guys superstore on the day *The White Album* was released in San Diego. It cost $8.99, and I had only $5.00. So, I had to ride back home, empty-handed. The next day at school, I told my sad tale to a friend. A couple days later, he presented me with a brand new copy. He had asked his parents for money to buy *The White Album*. Not only did they give him the money to buy it, they said to get one for me, too. That was a memorable moment, and I still have it (A 0541569) today.

Larry Clark (**A 0541569**)

I love the Beatles best as a garage band. I love them on the stage in the Cavern Club, on the creaky boards of Bruno Koschmider's Kaiserkeller. I love them when their playlist included "Hi Heel Sneakers," "Jambalaya," "Rock'n'Roll Music," and "Reelin' + Rockin'" (as they used to list it). I love the worn leathers, their penchant for insurrection and the tainted smell of their ramshackle tour van. That Beatles: that is my group.

But for a long time, the Beatles vanished. They were well varnished-over by the Epstein élan that gave us "the good boys"...the bow-at-the-waist Beatles who were palatable for the moms and dads of America.

Suddenly, in late August 1968, I found my group again – back from the land of polish and shine – back to the basics on the so-called B-side of their debut single on Apple. In the raucous opening riff of "Revolution" and its rasping, echoing scream, John proclaimed his rebirth. He was no longer the restrained entertainer that his manager had coerced him to be since December 1961. John was, once more, an opinionated Northern man.

Indeed, the lyrics of "Revolution" set John far apart from the run-of-the-mill anti-Vietnam protesters of that era. John wasn't about to burn the flag (or his bridges) recklessly; instead, he demanded that insurgents show him a plan, a better way forward. John stood against the tide of flippant, giddy "make love not war" mottos and boldly responded, "If you go carryin' pictures of Chairman Mao, you ain't gonna make it with anyone, anyhow!" He chided those who wanted to raze without having something worthwhile to replace what was destroyed. And while rioters popularly took to the streets in 1968, John suggested a more effective and organized way of changing the world. "You better free your mind instead!" he shouted. With those words, John Winston Lennon – the independent thinker, the loner, the rebel – was back again. Utterly revived.

With the release of *The White Album* a few months later, there could be no doubt. "Yer Blues" was Johnny Lennon at his level best, sweating out the devil and the will to die. His gritty, honest performance belied his constant public assertions that he was happier than he had ever been in his lifetime. Mouth to microphone, John belted out real pain, pain that surely accompanied his divorce and the separation from his son. He drew from his gut and released that emotion, straight onto vinyl.

Now, he was John – the real John, with warts and all – arrogantly sneering at the Maharishi in "Sexy Sadie." Having the last word, as Scousers are often wont to do, John hurled invective at the guru, warning him that "however big you think you are...you'll get yours yet."

Even in the quiet ballad "Julia," John was powerful. He offered an honest wail for the girl he had always loved more than anyone, even himself. "Half of what I say is meaningless, but I say it just to reach you, Julia." That was truth. It was the impetus for the soundtrack of his life...and thus, ours. John was no longer afraid to admit it.

The little boy who had been released by his mother, Julia, to his Auntie Mimi, was with us once again. His foray into the jungle-that-is-life under the bravado and guise of being a brave little hunter in "Bungalow Bill" was an allegorical, satirical throwback to the brash, clever Lennon Daily Howl of his infamous Quarrybank days. It is so typically John, without a single coat of shellac.

When the Beatles stated, "We really were a great little band," to me, the *Live At The BBC* band and the *White Album* band is the band to which they were referring: The Beatles without the frills. Yes, I sing along to "She Loves You." I dance to "Eight Days A Week." And now and again, I taste a bit of *Pepper*. But there's little that comes close to Lennon on *The White*. It's a darker shade of pale, to be sure, but at least he is back. Bungalow Bill has come home.

Jude Southerland Kessler, Author

After our world was transformed with *Sgt. Pepper*, we eagerly anticipated what the next Beatles surprise would be. I remember going to Caldor's that November and seeing the new Beatles album *The Beatles* sitting alongside the new Stones album *Beggar's Banquet*. I remember being shocked at the cost of the double album with 30 new tunes, but this was the Beatles and sure to be worth it. I was shocked at the plain white cover with the embossed Beatles written on the cover. Expecting something more ornate, it deepened the mystery. The local radio stations were having contests playing tracks from the album and asking fans to vote for their favorite. "Back In The U.S.S.R." and "Ob-La-Di, Ob-La-Da" were consistent winners. The wonder of the album was the versatility of the musical styles the band was presenting, I remember hiding the poster included with the album from my parents because of the embarrassment of the "nude" photos. I also remember not wanting to listen to "Revolution 9" in the dark. This album identified another Beatles skill, the genius of song sequencing. Even though this was supposedly a tension-laden album, it is one of my favorites from the Beatles gem-stocked catalog.

John Bezzini

I bought *The Beatles* the day it came out at Variety Records in Louisville, KY. One of the owners, Jim, was unpacking them himself. He saw me coming and handed me #0618157 straight out of the box. I love the album. It's full of sounds. I listened to the same copy of the album for years both over headphones and turned up loud in my room, sometimes both at once. To this day, my favorite memory is that when I played the whole album loud, I'd think the phone was ringing. So, I'd answer. There was never anyone there. Eventually I realized it was *The White Album* "calling."

Allan McGuffey (● **0618157**)

"I don't want Easter candy, I'd rather have a Beatles record!" I remember exclaiming as a 12-year old who was Chicago's biggest new Beatles fan of the 1970s. It was my intention to collect every Beatles song to play on my new vintage portable record player. Grandma took me to the nearby Musicland and I picked out my substitute for an Easter basket: The Beatles *White Album*. It sure gave me a lot of songs to check off my list. I was starting to decorate my room with Beatles pictures and I remember arranging the portraits included like a checkerboard on my wall, aside pictures from magazines and photo-copied out of library books. I made myself a "schedule" to learn the songs and diligently listened at least once a week, even "Revolution 9." When "Helter Skelter" came on, I recall my Grandma saying, "OK, time to put on the headphones." I remember impressing my friend by shutting off the turntable and moving the record backwards with my finger to hear what was supposed to be "Turn Me On Dead Man" on "Revolution 9." Although I was 10 years late for the album's release, I continue to enjoy the variety my favorite band offers on this special album.

Dr. Jennifer Sandi

In November 1968 I was a 13 year-old kid living in a small suburban town in northern Ontario, Canada. One evening, just before *The Beatles* hit the store shelves on November 25, a local AM station played the entire sprawling, beautiful mess uninterrupted, save some in-between-sides blather. While the rest of the family watched TV in another room, I sat glued to the floor in front of our Seabreeze hi-fi and took in the whole thing from start to finish. Wow. There's just no way to describe the experience without resorting to the usual clichés: This was a musical journey, and the journey is still crystal clear in my memory 50 years on.

Robert Woods

Trident Studios

Aug. 29, 1968 6:41 a.m.

Trident Studios

Aug. 29, 1968 4:50 a.m.

Trident Studios

Aug. 29, 1968 6:40 a.m.

EMI Studios

Aug. 16, 1968 1 a.m.

John leaving Trident on August 29 at 6:41 a.m; Paul leaving Trident on August 29 at 4:50 a.m.; George leaving Trident on August 29 at 6:40 a.m.; Ringo driving away from Abbey Road on August 16 at 1:00 a.m. Taken by Beatles fan Cathy Sarver during the 1968 recording sessions for The White Album.

I was 13 when I saw THE BEATLES with 74 MILLION OTHERS! I was hooked! I bought anything and everything I could lay my hands on! All thru school I eagerly awaited every new single, new album, magazine and other piece of music I could possess at that time (quite a lot actually). I loved *THE WHITE ALBUM* warts and all. It was a total time of experimentation, revolutionary sonic musing. I am still committed today as I was then! Even happier than before (if that is possible)!

Jim Scott

I'd like to say the following were my first impressions of the classic Beatles *White Album* in November of 1968. But the fact of the matter is, I was barely 12 years old when the album came out and the cover was a nice place to write phone messages from my friends!

But not too long after (OK, it was 10 years later!), I realized an amazing thing almost completely unique to the Beatles among all artists. They never rested on their laurels! Every album while they were together was trailblazing and completely unique with the boys being completely immune free to the influences musically of anyone but themselves! Not the media, the producers, the labels! Nobody but the Fabs were in control then and for the most part, even now. Who else can we say that about? They could've easily basked in the glow of the *Sgt. Pepper/Magical Mystery Tour* era for a good long time, but just they most assuredly surely did not.

The White Album showed that the Beatles were still on fire musically. Once again, they astounded and amazed the music world and their fans. The is an incredible well-paced two-album musical journey that dripped with creativity, diversity and quality. This is why *The White Album* is the favorite of so many fans to this day. The Beatles had certainly left behind the "hit singles" era that filled their great albums just a few short years

before. *The White Album* proved what we already knew! Only the Beatles could produce an album great enough that even a plain white cover couldn't keep the sales down! It sold in the millions in it's glistening white and that trend continues to this day! And were they done after this? No way, they had another masterpiece waiting the following year!

Perry Cox

The first memory I have of *The White Album* is my three older brothers and I taking a reel-to-reel tape player and listening to "Revolution 9" backwards. As a 12 year old, it messed up my mind and I lost sleep over it. Also, I tried listening to it played on a phonograph in the dark. I couldn't get through it all. PEACE AND LOVE.

Jim Ringo Martin

In the mid-sixties, I was a jazz drummer playing gigs at New York's Half Note Jazz Club as a member of the Zoot Sims/Al Cohn Quintet. I was also doing a lot of session work in New York, once again, primarily jazz. Although I obviously was aware of the Beatles from the start of Beatlemania, I never really took notice to what the Beatles were doing. That changed when I heard *The White Album*. It caused me to go back and research everything they did to hear the natural growth of the Beatles. I loved the controversy around Ringo being a great drummer or not. When I really researched his drumming on those early records I was amazed at how much swing he had, almost as if he came from a jazz background. Being friends with Ringo, I know that he had no jazz background, but he sure swings like a jazzer! His drumming was really so unique in the way that he fit the perfect drum part to the song. With Ringo's drumming, there is no ego involved.

Denny Siewell, drummer

My 15th birthday fell on November 14, 1968, and my gift was an AM-FM clock radio, a major upgrade! I lived near Boston, and the FM station I listened to was "underground" station WBCN. Just two weeks after my birthday, *The White Album* was released, and WBCN played it several times from start to finish. In one instance, the DJ said he didn't care much for "Back in the U.S.S.R.," so he began with "Dear Prudence." I also remember hearing a repeated "skip" in their well-worn vinyl during "Don't Pass Me By."

Dave Follweiler

I still remember the excitement of buying my first copy of *The White Album*. Not only was it a double album by my favorite group, but it came out on my birthday. Since it was a special day, I was able to convince my mother to drive me out to Sam Goody at the Garden State Plaza in New Jersey. Back then it was a huge outdoor mall, a dying breed along with most record stores. I paid for the record with my birthday money and rushed home to play it on my Zenith record player (another relic of the past).

I have bought many different copies of that album since then, and I have upgraded my stereo more times that I like to admit, but that album has never sounded better to me than on that fall day in November when I dropped the needle down and heard the opening notes of "Back In The U.S.S.R." come out of those tiny stereo speakers for the first time.

To this day, I still make sure I listen to "Birthday" at least once every November 22 and remember the days of outdoor malls, record stores, and being young enough to actually look forward to being another year older. I still have my original *White Album*, along with all the original inserts!

Frank Kobola (A2124399)

I was 13 in 1968 when *The White Album* was released and immediately got a copy, A1470447. I marveled over the stark white cover with the embossed "The BEATLES." Then discovering the 4 head shots of each Beatle AND a cool poster with the song lyrics on the back! (Still have everything in the record sleeves.) Even though the lyrics to "Rocky Raccoon" says "black mountain hills of Dakota" we still have arguments on the McCartney forum from those who hear "black mining hills!" Lol! All-in-all, a great double album (with the exception of "Revolution 9," which I think I have only listened to twice in 50 years!)

Nancy Riley (A1470447)

I brought home *The White Album* the day it was released in November 1968 at ATA Records and Appliances in North Hollywood, California. I had just turned 12 and remember like it was yesterday, rushing home from the record store on my little stingray bike for two miles... When I put on the turntable in my room for the first time, it was the first and only time ever that my Mom, and Dad huddled in my doorway and listened along for almost the entire album, all 4 sides. I'll never forget that — my Dad in particular took a liking to "Honey Pie," saying it reminded him of the music he grew up with in the 1920's.

Barry Silverman

As an avid Beatles fan, I eagerly anticipated the release of each single and album. But I must admit that I was disappointed with *The White Album*. Not only did I think several of the songs were below par for the group, but it gave me a very real sense that the group was falling apart. This was less of group effort, with each Beatle recording his own songs. I agree with George Martin's assessment that it would have been much better had it been a single disc with only the best songs on it.

Kelly Dude

Once in a while I'll sign an e-mail with "can't wait" when referring to my eagerness to attend an upcoming event with friends or a fun gig. And while my sentiment may be sincere, those mortgage payments, root canals, home repairs and other adult distractions tend to keep my mind diverted from mere mortal pleasures.

It was different for me and my friends when we were kids. Our worlds were small and the major events that had us counting the weeks, days, even hours were looming summer vacations and Christmas, when treasures untold would be heaped on us. And, whenever word hit the street that a new Beatles release was on the horizon our minds and spirits went absolutely bonkers.

They've dominated our culture for generations and it's easy to take them for granted. These days we can use our phones to access virtually any piece of music under the sun. Back then we listened to our transistor radios, begged our parents to drive us to stores to buy vinyl and rode our bikes to check out friends' record collections.

If you were there in the '60s you know what it was like. Just try and imagine hearing "I Feel Fine" or "Tomorrow Never Knows" for the first time. Every new 45 and LP by the Beatles brought us a new universe of sounds, attitudes and a joyous sense of how our lives would be forever changed. They were ours. We didn't know them personally but it felt as if they were friends, kindred spirits.

Growing up with John, Paul, George and Ringo made for countless Beatles-related memories but three moments stand out as if they happened yesterday.

In January of '64, I went with my mom to Joe's Records in Passaic, NJ. I'd already been nuts for their music from the radio, but I'd yet to see a picture of them. In the window of the shop was the 45 sleeve for "I Want To Hold Your Hand" with the iconic shot of the lads in their cardigan jackets. Wow. My psyche went numb.

And finding *Rubber Soul* in December '65 in the rack at Woolworth's in Perth Amboy, NJ hit me like a bolt of lightning. Their hair was a bit longer and they had a casual, yet knowing glare in that fisheye lens photo and exuded an air of impossible cool.

Flash forward to late November 1968. *The Beatles* was out and it was pretty much a given that I'd be receiving it for Christmas, which was still about a month away. Couldn't wait.

A lot had happened in three years. We'd been mesmerized by *Revolver*, "Strawberry Fields Forever" and *Sgt. Pepper*. We'd learned about their "trips," the Maharishi, Yoko Ono and Apple, their own new label. "Lady Madonna"/"The Inner Light," released in the spring of '68 was our last offering from the Beatles. What next?

We were teased by airplay on a few cuts on FM stations. And "Hey Jude" and "Revolution" already hipped us to a "new phase" Beatles sound earlier that summer. But the dee jays announced that this new DOUBLE ALBUM sported 30 TRACKS. COULD NOT WAIT!

Around that time, the family made a trip to Sears in New Brunswick, N.J. and, as was my wont, I made a beeline to the record department. There it was. Man. Fortunately, an unsealed copy awaited in the browser. I hovered around the others who perused this manna from heaven until I got my chance. I picked it up. It was heavy. Literally. The two slabs of vinyl and goodies contained inside the gatefold package made for a formidable grab. The stark, bare countenance of the plain white cover with the lopsided, embossed title and stamped serial number was unexpected and a bit of shock. But soon it struck me that it was a continuum of the band's artful sense of graphics and conceptualism. They'd done it again!

It was very cool to see the entire Apple label for the first time. The four headshots and colossal poster with lyrics and photo montage was revelatory and intriguing.

Ringo – with a beard? Dancing with Elizabeth Taylor?! Paul with slicked back hair and glasses? George sat familiarly and comfortably with his beloved guru. John had changed the most of the four, with his hair parted in the middle. The blue circular shot of him looked like a transmission from an interplanetary space craft.

My folks eventually came to "take me back where I came from." I'd have to wait a month to own a copy.

When I unwrapped this record under the tree on December 25, 1968, seismic shifts erupted in my soul. That may sound over the top. It was. I played it over and over and over in the days, weeks, months to come, savoring, discovering, learning. I'd dissect every morsel, every lyric with cousins and schoolmates.

Indeed, *The White Album* endures as an important record and a staunch favorite for many fans, including those born long after its release. After years of listening and oversaturation, I tend to skip over certain tracks. Yet my sense of wonderment and delight keeps me returning to those selections that speak to me the loudest.

I'm still tickled about the Beach Boys' nod in "Back In The USSR." In the day I had no idea that the Beatles held Brian Wilson and the Boys in such high regard and was ignorant about the February '68 Rishikesh TM summit with Mike Love in attendance.

The sheer melodious musicality of his "Martha My Dear" always gives me a lift. It's one of my go-to numbers when I'm blue. "I Will," with the vocal "duh" bass part, is irresistible, as are "Blackbird" and the pastoral "Mother Nature's Son." "Helter Skelter," a study in controlled chaos, is a musical raw nerve and stands as one of the great recorded achievements by a rock'n'roll band.

George's opus "While My Guitar Gently Weeps" tends to overshadow the quiet majesty and bombast of "Long, Long, Long," a real sleeper. "Savoy Truffle" still gasses me with those crunchy, compressed horns. "Not Guilty," which was cut during the *White Album* sessions, is a gem and its inclusion would have been welcome, and/or could have served as a suitable substitution for a song or two, in my humble opinion.

John's contributions struck a deep chord with me. I've always dug how he could craft a haunting, hypnotic and highly personal nugget like "Julia" and then concoct the gleeful jabbing of "Glass Onion." Or the brash, playful "Everybody's Got Something To Hide Except Me And My Monkey." It's a textbook example of a stunning hi-fi recording, where every instrument, every part snugly occupies its rightful space in the sonic picture. And I may be in the minority here, but I would miss "Revolution 9" were it excised from the program.

And speaking of whom, for my money, Ringo stands as one of the brightest "Starrs" of *The Beatles* and it's his impeccable drumming that makes me appreciate my favorite songs so much here (yeah, I know he's not on every track, but he's on most). His grooves are so damn perfect on "Sexy Sadie" and "Cry Baby Cry." The latter may be one of his finest and most imaginative recorded performances. He fashioned beats and patterns that were all his own. When producers direct drummers to "play like Ringo" in the studio – and they often do – they are referring to the feel heard on these cuts. My love for "Don't Pass Me By" increased exponentially when I heard the alternate mix on Anthology 3. What a groovy track!

The *Yellow Submarine* soundtrack album was issued on the heels of *The Beatles* and served as a bit of lagniappe, a bonus EP of sorts, sporting four previously unheard songs. "Hey Bulldog" and "It's All Too Much" can make for fun selections to add to one's custom alternate *White Album* playlist – should they defy Paul's rebuff of those who saw fit to futz with the original two LP concept! Shut up!

Dennis Diken, The Smithereens

The Beatles *White Album* is still so strange to me. It's not like anything they had done before, the variety and the experimentation in the music seems so organic, a lot of piano, organ and acoustic guitars. The stark contrast of influences shines through: the use of reggae or ska, electronic sound collages, blues, heavy rock and roll, country music, 1930's big band, full blown Hollywood orchestras. It's all Beatles music and it's all incredible.

I got the album in early 1969. I would stare at the gatefold sleeve, mesmerized at how I got this particular number, knowing that others had different numbers on their covers. It was so clever. I noticed the inside of the gatefold with all the song titles and how they formed a sentence in some cases: "Why Don't We Do It in The Road?"/"I Will"/"Julia" all on one line. As a kid, I wondered if they did that on purpose. There was "Revolution 1" and "Revolution 9" – what happened to "Revolution 2" through "8"? Upon hearing "Revolution 9" for the first time, it scared the hell out of me.

The Beatles always looked so cool. John in his granny glasses, unshaven Paul, George staring at camera and not knowing what he was thinking and Ringo looking great. I studied the poster with care. Is Paul naked? Is that Elizabeth Taylor dancing with Ringo? I also liked that they added the lyrics on the other side of the poster although I rarely read them having put the poster up on my wall. I later found out my cover, No. 2545410, was imported from the U.S., but the discs were pressed in Smith Falls, Ontario. I loved those Apple labels. My favourite song on the LP was and still is "Martha My Dear," so typically Paul with that wonderful catchy melody as an ode to his pet and a great piano exercise as well. I'm also very partial to side three of the LP. A an incredibly important album in the Beatles catalogue. And yes, I still have the original album bought all those years ago!

Yvan Tessier (№ **2545410**)

I got The Beatles *White Album* for Christmas 1968. It was a mono top loader, No. 0119535. I found the whole album incredible, hanging onto every single track. I don't think there was a track I didn't like, as there still isn't today. I was fascinated by "Wild Honey Pie" and "Why Don't We Do It In The Road?" I loved "Rocky Raccoon." But "Revolution 9," now there was something else! I hung onto every word, memorizing the words, and started to quote them to my friends. "Eldorado" I'd say, just out of the blue, or "The Watusi." I was so struck with "Revolution 9" that I taped it on my Dad's Grundig TK20 reel-to-reel tape recorder, and then twisted the tape at the play-head so that the whole thing was backwards! I then played that to my friends, it was after all 1968 and then 1969, and there was a wealth of weird and wonderful stuff out there.

In November 1972, I sold my *White Album* to a friend for £4. I was selling all my stuff as I was eloping to Rhyl in North Wales with my girlfriend Joan. We lived there for just over 10 months, during which time our friend Geoff came to visit us, and brought with him his copy of *The White Album*. A STEREO copy, and I freaked out. There was stuff here that I had NEVER heard before. What was happening? This was now 1973, five years down the road and I was experiencing *The White Album* all over again. I was 19 then, and it was just 21 years later, at a school reunion that my original copy of the White album was handed back to me. My original copy No. 0119535 came back home and has been in my collection of *White Albums* ever since, along with its original poster and photos, all now 50 years old, or near enough. Joan? Well she's my wife and has been with me now for 48 years, along with all my Beatles collection which began life in January 1963. Of course you can guess what I'm having for Christmas this year of 2018, can't you?

Garry Marsh (№ **0119535**)

When I first played *The White Album* in November 1968, I was struck by how different it was from previous Beatles albums. Still, it was another great Beatles album.

But there was also a mystery this new album posed for me. My favorite radio station, WLS in Chicago, played several new Beatles songs before the album's release, including "Hey Bulldog." When I played the album, I was surprised that "Hey Bulldog" was not on it. Where did this new Beatles song come from and go? Of course it surfaced several weeks later on the *Yellow Submarine* LP.

Years later when I mentioned my story to Bruce Spizer, I enjoyed his telling me that he had gone through a similar experience at that time when he heard "All Together Now" on a New Orleans radio station.

Michael Rinella (● **0751115**)

The White Album has always been my favorite LP, not only by the Beatles, but by anybody. I remember hearing it the very first time, with "Back in the U.S.S.R." coming from my stereo, moving from one speaker to the other, sounding like a jet plane taking off in my university room. I knew then that it was the most incredible album I'd ever heard. Its songs have many levels to them, which may not have been apparent at first. No other rock artists at the time (or I would argue, since) have been able to come up with such overall quality of material for four LP sides. My own belief is that the Beatles may well have been answering, in their own way (at a time when the political left was debating whether to answer government violence with violence in the 60's and the Vietnam War) their views on art and even politics. Could it be that the Beatles were saying, that they as artists, preferred to change society through their music and art? After all these years and hundreds of times experiencing it, I still discover something new in this revolutionary album.

Alan Chrisman

GREGORY

In 1968 I was 13 years old and still enjoying the thrill of *Sgt. Pepper* from June '67 and the joy of when I got *Magical Mystery Tour* for Christmas '67. And then, the third album in a row from the Beatles with a gatefold cover, the words to the songs and great pictures of "the boys!" Three Beatles albums in 17 months! A double album no less! All that GREAT music. Joy! A very happy & exciting memory. Thank you boys!

Brian J Moran (**A1586342**)

I was introduced to the Beatles through my sister's *Red* and *Blue* albums when I was 14 years old. For Christmas 1973, I received *The White Album* as a present. I loved the white cover, the poster and the pictures inside. I loved this eclectic collection, especially "Helter Skelter," "Birthday" and "Savoy Truffle." With each new reissue of *The White Album*, I listen to "Revolution 9" in its entirety and still find new effects or speech. I can't wait for the 50th Anniversary remix and bonus cuts.

Tom Drill

A Fan's Notes:
Fall 1968—A Video Time Capsule

by Bill King (originally published in Beatlefan #114 Sept-Oct 1998)

When I look back at the autumn of 1968, there are a number of personal milestones, images and memories that come to mind.

The pleasure and pain of being seriously in love for the first time ... reaching 16, the legal driving age, but facing several more months of driving with Dad before he pronounced me ready for a license ... the horrors of the nightly news from Vietnam being eclipsed by my own personal no-win quagmire known as Algebra III-Trig ... the thrill of my beloved Georgia Bulldogs winning the SEC football championship ... the disappointment of Nixon's victory ... the smell of Brasso as I polished the buttons and pins on my Junior ROTC uniform twice each week ... the fascination for me, a longtime space program buff, as NASA launched the Apollo program's final quest for the moon ... the excitement of my first professional newspaper job, doing sports rewrite on Friday and Saturday nights at my hometown morning daily.

I got a Swinger camera (finished black & white prints in 15 seconds!) for my birthday that fall. McDonald's introduced the Big Mac. The Atlanta Chiefs of the North American Soccer League won the city's first (and for many years only) professional sports title, while the NBA's Hawks had just arrived in town from St. Louis.

But, probably the most memorable images I carry with me from that fall are those two Sunday nights when the Beatles performed "Hey Jude" and "Revolution" on The Smothers Brothers Comedy Hour.

For some reason, I can't recall the first time I heard "Hey Jude" on the radio (while I do remember clearly catching its Apple Records companion, Mary Hopkin's "Those Were the Days," on the car radio via clear-channel WOWO out of Fort Wayne one night). I also remember how cool I thought that green Apple label was when I plunked down 77 cents each for the two singles, passing up Jackie Lomax's "Sour Milk Sea" because I hadn't heard it.

A few years back, I managed to obtain copies of those Smothers shows, complete with the old national commercials. Watching those now-familiar Beatles clips in their original context is like opening a video time capsule.

One thing that jumps out at you (because it's been so long since we've seen them) is the cigarette commercials. Kool Filter Longs ("Come up to the Kool taste"). Silva Thins. Tarreyton ("Tarryton smokers would rather fight than switch"). Pall Mall Gold.

Car manufacturers were the other big advertisers, with well-scrubbed Up With People types pushing Ford as "the going thing," and Volkswagen showing a sense of humor in its spots. The sexy blonde in the Noxzema Medicated Shave spot urged the shaver to "Take it off. Take it all off" while a Young Republican-looking model proclaimed, "I came back to Brylcream," and Don Drysdale of the Dodgers also bucked the fashion trend by pushing the "greaseless" look of Vitalis.

Because of the censorship battles Tom and Dick Smothers fought (and ultimately lost) with CBS, their show's radical legend has grown over the years. But, despite what passed for social commentary at the time (as quaint by today's standards as the Smothers' blazers and turtlenecks), it was essentially a classic '60s variety hour, with a mix of music and comedy performed by the hosts and guest star. (Then-unknown Steve Martin and Rob Reiner were among the show's writers.)

The running gag on the Smothers show that fall was regular Pat Paulsen's tongue-in-cheek campaign for president, and the October 6, 1968, show opened with the deadpan comic shilling for his book, only to be chastised by the Smothers, who proceeded to plug their own products in a very mild comment on commercialism. More to the point was a sketch in which the bereaved husband in Bobby Goldsboro's saccharine "Honey" turns out to be a charlatan running a tourist trap selling memories of Honey.

Nancy Sinatra, with enough makeup and hairspray for three women (but also a peace symbol pendant), sang "It's Such a Lonely Time" on a polka-dot set, and joined one-man-band Tom in a number that featured a "jugs" joke. (Sex humor, it seems, had an easier time getting past CBS than political or anti-war jibes.) Black ventriloquist Aaron Williams added reverse racism jokes that probably seemed stronger at the time. And, there was a clever bit using Lennon-McCartney's "The Word" that intercut vaudeville blackouts with a chorus singing dictionary definitions of "love."

There was no joking about, however, when it came time to introduce the Beatles, a measure of the status they held in those days. I remember how kids at school the day after "Hey Jude" was shown were talking about the audience joining in the extended ending, and how weird John Lennon now looked.

The following Sunday's show, featuring Barbara Feldon of Get Smart and former Righteous Brother Bill Medley as guests, had some mustache jokes (the brothers had grown them over the summer), more campaigning by Pat Paulsen (who sang a surprisingly straight rendition of "You'll Never Walk Alone"), a creaky (even then) Lady Godiva sketch ... And, of course, The Beatles doing "Revolution," with Tom making a reference to a censorship issue in his introduction.

Now, this was the new Fabs! While "Hey Jude," with its rainbow coalition sing-along crowd (old and young, black and white) had a warm feeling about it, the "Revolution" clip — featuring a TV-only combination of the single's fast tempo with the as-yet-unheard album version's backing vocals — was edgy, sexy and just too, too cool. From its silhouetted opening and closing to McCartney's scream, and the increasingly quick cuts by director Michael Lindsay-Hogg, it was a masterpiece.

My Mom, who'd always been indulgent (and even supportive) of my Beatles fandom, raised an eyebrow at Paul's shirt (which looked like an old-style button-up undershirt), the rather unkempt hair, and, especially, at John and his orgasmic grunting. Just in that morning's paper, we'd read about the *Two Virgins* nude LP cover controversy. "I think John's gone around the bend," Mom said, shaking her head.

But, while I was no teen rebel, I exulted in how unlike the cute Fab Four of Sullivan days they were now. Those other guys might have gotten it all started, but THESE were my Beatles!

Helter Skelter and the Manson Murders

I did not originally intend to write about the connection between *The White Album* and Charles Manson. But after talking to younger fans, I realized that many of them had learned about the Manson murders prior to hearing the album. This even caused some fans to postpone experiencing the two-disc set, which they considered "creepy" due to its ties to the heinous killings.

Although the murders took place less than a year after the album's release, their association with the Beatles was not fully exploited until the broadcast of an electrifying two-part mini-series titled *Helter Skelter*. The made-for-television film, which aired in America on the CBS television network on April 1 and 2, 1976, received the highest ratings ever for a TV-movie at the time. It was based on the best-selling book of the same name co-written by Vincent Bugliosi, the Los Angeles District Attorney who prosecuted Charles Manson and his "family" for the grisly Tate/LaBianca murders in August 1969.

The media gave extensive coverage to the two-night crime spree, which began on August 9, 1969, with the murder of actress Sharon Tate and four others at the Hollywood home of her husband, film director Roman Polanski. Three victims, including coffee heiress Abigail Folger, were found dead outside the home. Tate, who was eight-months pregnant, and a friend were killed inside the house. One victim was shot. The others were brutally beaten and stabbed. The word "PIG" was written on the wall with Sharon Tate's blood.

The next evening, supermarket chain president Leno LaBianca and his wife were brutally murdered in their Los Angeles home. This time the killers wrote the words "DEATH TO PIGS," "RISE" and "HELTER SKELTER" on the walls in blood.

Although the police did not initially connect the murders, they later got a break in the case through jail-house bragging. Charles Manson and several of his followers were in jail after being arrested for arson. When Manson family member Susan Adkins told fellow inmates about her participation in the murders, one of them went to the police. Although Adkins made a deal to co-operate with prosecutors, she later backed out. Another family member, Linda Kasabian, who was present at the crimes but did not kill anyone, began feeling remorseful and agreed to testify against Manson and four others involved in the murders. The trial dragged on for months and was constantly disrupted by the defendants. All five were found guilty and sentenced to death; however, their sentences were reduced to life-in-prison when California later abolished the death penalty.

Manson's motive was as bizarre as the murders were gruesome. He believed that there would be a great battle between whites and blacks leading to the extermination of the white race. He thought that he and his followers, who lived in a remote desert area, would survive the conflict. From the book of Revelation, Manson envisioned himself as the Fifth Angel, the gatekeeper of Hell, who would be chosen by the blacks to be their leader due to his superior nature. His plan was to commit high profile murders of whites so that blacks would be blamed, triggering the racial war.

Manson, who was a musician and songwriter of limited ability, considered the Beatles to be prophets and believed their songs foretold the future. In his twisted mind, the Beatles White Album bore the guidelines of the upcoming revolution between blacks and whites. "Revolution 9," with its chaotic screaming, gunshots and

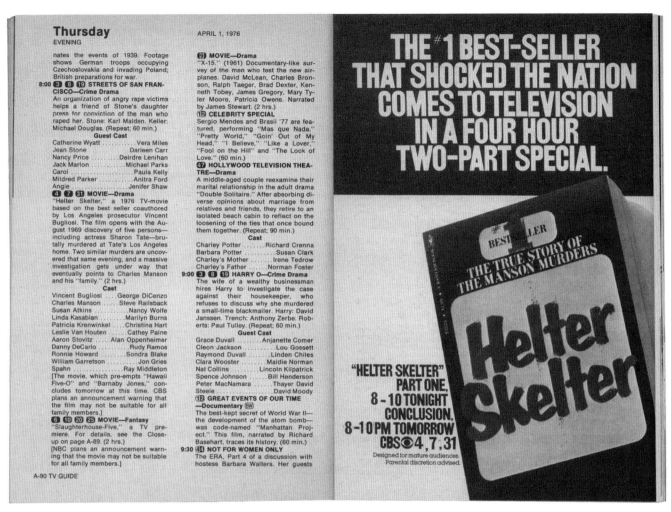

moans, was seen as an audio soundtrack to the ninth chapter of the book of Revelation predicting the apocalypse. "Piggies," vilifying the establishment as pigs, contains the line "What they need's a damn good whacking." The word "PIG" was written in blood at the first murder scene and the phrase "DEATH TO PIGS" at the second. Manson believed "Blackbird" was written for blacks, encouraging the race to revolt with the line "You were only waiting for this moment to arise." The word "RISE" was scrawled in blood at the second murder scene. Manson referred to family member Susan Adkins as Sadie Glutz, a reference to the song "Sexy Sadie." As for "Helter Skelter,"

he thought that it was the name given by the Beatles for the great conflict. Although the term helter-skelter, which dates back to the 16th century, means disorderly confusion or turmoil, Paul had a less chaotic image in mind. His lyrics were inspired by another meaning of the phrase: a tall spiral fairground slide ("When I get to the bottom I go back to the top of the slide").

Although Manson drew inspiration from the album, neither the Beatles nor the LP caused Charles Manson to order these murders. He was a deranged cult-leader who would have sent his followers to murder for him even had he never heard of the Beatles.

A Revolutionary Return to Simplicity—
The White Album Packaging

Although the official name of the Beatles 1968 album is *The Beatles*, it is more commonly referred to as *The White Album* due to its pure white cover. Its simplicity and elegance make the jacket as revolutionary as the group's more complex and innovative covers.

Prior to embracing the minimalist concept of the all white cover, the Beatles considered different ideas, including a transparent front cover that would expose a color photo when the record was removed from the jacket. There was also talk of having the records pressed with white or clear vinyl, but EMI indicated that was not possible (although ten years later EMI issued a limited edition white vinyl pressing of *The White Album*).

The group also considered naming the album after Henrik Ibsen's novel, *A Doll's House*; however, this idea was dropped when the British group Family named its debut LP *Music In A Doll's House*, which was issued in July 1968. Scottish artist John "Patrick" Byrne prepared a drawing that may have been under consideration for its cover. It later appeared in the 1969 book *The Beatles Illustrated Lyrics* by Alan Aldridge and later as the cover to the 1980 compilation album *The Beatles Ballads*. Although the album was released in the U.K., Canada, Mexico and other countries, it was not issued in the U.S.

Many people assumed that John and Yoko were responsible for the album's all white cover; however, the idea came from pop artist Richard Hamilton, who was approached by Paul on the advice of Robert Fraser. Hamilton's concept was to do something that was the opposite of the elaborate cover to *Sgt. Pepper* by having the album issued in a plain white jacket. There was also discussion of having a simulated coffee cup ring or apple stain on the cover, but these ideas were dismissed as being flippant and difficult to print accurately.

It was also Hamilton's idea to title the album *The Beatles*, following an elaborate title (*Sgt. Pepper's Lonely Heart's Club Band*) with a simple one. After Paul expressed reservations about an all white cover, the artist suggested embossing "The BEATLES" onto the jacket. He also suggested that each cover be sequentially numbered "to create the ironic situation of a numbered edition of something like five million copies."

The back cover is completely blank white save for a small "Stereo" notation in the upper right corner of the U.S. and stereo U.K. jackets. The inside gatefold is white with gray song titles printed on the lower left panel and four John Kelly portraits on the right.

While Hamilton was pleased with his concept, he began to feel guilty about putting the group's double album out in a plain white jacket. He suggested that the package "could be jazzed up with a large edition print, an insert that would be even more glamorous than a normal sleeve." Paul was recruited to collect pictures of the Beatles to incorporate into a huge collage. After selecting the images for the poster, Hamilton had many of the pictures re-sized. He then laid out the photos on a sheet of paper that was the same size as the poster insert. His composition was complicated by the fact that the poster would be a folded insert. This would create six separate squares, with the top right and top left sections needing to stand on their own, serve as a double spread and fit in with the four lower sections.

The final product achieved the artist's goal of creating a print that "would reach and please a large audience" while including "some arcane touches which only the Beatles' more intimate associates were likely to smile at." Included in the poster are photos of Paul lying in a bathtub, John and Paul in black leather jackets (taken in Paris), a bearded Ringo Starr dancing with Elizabeth Taylor at London's Dorchester Hotel and the band performing for the "Revolution" video.

The poster caused a bit of controversy at the Capitol Tower. Some of the company's employees were concerned about the sexual nature of a few of the images. John's tiny drawing of he and Yoko standing naked was altered by the removal of pubic hair. Then there was a small photo of a naked person located to the left of the picture of Ringo dancing with Elizabeth Taylor. Although the person's genital area was blocked out by a pole, Capitol found it necessary to airbrush the image to remove the pubic hair. Oddly enough, the biggest concern was over a picture of John sitting naked in bed while talking on the phone. Although John's arm blocked the view of his crotch, some Capitol executives were disturbed by the closeness of Yoko's head to John's legs. After much discussion, Yoko was allowed to remain in bed. Although she was not airbrushed out of the poster, her face may have been darkened.

Although no alterations were made to the U.K. poster, it created a bit of a stir in the British dailies, where it was reported that the naked person in the poster was actually Paul McCartney. Never mind that the photograph was small and a pole strategically blocked his pole — it was Paul in the nude! Alan Smith, writing in the November 30, 1968, New Musical Express, commented that it was hardly any more offensive than bathing suits. Smith speculated that Paul likes to shock. It was a natural part of his humor and the enjoyment he gets from watching the reaction of conventional people when their social patterns and thoughts are put into question. The "Paul goes nude" comments prompted Apple Press Officer Derek Taylor to lament: "All this work, all these tracks, all this talent — and all their dirty little minds focus on is one tiny picture!"

The Beatles followed their *Sgt. Pepper* practice of giving their fans good value for their money. *Sgt. Pepper* had the song lyrics printed on its back cover; *The White Album* had its lyrics on the back of the poster. *Sgt. Pepper* came with an insert sheet of cutouts; *The White Album* contained glossy John Kelly color portraits of each Beatle (see pages 102-105). The U.K. portraits measured 8" x 13½". The U.S. were 7¾" x 10¾".

The embossed and sequentially numbered covers and their enclosures created challenges for EMI and Capitol to complete the packaging in time for the album's late November release. EMI director of sales John Fruin described it as a "nerve shattering experience." Because the covers and inserts would not be ready until mid-November, EMI could not wait for the covers to begin manufacturing the records. The company's Hayes factory started pressing the discs in early November. As the records came off the pressing machines, they were placed into black inner bags and stored until the covers arrived. As EMI had no equipment capable of inserting records into double pocket sleeves, the discs had to be inserted into the covers by hand. EMI supplemented its staff by hiring disabled ex-servicemen to help with the tedious task of placing records and inserts into sleeves.

Internal Capitol documents indicate that the art work was not sent to the printers until October 22 and November 1, 1968. Capitol's national director of purchasing Curt Kendall recalled that "*The White Album* was an enormous undertaking. The quality control involved in the printing of that job was incredible."

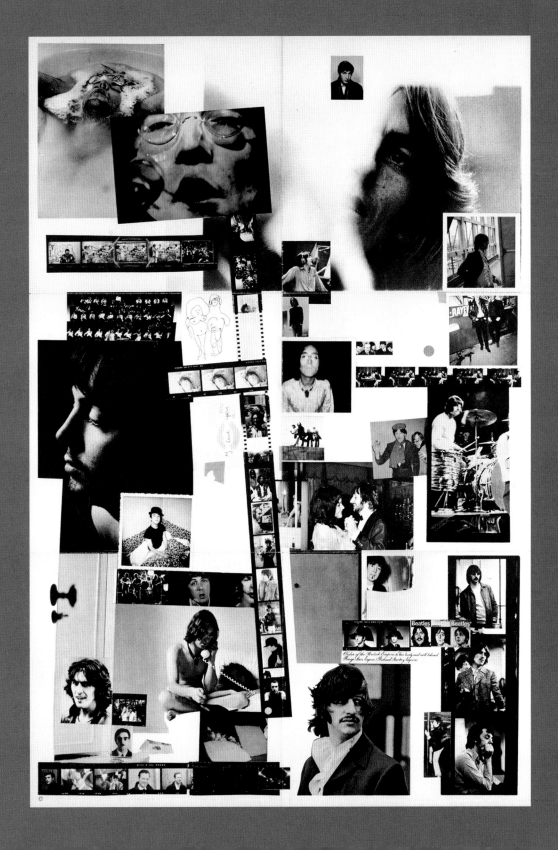

Obsessed with numbers

by Professor Frank Daniels (A16964179)

Although the sequential numbering of the covers for the Beatles double album presented challenges for all involved, EMI affiliates were so enamored with the group that they happily set about trying to determine how on earth they could number each cover. They selected an automatic numbering machine known as a "Bates-type" stamper (named after the well-known company, Bates, that manufactured them). It is clear from the relatively fixed locations of the numbers that they secured the stampers and covers so that the covers would be in the same position each time they were stamped. The stamp would automatically advance to the next number.

In the U.K., printer Garrod and Lofthouse did the numbering in batches – assigning the first 300,000 numbers to mono LPs and the next 300,000 numbers to stereo albums. At least that was the plan. The numbers were seven digits long, with zeros preceding the sequential numbers. On most British covers, the numbers have a № prefix. Since the printer had to work fast, there may have been multiple machines – each assigned a group of numbers. The numbering wasn't a science. If they ruined a cover, they tossed it and did not reuse its number. If the numbering went wrong, again they skipped to the next number, and they paid no attention to whether or not they were using every number in the set.

Exceptions were made for the lowest numbers. It seems that someone decided that there could be multiple copies of the low numbers – for the Beatles, their friends, record-company executives and so on. If they decided to duplicate a mono number for stereo, they would, and apparently when they reused a low number sometimes they used a large dot as the lead character instead of the usual № prefix. For example, number 5 covers can be found with № **0000005** or ● **0000005**.

As soon as the initial demand for the LP ran out, the printer used numbers originally allocated for mono and stereo as it saw fit. This led to stereo covers with numbers in the 200,000 to 300,000 range and mono covers with numbers above 300,000, including some in the 600,000 to 600,030 range. All told, EMI numbered over 624,000 copies of *The White Album* in the U.K., some of which were exported to other countries.

While EMI had only a single factory in Hayes in Middlesex manufacturing its discs, Capitol had three factories pressing copies of *The White Album*. Its three pressing plants each received the bulk of their covers from different printers and album cover manufacturers. The covers for Capitol's main plant in Scranton had their cover slicks printed by Queens Litho in Queens, New York. The company's Los Angeles factory generally used covers printed by Bert-Co Enterprises in Los Angeles. Capitol's new pressing plant in Jacksonville, Illinois had its White Album covers printed by Gugler Litho in Milwaukee, Wisconsin.

As the album was only issued in stereo in America, Capitol did not have to assign different number blocks to mono and stereo albums. However, to ensure there were no duplicate numbers, separate blocks of numbers were assigned to the three different printers used by its three factories. Bert-Co was assigned the numbers 1 through 580,000 for covers printed for the Los Angeles factory. Gugler Litho was allocated numbers 580,001 through 1,380,000 for the Jacksonville plant. Queens Litho had numbers 1,380,001 through 2,000,000 for Scranton. All three factories were later assigned different blocks of numbers above the 2,000,000 mark.

Bert-Co printed 25 specially numbered covers for Capitol to send to Apple. These covers utilized all of the wheels on the stamper, having seven digits preceded by a wide **A**. The numbers ran from **A 0000001** through **A 0000025**. (The **A** did not stand for America, but rather was from the first wheel of the stamper, which had the letters A through J.)

Capitol president Stan Gortikov sent these special covers to the London Savile Row headquarters of Apple. Gortikov sent a letter to George Harrison stating: "I am sending under separate cover those copies of the new U.S. Beatles album that are serially numbered 'A0000001 through A0000025' as personal souvenirs for you and selected friends. I have personally stolen number 'A0000005,' because I am a friend too. Beside, I love the music!"

For its initial standard batch of covers, Bert-Co did not use the **A** prefix. The company started over at one, limiting the first hundred covers to three digits, appearing as **001** through **100**. (The numbers **007**, **009**, **027**, **034** and **100** have been confirmed.) Thereafter, all of the numerical wheels of the stamper were used, repeating 100 as **0000100** and continuing through about **0210000**. Bert-Co later returned to using the **A** prefix, with numbers such as **A 0218735** and **A 0578465**. Some Bert-Co covers above two million are preceded by a **Nº** abbreviation rather than an **A**, such as **Nº 2672056**. Bert-Co's last run of numbered covers have numbers in excess of three million, with **A 3133802** being the highest confirmed.

Gugler Litho was assigned the batch running from 580,001 through 1,380,000. The numbers for these covers have a large dot preceding the number. Examples include ● **0597774** and ● **1338912**.

The first batch of Queens Litho covers run from 1,380,001 through 2,000,000. The numbers for these covers are preceded by a thin **A**, such as **A14704470**. Some of the Queens Litho covers with numbers above two million have a **Nº** abbreviation rather than an **A**, such as **Nº 2273151** and **Nº 2924360**.

As was the case in the U.K., no effort was made to ensure that all numbers were used. It appears that no albums were numbered in the 2,700,000s. There were some duplicate numbers after two million, apparently caused by the same small batch of numbers being mistakenly allocated to two printers.

Capitol stopped numbering the covers in the summer of 1971. By this time, the numbers had exceeded 3,133,000. Even accounting for the 100,000 numbers never used, Capitol sold over three million numbered copies of *The White Album*, living up to designer Richard Hamilton's "ironic situation of a numbered edition" in the millions.

It is interesting to note that two numbers were deliberately used on multiple covers. Capitol was excited about the prospect of the double album selling in excess of two million units. Capitol's Curt Kendall instructed Queens Litho to make a dozen or so covers with the number **A2000000** to commemorate this milestone. The **A2000000** covers were given to key Capitol executives. An employee of Queens Litho was inspired by this Capitol idea and made a half-dozen or so instant collector's item covers with the number **A0000001** for himself and a few of his friends.

The White Album was not the first rock double LP. The first was *Freak Out!* by the Mothers of Invention (led by Frank Zappa), whose double disc set preceded Bob Dylan's *Blonde On Blonde* by a few weeks in the summer of 1966. Nor was it the first rock double album to hit number one on the LP charts. That honor went to *Diana Ross And The Supremes Greatest Hits*, which topped the charts for five weeks starting on October 28, 1967. The next double LP to top the charts was Cream's *Wheels Of Fire*, whose five weeks at number one began on August 10, 1968. Jimi Hendrix's double masterpiece, *Electric Ladyland*, spent two weeks at top beginning on November 16, 1968. But no rock double album sold so many copies so quickly as *The White Album*. And it did so without any singles being pulled from the LP to push sales. It hit number one on December 28, 1968, and topped the charts for a total of nine weeks.

EMI affiliates in most countries tried to release the record as a "numbered limited edition," with several early pressings of the album being numbered. Richard Hamilton's numbering concept was so widespread that it became part of the legacy of *The White Album*.

When EMI first issued *The White Album* in the compact disc format in August 1987, the included CD inserts were sequentially numbered in several countries, including America and Great Britain. EMI also numbered special reissues.

While the industry was no stranger to numbered limited editions – Capitol's own set of Stan Kenton LPs had been a numbered edition back in February 1955 – the concept of numbering a regular-issue album seems to be permanently connected to *The White Album*.

Collectors place a premium on the low-numbered original covers. Although there a multiple copies of the Queens Litho **A0000001** covers, they are still the most desirable of the U.S. covers other than the original

batch **A 0000001** sent to Apple by Capitol president Stan Gortikov. The location of that album remains unknown, although it was surely originally owned by a Beatle. Ringo's personal U.K. copy of *The White Album*, №**0000001**, sold for $790,000 at auction in 2016.

The special Bert-Co covers (**A 0000001** through **A 0000025**) and the three didgit Bert-Co covers (**001** through **100**) are both extremely desirable and extremely rare. It is not known how many of these covers survived. Beatles historian Bruce Spizer has number **027** in his collection, which is rarer than his **A0000001** cover. The cover **007** is cool for its James Bond reference.

While the ultra-low numbers are not affordable to most collectors, there are some rare hidden gems out there that would probably not command high prices as their significance is unknown to most. For example, the U.K. cover № **0300001** would be the first stereo cover. Anything close to that number would be one of the first U.K. stereo covers. In the U.S., ● **0580001** and **A1380001** would be first covers from the Jacksonville and Scranton factories. They would just as "low" as **001**, but obviously not as desirable.

Other games involve searching for numbers that represent a particular date, such as one's birthday. August 22, 1986, could be associated with *White Album* numbers **0082286** (U.S. order) or **0220886** (European order). If you wanted to put the year of birth first, you could satisfy your quest by finding number **A1986822**.

You could also search for covers that contain a historically significant date. For example, American Independence Day would be ● **0741776** (July 4, 1776). The Beatles first appearance on The Ed Sullivan Show would be **A 0291964** (February 9, 1964).

What if the *White Album* number was part of your phone number, past or present? While you couldn't find a seven-digit phone number, you might look for all but the first digit. Thus, Jenny might go for *White Album* number ● **0675309**. Street addresses are also possible, but these would normally require lower numbers. While a cover representing Apple headquarters at 3 Savile Row would be near impossible to come by, perhaps its New York address of 1700 Broadway could be found (**A 0001700**).

Then there are numerical oddities such as the sequence ● **1234567**. That would be pretty darn cool. And how about a nice Palindromic Number? That would be a number that reads the same backwards and forwards, such as **0125210**.

And let's not forget numbers associated with other Beatles records or records by other artists. Someone might go for album number **0007067** (the catalog number for the first LP in England), or **0005150** (Van Halen), **0008701** (Usher), or **0002112** (Rush). What's the point of this madness? Sometimes collecting numbered White Albums means collecting their numbers.

Finally, it should be pointed out that even the catalog number of *The White Album* is significant. In early fall 1968, Capitol faced a day of reckoning of sorts. They had released album number 1, *Songs By Johnny Mercer*, all the way back in 1944 – inaugurating their main series. In 1949, when they began releasing popular albums in the LP format, they kept their existing series intact. When twelve-inch LPs gradually replaced ten-inchers, Capitol continued their numbering system. When stereo came along, they merely added an "S" to the prefix – keeping their series going.

Meanwhile, Capitol had been using high numbers for albums in other series, and for albums by subsidiary companies. For example, the Beatles own label, Apple Records, began with 3350. Tower Records was using the 5000s, the Beach Boys Brother Records began with 9001 and Sidewalk started with 5901. As a result, when the numbering of their main series reached 3000, they had to jump to another number. Capitol execs realized that most of the numbers below 1000 were out of print in 1968 and had never been used for stereo records. Therefore, they decided that their new beginning would be numbered 101. Aware that a new Beatles album was coming, they reserved number 101 for the album that became famous in part for its numbering.

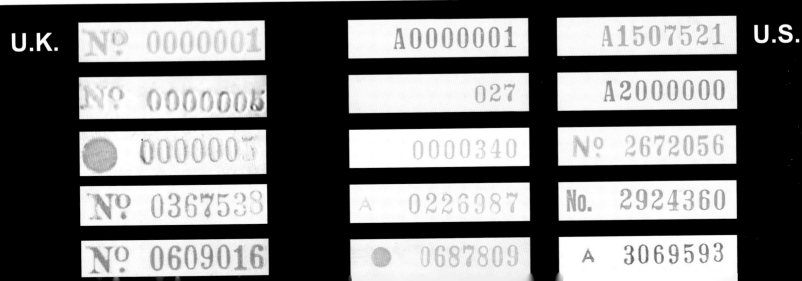

U.K.

		U.S.
№ 0000001	A0000001	A1507521
№ 0000005	027	A2000000
● 0000003	0000340	№ 2672056
№ 0367538	A 0226987	No. 2924360
№ 0609016	● 0687809	A 3069593

The Esher Demos

In late May 1968, the Beatles gathered together at Kinfauns, George Harrison's bungalow in Esher, Surrey, England, to rehearse songs for their upcoming recording session set to begin at Abbey Road on May 29 (although the first day ended up being May 30). The group ran through 27 songs which were either recorded on or transferred to Harrison's Ampex four-track reel-to-reel tape recorder. Harrison mixed the songs in mono and gave each of his bandmates a copy of the demo tape in advance of the proper recording session.

Many of the songs recorded at Kinfauns were written by John, Paul and George during their stay in Rishikesh, India, at the ashram of Maharishi Mahesh Yogi. The group traveled there in February 1968 to study Transcendental Meditation with the Maharishi. In his Playboy interview, John gave the following summary of the trip: "We got our mantra, we sat in the mountains eating lousy vegetarian food and writing all those songs. We wrote *tons* of songs in India." Some of these songs were inspired by the Maharishi's lectures, the beautiful surroundings, characters at the ashram and even the Maharishi himself.

Although the exact date that these recordings were made is unknown, it recently came to light that John and Ringo went to George's house for a rehearsal on May 28 that Paul did not attend. In all likelihood, all of the Beatles got together before that date.

Of the 27 Esher demo songs, 19 were included on the group's next LP: "Back In The U.S.S.R.;" "Dear Prudence;" "Glass Onion;" "Ob-La-Di, Ob-La-Da;" "The Continuing Story Of Bungalow Bill;" "While My Guitar Gently Weeps;" "Happiness Is A Warm Gun;" "I'm So Tired;" "Blackbird;" "Piggies;" "Rocky Raccoon;" "Julia;" "Yer Blues;" "Mother Nature's Son;" "Everybody's Got Something To Hide Except Me And My Monkey;" "Sexy Sadie;" "Revolution;" "Honey Pie;" and "Cry Baby Cry."

Details regarding the demos for these songs are included in the description of each song in the Recording Sessions section of the book. The demos of some of the songs, such as "Blackbird," "Julia," "Mother Nature's Son," "Bungalow Bill" and "Dear Prudence," are essentially the same as the recording on the album minus their embellishments. Other demos, such as "Cry Baby Cry" and "Ob-La-Di, Ob-La-Da," were complete, but would be rearranged during the recording sessions. Still others, such as "Back In The U.S.S.R." and

"Revolution," were close to complete, but were missing third verses. "Yer Blues," "Glass Onion" and "While My Guitar Gently Weeps" would go through lyrical revisions before they were recorded for the LP. "Happiness Is A Warm Gun" was in its embryonic state, with only its "I Need A Fix" and "Mother Superior Jumped The Gun" sections in place. The title section would not evolve until the recording session.

Although the group went through over 100 numbered takes of George's "Not Guilty," the song was left off the album. The demo, which has a jazzy feel to it, has George's vocal double-tracked and contains some lead guitar. George later recorded the song for inclusion on his 1979 *George Harrison* album. John's "What's The New Mary Jane" was recorded and mixed for stereo and mono, but is not on the LP. Both of these songs were included on *Anthology 3*.

George's "Sour Milk Sea" was given to Jackie Lomax and became one the first four singles released by Apple in late August 1968. Paul provides harmony on the chorus and George vocalizes the solo. Paul and Ringo joined George for Lomax's recording of the song, which was produced by George.

"Circles" was another of George's songs not recorded for the album. The slow tempo demo has Harrison singing over an organ backing. He later recorded the song for his 1982 LP *Gone Troppo*.

Two of John's songs, "Mean Mr. Mustard" and "Polythene Pam," later became part of the medley on Side Two of *Abbey Road*. Both demos have double-tracked Lennon vocals. "Mean Mr. Mustard" has both verses in place, but the sister's name is Shirley, not Pam. "Polythene Pam" has a line that is not in the recorded version: "Well it's a little absurd, but she's a nice class of bird."

John's "Child Of Nature" was not recorded during the album sessions, perhaps because its theme was similar to Paul's "Mother Nature's Son." Although later rehearsed during the *Get Back* sessions, the song was never properly recorded by the group. John liked the melody, so he started over with new lyrics. The song morphed into "Jealous Guy," which was included on his 1971 *Imagine* LP.

The music and arrangement for Paul's "Junk" were in place, but the lyrics were incomplete. The demo has Paul double-tracked with one of his voices often laughing or scatting. Paul finished the song for his first solo album, *McCartney*.

All of these demos are on *The White Album* deluxe edition.

The Recording Sessions

The sessions for what would later be known as *The White Album* began at EMI Studios on Abbey Road on May 30, 1968, and continued through October 14, 1968, with mixing and banding completed on October 17. Nearly all of the recording took place at Abbey Road, although the group did spend some time at Trident Studios, Trident House, St. Anne's Court, Wardour Street, London. George and Paul were familiar with Trident having produced sessions there respectively with Jackie Lomax and Mary Hopkin.

In addition to providing a change of scenery, Trident had a then state-of-the-art eight-track recorder. Abbey Road was still using four-track recorders. Although EMI had recently purchased an eight-track, it was undergoing testing. When the Beatles learned of this in early September, they insisted that the new machine be brought to Studio Two for their use. Engineer Ken Scott arranged for its installation in Studio Two while George Martin was on vacation. The first Abbey Road eight-track session took place on September 3, 1968, for "While My Guitar Gently Weeps."

By the time the sessions started on May 30, the dynamics of the band had changed dramatically. Less than two weeks earlier, John had invited Yoko Ono to his home in Surrey. They taped a series of sound collages that would later be released on the album *Two Virgins*, and then made love together for the first time. When John showed up at Abbey Road, he brought Yoko with him, breaking the unwritten rule that wives and girlfriends generally did not attend recording sessions. From that point forward, Yoko was nearly always at John's side. The group camaraderie of prior recording sessions was starting to fade away.

Those in the studio could feel the tension. Geoff Emerick, who had won Grammy awards for best engineered non-classical album with *Revolver* and *Sgt. Pepper's Lonely Hearts Club Band*, grew weary of the deteriorating atmosphere in the studio and abruptly quit during the recording of "Cry Baby Cry" on July 16. He was replaced by Ken Scott. Even George Martin was fair game for attack, with Paul reportedly sniping at him during the recording of "Ob-La-Di, Ob-La-Da." When Martin made a suggestion regarding his vocal, Paul sarcastically suggested Martin come down and sing it. Although he remained the group's producer, Martin took a vacation for the entire month of September, during which time Chris Thomas stepped in.

The bad vibes were there from the start and even evident to visitors. Beatles Book editor Sean O'Mahony (who went by the name of Johnny Dean) brought his photographer, Leslie Bryce, to the June 4 session. Yoko Ono, who made her debut on May 30, was there, as was Paul's new girlfriend, Francine Schwartz. Sean recalled, "Everything was wrong. I told Leslie to shoot a few pictures quickly and then Mal Evans came over and suggested we leave." The dour faces, as seen in Bryce's photo shown on the next page, conveyed the uptight atmosphere, even on a tea break.

Sometimes the tension sparked great performances. Fed up with Paul's perfectionist approach to "Ob-La-Di, Ob-La-Da," John showed up for the session late and somewhat stoned. His distinctive pounding piano opening for the song was a result of his frustration with doing a re-make of a song he loathed.

When George had trouble getting the group engaged for the recording of "While My Guitar Gently Weeps," he invited his friend Eric Clapton to attend the session and play lead guitar. Impressed by Clapton's presence, the band turned in a spectacular performance.

Sometimes the tension became too much. When Ringo grew tired of Paul's criticism of his drumming on "Back In The U.S.S.R.," he quit the group for a week and a half. Paul ended up playing drums on that song and on "Dear Prudence."

But despite the bad vibes that surfaced from time to time, there were tender moments as well, such as John teaching and accompanying Ringo on his lullaby, "Good Night." The storm clouds often blew away, allowing the mature Beatles to become the boys again, laughing their way through the end of "Ob-La-Di, Ob-La-Da" and "going to a party, party" on "Birthday" and "Bungalow Bill." Listening to the outtakes on the deluxe anniversary edition of *The White Album*, it is clear that the sessions were full of wonderful and magical moments.

After the group's breakup became public, John offered the following view of *The White Album*: "Every track is an individual track — there isn't any Beatles music on it.... It was John and the Band, Paul and the Band, George and the Band." And while *The White Album* is in many ways an elaborate compilation of solo-led recordings, the final product shows that John, Paul, George and Ringo recorded some incredible music.

Back In The U.S.S.R.

Recorded: August 22 (basic track) & August 23 (overdubs)
(Abbey Road Studio 2)
Mixed: August 22 (mono) & October 13 (stereo)

Producer: George Martin
Engineers: Ken Scott & John Smith

Paul: Lead and backing vocals; drums; bass guitar (Rickenbacker); lead guitar (Casino); piano; hand claps
John: Backing vocal; bass guitar (Fender VI); drums; hand claps
George: Backing vocal; lead and rhythm guitar; bass guitar (Fender Jazz); drums; hand claps
Ringo: Drums (early session only; not on recording)
Sound effects: Airplane revving up and taking off

The album's opening track, "Back In The U.S.S.R.," was written by Paul in Rishikesh. It is a clever parody of Chuck Berry's "Back In The U.S.A.," which was released in the U.S. on Chess 1729 and peaked at number 37 on the Billboard Hot 100 and at 16 on Billboard's Hot R&B Sides chart in 1959. In the song, Berry sings about how good it feels having "just touched ground on an international runway, jet-propelled back home from overseas to the U.S.A." He sings about how he missed the cities, skyscrapers, drive-ins, hamburgers and juke boxes, and how glad he is to be living in the U.S.A. Paul took the concept and wrote a tongue-in-cheek song about a Russian who flew in from Miami Beach and is glad to be back home. He may not have a lot, but he's still every bit as proud as an American would be. At Beach Boy Mike Love's suggestion, Paul added the bit about the Ukraine and Moscow girls, giving the lyrics a touch of the Beach Boys' "California Girls." The song is full of in-jokes, including the line "That Georgia's always on my mind," which serves as a tribute to both the Soviet republic of Georgia (now an independent country since the breakup of the U.S.S.R.) and the Ray Charles tune "Georgia On My Mind." There is also a bit of irony in the lines "You don't know how lucky you are boys/Back in the U.S., back in the U.S., back in the U.S.S.R." Whether you're from the U.S. or the U.S.S.R., it's still great to be back home.

The Esher demo of the song is propelled by acoustic guitars and Paul's double-tracked vocal. The arrangement is essentially the same as the later studio recording, except for different Beach Boys-style backing vocals in the bridge and Paul resinging the first verse, as he had yet to write the song's third verse.

The Beatles began recording "Back In The U.S.S.R." on August 2. During the early stages of the session, Paul and Ringo got into an argument over the drumming, which prompted Ringo to quit the group for a spell. The band continued work on the song, laying down a rhythm track with Paul on drums, George on guitar and John on the Fender VI bass guitar. The fifth and final take was deemed the best and given numerous overdubs the next evening. Paul added piano, Rickenbacker bass fills and a lead guitar solo. George overdubbed additional guitar and bass on a Fender Jazz bass. John and George added drum parts. According to Paul, he sang the lead in his "Jerry Lee Lewis voice." Beach Boys-style backing vocals by John, Paul and George were added on the bridge. The three also added hand claps. As a finishing touch, the sound of an airplane was faded in and out of the mix, primarily to open and close the song. The sound effects are from a recording made at London airport of a Vickers Viscount turbo prop revving up and taking off. *The White Album* deluxe edition contains the basic backing track of Take 5 prior to vocal overdubs. The track was recorded in the key of G and sped up at some point to where the finished master is in the key of A.

Dear Prudence

Recorded: August 28 (basic track) & August 29 - 30 (overdubs)
(Trident Studios, 8-Track)
Mixed: October 5 (initial mono mix at Trident);
October 13 (final stereo and mono mixes at Abbey Road)

Producer: George Martin
Engineers: Barry Sheffield and unknown second engineer

John: Lead and backing vocals; lead guitar (Casino); hand claps; tambourine
Paul: Backing vocal; drums; bass guitar (Rickenbacker); hand claps; piano; flugelhorn
George: Backing vocal; lead guitar (Les Paul); hand claps
Additional participants: Mal Evans (backing vocal, hand claps, tambourine); Jackie Lomax (backing vocal, hand claps); John McCartney (backing vocal, hand claps)

The sound of the airplane at the end of "Back In The U.S.S.R." cross fades into the opening guitar notes of the album's second track, "Dear Prudence." John wrote the song in Rishikesh for Prudence Farrow, the sister of actress Mia Farrow. Prudence had become dangerously obsessive about practicing Transcendental Meditation, and was spending all of her time meditating in her room. The opening line "Dear Prudence, won't you come out to play" was simply a plea by John for her to take a break from her excessive meditation and join the others.

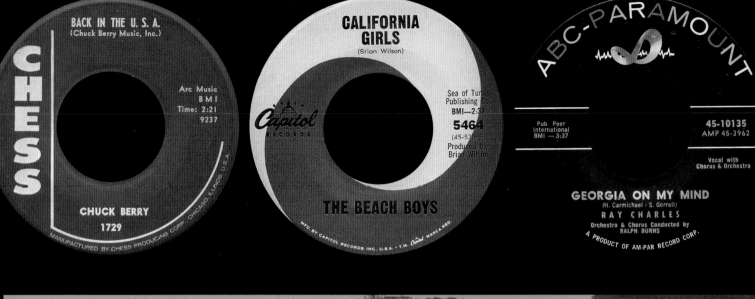

CHESS
BACK IN THE U.S.A.
(Chuck Berry Music, Inc.)
Arc Music
B M I
Time: 2:21
9237
CHUCK BERRY
1729
MANUFACTURED BY CHESS PRODUCING CORP., CHICAGO, ILLINOIS, U.S.A.

CALIFORNIA GIRLS
(Brian Wilson)
Capitol RECORDS
Sea of Tunes Publishing Co.
BMI—2:37
5464
(45-53846)
Produced by:
Brian Wilson
THE BEACH BOYS
MFD. BY CAPITOL RECORDS, INC., U.S.A. • T.M. Capitol MARCA REG.

ABC-PARAMOUNT
Pub. Peer
International
BMI — 3:37
45-10135
AMP 45-3962
Vocal with
Chorus & Orchestra
GEORGIA ON MY MIND
(H. Carmichael - S. Gorrell)
RAY CHARLES
Orchestra & Chorus Conducted by
RALPH BURNS
A PRODUCT OF AM-PAR RECORD CORP.

BOAC Vickers Viscount Turbo Prop

The Esher demo of the song has essentially the same lyrics and arrangement as the finished master. Towards the end of the performance, John gives the following explanation while continuing his guitar playing: "No one was to know that sooner or later she was to go completely berserk under the care of Maharishi Mahesh Yogi. All the people around were very worried about the girl because she was going insane. So, we sang to her." John later speculated that Prudence was "trying to reach God quicker than anyone else."

"Dear Prudence" was recorded in three straight days, starting August 28, on Trident Studio's eight-track. The basic backing was taped that first evening with John's finger-picking guitar style on his Epiphone Casino, George on his Gibson Les Paul guitar and Paul on drums because Ringo was still on his "vacation" from the group. John added a second Casino guitar, and George overdubbed a distorted lead guitar part. The group's use of Fender Twin-Reverb amplifiers gave Lennon's guitar a sharp, clean sound, and Harrison's Telecaster a tough, gritty sound. The next day more overdubs were added to Take 1: Paul's distinctive Rickenbacker bass guitar, tambourine by John and Mal Evans, John's double-tracked lead vocal, and backing vocals and hand claps by John, Paul, George, Mal Evans, Paul's cousin John McCartney and Apple recording artist Jackie Lomax. Finally, on August 30, Paul added the rippling piano heard at the end of the song and a brief bit of flugelhorn. *The White Album* deluxe edition contains a stripped-down version of the song.

Glass Onion

Recorded: September 11 (basic track) & September 12, 13, 16 & 26 (overdubs) & October 10 (orchestra) (Abbey Road Studio 2)
Mixed: October 10 (stereo and mono)

Producer: Chris Thomas (except George Martin on October 10)
Engineers: Ken Scott, John Smith (September 11, 12 & 13 & October 10) & Mike Sheady (September 16 & 26)

John: Lead vocal; acoustic guitar (Jumbo)
Paul: Bass guitar (Fender Jazz); piano; recorder
George: Lead guitar (Stratocaster)
Ringo: Drums
Embellishment: Tambourine
Outside musicians: Henry Datyner, Eric Bowie, Norman Lederman and Ronald Thomas (violins); Eldon Fox and Reginald Kilby (cellos); John Underwood and Kieth Cummings (violas)

"Glass Onion" was described by John Lennon in his Playboy interview as one of his "throwaway" songs. It is full of references to other Beatles songs ("Strawberry Fields Forever," "I Am The Walrus," "Lady Madonna," "The Fool On The Hill" and "Fixing A Hole") and interesting wordplay images (bent backed tulips, cast iron shore and dovetail joint). "Looking through the bent backed tulips to see how the other half live" refers to a floral arrangement at the posh London restaurant Parkes. The Cast Iron Shore is a name for Liverpool's beach and a dovetail joint is a type of construction wood joint.

The line that later drew the most attention was "And here's another clue for you all, the Walrus was Paul." When the "Paul is dead" rumor surfaced in late 1969, people claimed that John's revelation was a vital clue proving Paul's death because the walrus was a symbol of death. In the "I Am The Walrus" sequence from *Magical Mystery Tour*, John was the Walrus, not Paul. According to Lennon, "I threw the line in...just to confuse everyone a bit more." As for Glass Onion, it is British slang for a monocle and was one of the names suggested by John for the Iveys, an Apple act that changed its name to Badfinger.

The Esher demo of "Glass Onion" shows that the song was far from being complete prior to the album sessions. With only a few lines to work with, John sings the first verse three times. And even its lyrics differ from the finished song as John opens with "I told you about Strawberry Fields, well here's a place you know just as real." Lennon's vocal is double-tracked throughout. Beginning with the second verse, he mumbles some gibberish-sounding phrases. The performance moves to shifting tempos for the third verse, with a tambourine in the background. Towards the end, one of the Beatles yells "Help!" The tape concludes with Lennon vocal non sequiturs and singing "Chicago, Chicago, what a wonderful town."

"Glass Onion" was recorded on Abbey Road's eight-track tape machine during a time in the sessions when Chris Thomas was subbing as producer for the vacationing George Martin. The Beatles ran through 34 takes of the song on September 11, with John on his Gibson Model J-160E "Jumbo" acoustic guitar, George on his Fender Stratocaster, Paul on his Fender Jazz Bass and Ringo on drums. *The White Album* deluxe edition contains Take 10, which has a Lennon guide vocal in which he sings "Looking through a hole in the ocean" rather than "Fixing a hole." The next day, John's double-tracked lead vocal and a tambourine were superimposed onto Take 33. The following day, Paul added piano, while Ringo overdubbed his snare drum on the off-beats.

On September 16, embellishments were recorded as musical references to two of the songs mentioned in the lyrics. Although not

Although Prudence Farrow wouldn't come out to play, she did come out for this group picture at the Maharishi Mahesh Yogi's ashram. Left to Right: Prudence (front row far left in chair), Ringo, Maureen, Jane Asher, Paul, George, Pattie, Cynthia, John and Mike Love (seated in a chair). The Maharishi is sitting behind and above Paul and George.

used in the final mixes, a brief bit of mellotron was added after the line about Strawberry Fields. Paul double-tracked a short recorder part after the song's reference to "The Fool On The Hill." One of the recorder parts was punched in over Ringo's superimposed snare drum. Because engineer Ken Scott hit the record mode too early, Ringo's double-tracked snare becomes a single snare at the 1:20 mark seven seconds before the brief recorder solo.

A bizarre mono mix of the song was completed on September 26, while George Martin was still on holiday. John assembled a four-track tape of special effects including a ringing telephone, a sustained organ note, BBC soccer commentator Kenneth Wolstenholme shouting "It's a goal" over the sounds of a roaring crowd and breaking glass. These effects were brought into the mix at various times during the song. The ringing telephone opens the song and is also heard after the middle break and during the ending coda. The soccer broadcast and breaking glass tape loops are used to end the track. This version of the song is on *Anthology 3*.

Upon his return from vacation, Martin was not impressed with the track and suggested adding orchestration in lieu of the special effects. On October 10, Martin's score of four violins, two violas and two cellos was superimposed onto Take 33. The song was mixed for mono and stereo later that day.

Ob-La-Di, Ob-La-Da

Recorded: July 3, 4 & 5 (reggae version); July 8, 9, 11 & 15 (re-make) (all Abbey Road Studio 2 except July 9 & 11 Studio 3)
Mixed: July 15 (mono not used); October 12 (stereo & mono)

Producer: George Martin
Engineers: Geoff Emerick & Richard Lush

Paul: Lead vocal; acoustic guitar (distorted bass part); bass guitar (Rickenbacker); percussion; hand claps
John: Backing vocal; piano; hand claps
George: Backing vocal; acoustic guitar; hand claps
Ringo: Drums; maracas; conga drum; percussion; hand claps

Outside musicians: Jimmy Scott (bongos) & James Gray, Rex Morris & Cyril Reuben (saxophones) (reggae version); three saxophones

"Ob-La-Di, Ob-La-Da" was another song Paul worked on while in Rishikesh. In Barry Miles' *Many Years From Now*, Paul recalls walking through the Indian jungle with his guitar singing "Ob-La-Di, Ob-La-Da, life goes on, bra." Paul took the phrase from Jimmy Scott,

a Nigerian conga player who had been part of the London music scene since the fifties. In Scott's native Yoruban language, "Ob la di ob la da" is an expression meaning "life goes on." The song was another of Paul's fantasy stories, this time inhabited by Desmond and Molly in their barrow in a Caribbean market place.

The rehearsal of the song at George's house reveals that Paul had completed his lyrics and initially envisioned the song as an acoustic guitar-dominated, Jamaican-flavored song. After the first line in the song's bridge, Paul vocalizes instruments with a "chick-a-boom, chick-a-boom, chick-a-boom, boom" refrain that was used in the first version of the song recorded at Abbey Road on three consecutive evenings beginning on July 3. The first session started with seven takes of a rhythm track featuring Paul on acoustic guitar and guide vocal, and Ringo on drums. Paul added another acoustic guitar and his lead vocal to Take 7, but then decided that Take 4 was a better performance. He added acoustic guitar to Take 4 before calling it a night. The following evening, Paul recorded his lead vocal, with John and George adding background "la-la" vocals. The tape was given a reduction mixdown and designated Take 5, to which Paul superimposed another lead vocal. The next day, the track was embellished by outside musicians, including three saxophonists and Jimmy Scott on bongos. Later that evening, a piccolo was added, but Paul shortly thereafter recorded over the piccolo track with another guitar part played and recorded to sound like a bass.

Although this reggae version of the song is quite charming, Paul, as he had done with "I'm Looking Through You," rearranged the tune. The remake was started on July 8, with John on piano, George on acoustic guitar, Paul playing the bass part on acoustic guitar (distorted) and Ringo on drums. Ironically, it was John's resentment at doing a remake of the song that gave the tune its distinctive opening. John arrived at the studio late and stoned. He sat behind the piano and aggressively banged out the opening chords at a fast pace that was carried throughout the performances. The group ran through 12 takes of the song before Paul was satisfied. After a reduction mix of Take 12 was designated Take 13, the group added lead and backing vocals and percussion onto the open tracks. Paul left the studio at 3:00 a.m. with a mono mix of the song.

Apparently dissatisfied with the remake, Paul worked on two takes of a re-remake (designated Takes 20 and 21) the next evening. Mark Lewisohn speculates that this version was recorded with Paul on drums prior to Ringo's arrival. After spending five hours on the second remake, Paul decided to abandon the new version

Paul and John run through *Ob-La-Di, Ob-La-Da*
while Ringo looks on in this photo from Paul Saltzman's book *The Beatles In India*.

and return to the July 8 remake. Paul, John and George recorded over the vocals on Take 13, this time adding laughter and humorous asides. This lighthearted approach probably originated from Paul accidentally reversing the roles of Desmond and Molly in the last verse. Take 13 was given a reduction mix, identified as Take 22, and embellished with hand claps and additional vocals and percussion.

On July 11, the recording resumed with overdubs of three saxophones by outside musicians and a second bass part by Paul played at an octave lower than his first bass part. The best of two mixdowns, Take 23, was further embellished before two mono mixes were made. The next night, two new mono mixes were made. On July 15, after listening to an acetate of the mono mix over the weekend, Paul decided to re-record his lead vocal onto Take 23. Once this task was completed, ten mono mixes were made. "Ob-La-Di, Ob-La-Da" was mixed for stereo on October 12, at which time another mono mix was made. The track was sped up a semitone to B flat.

The rejected reggae version of "Ob-La-Di, Ob-La-Da" was later slated to appear on the aborted *Sessions* LP of the mid-eighties and was nearly released as the B-side to the canceled "Leave My Kitten Alone" single. It was finally released on *Anthology 3*. The *Anthology* version is preceded by Paul shouting "Yes sir, Take 1 of the Mighty Jungle Band" in a mock-Jamaican accent. At the song's conclusion, John shouts "Ob-la-di, ob-la-da, brother." *The White Album* deluxe edition has Take 3 of the song.

Wild Honey Pie

Recorded: August 20 (Abbey Road Studio 2)
Mixed: August 20 (mono); October 13 (stereo)

Producer: George Martin
Engineers: Ken Scott & John Smith

Paul: Lead vocal; acoustic guitars; drums

"Wild Honey Pie" also had its origin in Rishikesh, starting out as a simple sing-along. Paul recorded the song by himself in Abbey Road's Studio Two on August 20, 1968, while George Harrison was in Greece, and John and Ringo were in Studio Three recording an edit piece for "Yer Blues" and supervising the mono mix of "Revolution 9." Paul described "Wild Honey Pie" as "a little experimental piece" built up in the studio over one basic rhythm track. He started with acoustic guitar parts, featuring "a lot of vibrato on the strings." In addition to playing three guitars, Paul added three vocals and played drums. The 53-second track was mixed for mono at the end of the session, and for stereo on October 13.

The Continuing Story Of Bungalow Bill

Recorded: October 8 (Abbey Road Studio 2)
Mixed: October 9 (stereo & mono)

Producer: George Martin
Engineers: Ken Scott & Mike Sheady

John: Lead vocals & whistles; acoustic guitar (Jumbo); organ
Paul: Backing vocals; bass guitar (Rickenbacker)
George: Backing vocals; acoustic guitar (Gibson J-200)
Ringo: Backing vocals; drums
Chris Thomas: Mellotron (mandolin, bassoon & guitar effects)
Embellishments: Tambourine; hand claps, whistles and vocals (including Yoko Ono, Maureen Starkey and others)

"The Continuing Story Of Bungalow Bill" was written in India. John wrote the song "about a guy [American Richard A. Cooke III] in Maharishi's meditation camp who took a short break to go shoot a few poor tigers, and then came back to commune with God." The Bungalow Bill name is a mutation of American showman Buffalo Bill and the bungalow living quarters in Rishikesh. John described the tune as "a sort of teenage social-comment song and a bit of a joke."

The Esher demo, featuring John on lead vocal and acoustic guitar, has the same basic arrangement and lyrics as the finished master. The background hand claps and vocals of jungle sound effects give the performance a party atmosphere that carried over to the recording of the song at Abbey Road more than four months later. The tape ends with John asking, "What did Bungalow Bill kill?"

"Bungalow Bill" was recorded in three takes at the end of a productive 16-hour session held on October 8 that also produced John's "I'm So Tired." The backing track consists of John and George on acoustic guitars, Paul on his Rickenbacker bass and Ringo on drums. *The White Album* deluxe edition contains Take 2, with only John and Yoko on the chorus and no "All the children sing." Yoko plays the role of Bill's mommy singing "Not when he looked so fierce" and "If looks could kill it would have been us instead of him." Overdubs to Take 3 include John on organ, Chris Thomas on mellotron (mandolin sounds on the first part of the song and then bassoon, heard prominently during the ending breakdown of the song), Paul on a second bass part (heard only at the end of the third verse) and tambourine. John gives a spirited lead vocal performance and is backed by singing, hand claps and whistles provided by Paul, George, Ringo, Yoko and others at the studio, including Ringo's wife Maureen. The song's opening flamenco-style guitar sound (one of the mellotron's pre-recorded samples) was edited to the front of the master tape. The track ends with John shouting "Eh up!"

Deep in the jungle where the mighty tiger lies
Bill and his elephants were taken by surprise
So Captain Marvel zapped him right between the eyes

While My Guitar Gently Weeps

Recorded: July 25 (demo); August 16 & September 3 & 5 (first band version); September 5 & 6 (remake) (Abbey Road Studio 2)
Mixed: October 14 (stereo & mono)

Producer: George Martin (July 25 & August 16 only)
Engineers: Ken Scott & John Smith (except Richard Lush on July 25)

George: Lead vocal; acoustic guitar (J-200); organ; lead guitar and backwards guitar (on first band version only)
Paul: Backing vocal; piano; bass guitar (Fender Jazz); harmonium (on demo only)
John: Organ (on first band version only)
Ringo: Drums; castanets; tambourine
Outside musician: Eric Clapton (lead guitar on Les Paul)

Lennon's "Eh-up!" effectively links "Bungalow Bill" to "While My Guitar Gently Weeps." In his book, *I Me Mine*, Harrison explains that he was reading *The I Ching*, the Chinese book of change, around the time he wrote the song. The book is based on the Eastern concept that everything is relative to everything else, as opposed to the Western view that things are merely coincidental. While visiting his parents, he decided to write a song on the first thing he saw upon opening a book "as it would be relative to that moment, at *that* time." George randomly opened a book and saw the phrase "gently weeps." He then began writing the lyrics.

The Esher demo, which lasts just over two and a half minutes, is structurally similar to the finished master, but has a totally different feel. The stark arrangement features George on acoustic guitar, playing in the finger-picking style the group learned in India. The lyrics to the third line of the first verse differ from the finished master, with George singing "The problems you sow and the troubles you're reaping." In addition, the demo contains a third verse absent from the finished master. The deleted lyrics are: "I look at the trouble and hate that is raging/while my guitar gently weeps/As I'm sitting here doing nothing but aging/still my guitar gently weeps."

The first studio recording of the song took place at Abbey Road on July 25. After several rehearsals, a beautiful solo performance of George singing and playing acoustic guitar was recorded, apparently for demo purposes. Paul added a simple but effective harmonium part towards the end of the song. This early acoustic take is one of the highlights of *Anthology 3*. It runs for about three and a half minutes and contains a third verse with lyrics different than the Esher demo: "I look from the wings at the play you are staging/while my guitar gently weeps/As I'm sitting here doing nothing but aging/still my guitar gently weeps."

On August 16, the band recorded 14 takes of the song with George on acoustic guitar, John on organ, Paul on bass and Ringo on drums. *The White Album* deluxe edition contains Take 2, which has the July 25 lyrics. Take 14 was run at 42½ cycles per second to form Take 15. The next day, George left for a long weekend in Greece, resulting in the song being ignored for a few weeks.

By the time the group returned to the song in September, they had recorded "Dear Prudence" on Trident's eight-track. Upon learning that EMI had an eight-track recorder being held for quality review, the Beatles persuaded Ken Scott to have the new recorder installed in Studio Two. "While My Guitar Gently Weeps" was the first song recorded on Abbey Road's new eight-track. On September 3, Take 15 was transferred to eight-track tape and renamed Take 16. George spent several hours recording a backwards guitar solo. George Martin was on vacation for these September sessions.

On September 5, Harrison got a ride into London with Eric Clapton. During this car ride, he asked Clapton to play lead guitar on "While My Guitar Gently Weeps." It is not clear if Clapton was in the studio when the group recorded additional parts to Take 16, including two Harrison vocals, maracas, drums and another guitar solo. Upon hearing the playback, Harrison was not pleased with how the song was going, so he decided to start over again.

By this time, Clapton was definitely in the studio. Harrison, on acoustic guitar and vocal, led the group through 28 takes numbered 17 through 45, with Clapton playing lead guitar on his Les Paul, McCartney on piano (or, on some takes, organ) and Ringo on drums. Clapton's playing that evening was brilliant, giving the song the gently weeping guitar called for in its title. His presence inspired the group to take George's song seriously and perform at their best.

Although Take 25 would later be deemed the best and given overdubs, the band played on. The deluxe edition has Take 27, which breaks down when George flubs his vocal. John, who apparently is in the control room, interrupts the performance with "Hold it, Hari." George replies, "I tried to do a Smokey and I aren't Smokey," referring to Motown singer Smokey Robinson. On September 6, the group overdubbed George's double-tracked lead vocal, Paul's bass, organ and backing vocal, and Ringo's castanets and tambourine.

Although stereo and mono mixes were made on October 7, the song was remixed a week later on October 14 to alter Clapton's lead guitar. Apparently the guitarist was concerned that his playing didn't have enough of a Beatles sound. Chris Thomas wobbled the oscillator during the mix, giving the guitar its distinct sound. Because Harrison's organ part was on the same track as Clapton's guitar solo, it also has the same flanged sound.

Happiness Is A Warm Gun

Recorded: September 23, 24 & 25 (Abbey Road Studio 2)
Mixed: September 25 & 26 (mono); October 15 (stereo)

Producer: Chris Thomas
Engineers: Ken Scott & Mike Sheady

John: Lead and backing vocals; guitar (Casino); organ
Paul: Backing vocal; bass guitar (Rickenbacker)
George: Backing vocal; lead guitar (fuzz in "I Need A Fix" section)
Ringo: Drums, including overdubbed hi-hat and snare; tambourine
Embellishments: Piano; tuba(not heard in mix)

The final selection on Side One, "Happiness Is A Warm Gun," is one of the most interesting tracks on the album. It consists of three separate parts: "I Need A Fix," "Mother Superior Jumped The Gun" and "Happiness Is A Warm Gun." At the time the Esher demo was recorded, John had only written what would be the ending lines for the "I Need A Fix" section and the one-line "Mother Superior Jumped The Gun" section. "Mother" was one of John's names for Yoko. After going through both existing elements of the song, John sings "Yoko Ono, oh no, Yoko Ono, oh yes" before returning to "I Need A Fix" and "Mother Superior Jumped The Gun."

The lyrics to the first part of the song came from phrases supplied primarily by Derek Taylor during an evening get together of Derek, John, Neil Aspinall and Pete Shotton. John told the gang he had a half-written song and needed help finishing the lyrics. He wanted a way to describe a really smart girl, and Taylor gave him the song's opening line, "She's not a girl who misses much." Taylor told of a man who enjoyed wearing moleskin gloves during sex and supplied the image of a lizard's quick movement on glass windows. This became "She's well acquainted with the touch of the velvet hand like a lizard on a window pane." "The man in the crowd with the multicolored mirrors on his hobnail boots" was inspired by a newspaper story about a soccer fan who had been arrested by the police for having mirrors on the tips of his shoes so he could look up ladies' skirts. The next line, "Lying with his eyes while his hands are busy working overtime," was drawn from another news story about a man who used a set of fake hands to divert attention away from his real hands as he stole items from a counter case. The line about eating something and donating it to the National Trust was a reference to defecating on public property. John artfully tied all of these images together to complete the "I Need A Fix" segment.

The "Happiness Is A Warm Gun" section was the final piece of the puzzle. The phrase "Happiness is a warm gun" came from the title of an article appearing in May 1968 issue of The American Rifleman, the official magazine of the National Rifle Association, which was shown to John by George Martin. (The NRA-inspired phrase was a takeoff on Charles Schulz's Peanuts comic strip book *Happiness Is A Warm Puppy*.) Part of this section was lifted from an unused half-spoken bit from "I'm So Tired." Towards the end of the Esher demo of "I'm So Tired," John sings "When I hold you in your arms, when you show me each one of your charms, I wonder should I get up and go to the funny farm," followed by "no, no, no" and then returning to the song's bridge. For "Happiness Is A Warm Gun," John slightly altered the first line and rewrote the remaining lines to fit the warm gun motif. In his Playboy interview, John admitted that the line "When I hold you in my arms and I feel my finger on your trigger" had a double meaning as he was fresh in his relationship with Yoko and "very sexually oriented" at the time.

Recording on "Happiness Is A Warm Gun In Your Hand" (as it was initially titled) got underway on September 23 utilizing the eight-track machine under the production of Chris Thomas. The song's changing tempos caused problems for the band, resulting in 45 unacceptable takes that evening alone. The next night Takes 46 through 70 were recorded. All of these takes featured John on guide vocal and his Epiphone Casino, George on electric guitar, Paul on his Rickenbacker bass and Ringo on drums.

After listening to the tapes, it was decided that the first two parts of Take 53 (up through 1:34) and the third and final part of Take 65 were the best performances. On September 25, these two takes were edited together and named Take 65. That evening the following parts were superimposed onto Take 65: John's lead vocal (triple-tracked in some places); "happiness, bang, bang, shoot, shoot" backing vocals by John, Paul and George; additional bass by Paul; organ; piano; tuba (all but mixed out in the final masters); tambourine; and Ringo's hi-hat and song-ending snare drum couplet.

The song was mixed for mono on September 25 and 26, and for stereo on October 15. At the mixing stage, the first "I need a fix 'cause I'm going down" line was deleted to provide a brief instrumental passage. A careful listen 57 seconds into the stereo version reveals John singing "down" as his vocal was brought back into the mix a tad too early. *The White Album* deluxe edition contains Take 19. John's guide vocal is interesting (one time singing "When I feel my finger on your arms"), but not as strong as the finished master.

John considered "Happiness Is A Warm Gun" one of his best songs. Paul and George reportedly said the track was their favorite on the album.

HAPPINESS IS A WARM GUN

Primer popping with pop from early boyhood

By WARREN W. HERLIHY

IN my gun cabinet two "little guns" have a special place of honor. One is a Remington Model 514 single-shot .22; the other, a Winchester Model 37 boy's 20 ga. shotgun.

The bores are clean and the barrels have a good bit of their original bluing. Sometimes I open the cabinet to admire their polished stocks and well-oiled metal. They bring back memories.

I remember a little boy, my son, now a strapping man of 18, and his joy when he got his first gun. I remember those grand times we had over the years, father and son, each as enthusiastic about guns as the other.

It is hard to believe, that it was 11 years ago when I was getting ready to go off on a Sunday afternoon for a few hours shooting with some buddies.

I was on the way to the car, loaded down with guns, shooting mat, the works, when a little voice said, "Dad, take me."

It was son John, then all of 7 years old. I pondered a moment: sure, he was young, but—off we went. And what a time we had that Sunday. I let him shoot an M1 carbine. The stock was short, the recoil mild, and John enjoyed every shot he cranked off.

Lots of shooting

He was hooked, no doubt about it. So we went off to a nearby quarry and shot, shot, shot for the next few months. He loved shooting, and had so much fun that there was only one thing to do: get him a gun of his own.

I decided on a Remington Model 514, the one that's still in my cabinet. It was a real sweetheart just as it came out of the box, but I thought John would have better luck with it if a few modifications were made.

The stock was shortened to fit John, the trigger smoothed up and adjusted for a 3-lb. pull, and a Lyman receiver sight and a Redfield front sight with interchangeable elements were mounted. Finally, we fitted it with a small sling.

The day it was ready we took off for the quarry, loaded down with ammo. John got the feel of the little Reming-

ton right off and in no time flat he was putting round after round into the black at 50 yds.

We banged away in the quarry for a few weeks until it was quite clear John was ready for a hunt up Crow Canyon for squirrels. That was real shooting. Warm sun, big, puffy clouds chasing across the sky, and all the squirrels anyone could ask for.

John really had the bug. Every weekend it was the same story. "Let's go shooting, Dad." And, since I sort of like to shoot myself, we went.

By the time he was 8, I figured John was ready for a shotgun. But how much recoil could he take? What gauge would be best? That's where shooting friends come in. After lots of jaw-boning with gunsmiths, sporting goods store owners and shotgunners, I decided on a Winchester Model 37. With its short stock, recoil pad and swell workmanship, the 20-ga. was a real rugged field gun, just the thing to start a lad off with.

Clay bird practice

Long and hard we practiced. I'd throw the clay birds by hand, John would try to knock them down. Once he could hit the clay birds more times than not, it was off to the local trap range. I'll tell you, it did me a world of good to watch John work that little Winchester. Pretty soon he was popping the discs while I was missing them.

It was fall before we knew it, and time for pheasant hunting. Opening day of the season we tried our luck. Poor old dad missed his chances, but not John. He connected with a big rooster with long spurs, flushed by his dog, Happy.

The years went by. Happy years. Hunting ducks and geese in mud up to the arm pits, rain streaming down our necks. Through those years that kid of mine made kills that would turn a veteran shotgunner blue—not with cold but with envy.

Soon John was old enough to take the NRA Hunter Safety course. Maybe he did know a good bit about guns and safety, but it was a chance to let him hear it from someone else. It's a fine course and he learned a lot from a good instructor.

Boys have a way of growing up. And one day, just before bird season, John announced that the 20-ga. was too small. Now he wanted a "big" gun. We shopped around, checking out weight, stock fit, swing, action. We set-

The Herlihys ate pheasant after young John's first wildfowl hunt.

tled for a pump gun, a Hi-Standard 12-ga. Model 200 with ventilated rib. It suited John to a tee. He got his limit with it that year and has done real well with it ever since.

John has other "big" guns now. For rifles he has a fine old .30-30 Winchester Model 94 and a Remington Model 700 with a 6X Weaver scope. He handles them like a man, which is natural because he is a man now.

But we still keep those "little" guns because they stand for something. To me, they stand for the comradeship and good times a father and son can have when they share a love of guns and shooting. I'm never sorry I gave in when John pleaded, "Take me, Dad." ∎

Martha My Dear

Recorded: October 4 (Trident Studios)
Mixed: October 5 (mono & stereo); October 7 (EQ changed)

Producer: George Martin
Engineers: Barry Sheffield & unknown

Paul: Lead vocal; piano; bass guitar (Rickenbacker); electric guitar; hand claps
George: Guitar (Casino)
Ringo: Drums

Outside musicians: Bernard Miller, Dennis McConnell, Lou Sofier & Les Maddox (violins); Leo Brinbaum & Henry Myerscough (violas); Reginald Kilbey & Frederick Alexander (cellos); Leon Calvert (trumpet & flugelhorn); Stanley Reynolds & Ronnie Hughes (trumpets); Tony Tonstall (French horn); Ted Barker (trombone); Alf Reece (tuba)

Side Two opens with Paul's piano-driven ballad "Martha My Dear." While the song was definitely named for Paul's sheep dog, Martha, there is debate as to who was Paul's inspiration — former girlfriend Jane Asher or his sheep dog. In The Beatles Book (No. 64, November 1968), Mal Evans reported: "NOT dedicated to Paul's Good Dog Martha! Theme is You Were Meant For Me." In other words, a sentimental love song inspired by a woman. But in Miles' *Many Years From Now*, Paul said: "I'm not really speaking to Martha. It's a communication of some sort of affection but in a slightly abstract way 'You silly girl, look what you've done...' Whereas it would appear to anybody else to be a song to a girl called Martha, it's actually a dog, and our relationship was platonic, believe me."

The song was recorded at Trident Studios on October 4 in one take and several overdubs. It features Paul on piano and vocals. Although it has been speculated that Paul played drums on the song, Mal stated in his report that Ringo bashed a hole in his brand new bass drum skin that night.

George Martin's score, consisting of four violins, two violas, two cellos, three trumpets, French horn, trombone, tuba and flugel-horn, was recorded onto Take 1. After the musicians left the studio, Paul re-recorded his vocal and added hand claps. The following night, Paul added bass and guitar to the song. Mono and stereo mixes were made that evening, although the equalization was changed at Abbey Road on October 7 when the tapes were copied. *The White Album* deluxe edition contains a stripped-down mix without the strings or brass.

I'm So Tired

Recorded: October 8 (Abbey Road Studio 2)
Mixed: October 15 (stereo and mono)

Producer: George Martin
Engineers: Ken Scott & Mike Sheady

John: Lead vocal; guitar (Casino); organ
Paul: Backing vocal; bass guitar (Rickenbacker); electric piano
George: Guitar (Stratocaster)
Ringo: Drums
Unused embellishment: Harmony vocals by John, Paul and George

"I'm So Tired" is another of John's songs written while in India. According to John, the all-day meditation regime in Rishikesh prevented him from sleeping at night. On top of that, he was missing Yoko. The line "You know it's three weeks, I'm going insane" indicates that the song may have been written at the three-week mark of John's stay in India.

The Esher demo shows that the song was complete by the time the group began rehearsals for the upcoming album. As discussed above, the demo contains a spoken segment that was dropped from the song and rewritten to form the final section of "Happiness Is A Warm Gun."

"I'm So Tired" was started and finished in 14 takes on October 8 on Abbey Road's eight-track tape machine. The live basic track features John on lead vocal and electric guitar, George on his Fender Stratocaster, Paul on his Rickenbacker bass and Ringo on drums. Overdubs added to Take 14 include electric piano, organ and additional vocals from John and Paul. George overdubbed a guitar part on his Fender Stratocaster answering John's vocal during the verses, but it is not present in the mix. At the end of the recording, John mumbles "monsieur, monsieur, how about another one?" When played backwards, it sounded like "Paul is dead man, miss him, miss him" to those looking for clues of Paul's death. The song was mixed for stereo and mono on October 15.

Anthology 3 has an edit of Takes 3, 6 and 9. Take 7 is included on *The White Album* deluxe edition. At the end, John says "If you think it was good. If not, scrap it." The deluxe edition also has the master Take 14, but with George's lead lines mixed back in.

John considered "I'm So Tired" as one of his favorites, saying "I just like the sound of it, and I sing it well." Paul liked the line "And curse Sir Walter Raleigh/He was such a stupid git," stating "That's a classic line and it's so John that there's no doubt who wrote it."

Blackbird

Recorded: June 11 (Abbey Road Studio 2)
Mixed: October 13 (stereo & mono)

Producer: George Martin
Engineers: Geoff Emerick & Phil McDonald

Paul: Lead vocal; acoustic guitar; foot-tapping
Sound effects: European Blackbird

"Blackbird" was written by Paul at his Scotland farm. According to Paul, he developed the melody on guitar based on a Bach composition and took it to another level, fitting words to it. In Miles' *Many Years From Now*, McCartney states that he wrote the song with a black woman in mind, relating to the civil rights movement in the United States. He kept the song symbolic so others could apply the song's empowerment message to their particular problems.

The Esher demo has the same lyrics and arrangement as the finished master, except that its ending is a bit different. The song was recorded on June 11 by Paul in Abbey Road's Studio Two. Although John was in Studio Three that evening working on tape loop sound effects for "Revolution 9," film shot by a camera crew shows that John was present and participated in the session, even briefly playing acoustic guitar (though not recorded). George Martin's suggestion that the song come to a complete halt before the final verse was accepted by Paul, but Martin's idea for orchestral embellishments was rejected. The discussion would prove fruitful when McCartney briefly played another of his folk guitar songs, "Mother Nature's Son," and realized that brass would be effective on that song.

Paul sang and played acoustic guitar through 32 takes (of which 11 were complete) before being satisfied. While it has been written that he was accompanied by a metronome, that is not correct. The percussion-like sound keeping the beat is actually Paul tapping his foot on the studio floor (which was separately miked onto one of the tracks). Although a separate microphone was used to pick up the room's ambient sound, this track was wiped when Paul double-tracked his vocal on parts of the song onto Take 32. The song was mixed for mono at the end of the session.

When the song was mixed for stereo on October 13, Paul decided that he wanted to add bird sound effects from the EMI tape library. After the mix was completed, Ken Townsend noticed that the sound of a thrush had accidentally been used. The song was mixed again, this time with the sound of a European Blackbird. The song was also given a mono remix to incorporate the blackbird

sound effects. *Anthology 3* contains Take 4, an equally effective performance. *The White Album* deluxe edition contains Take 28, which has additional humming, vocalization and studio banter.

Piggies

Recorded: September 19 & 20; October 10 (Abbey Road Studio 2)
Mixed: October 11 (mono & stereo)

Producer: Chris Thomas (September 19 & 20); George Martin (October 10 orchestral overdubs)
Engineers: Ken Scott; Mike Sheady (September 19 & 20); John Smith (October 10)

George: Lead vocal; acoustic Guitar (J-200)
Paul: Backing vocal; bass guitar (Rickenbacker)
John: Backing vocal
Ringo: Tambourine
Chris Thomas: Harpsichord
Sound effects: Pig sounds
Unused vocals: Laughter (all four Beatles); pig snorting (George)

Outside musicians: Henry Datyner, Eric Bowie, Norman Lederman and Ronald Thomas (violins); Eldon Fox and Reginald Kilby (cellos); John Underwood and Kieth Cummings (violas)

"Piggies" is a George social commentary songs dating back to 1966. Its stinging lyrics bring back memories of "Taxman." Although "pig" was a sixties derogatory term aimed at police, his target was the upper class. His mother supplied the line "What they need's a damn good whacking" to rhyme with "backing" and "lacking."

The Esher demo features George on acoustic guitar and double-tracked lead vocals. At that stage the song's last line was "Clutching forks and knives to cut their pork chops." John improved on this with "Clutching forks and knives to eat their bacon."

The rhythm track was recorded at Abbey Road on September 19 with Chris Thomas subbing as producer. It was completed in 11 takes on a four-track machine. The backing track features George on his Gibson J-200 acoustic guitar, Thomas on harpsichord, Paul on his Rickenbacker bass and Ringo on tambourine. Apparently John did not attend the session. The next night, the four track tape was copied to an eight-track tape (designated Take 12) to allow for over-dubs. Three Harrison vocals and backing harmony vocals from John and Paul were recorded onto some of the open tracks. John put together a tape loop of pig sounds taken from the EMI sound effects tape library, which were superimposed onto Take 12.

PIGGIES

(1) HAVE YOU SEEN THE LITTLE PIGGIES, CRAWLING IN THE DIRT? AND FOR ALL THE LITTLE PIGGIES LIFE IS GETTING WORSE — ALWAYS HAVING DIRT TO PLAY AROUND IN.

(2) HAVE YOU SEEN THE BIGGER PIGGIES IN THEIR STARCHED WHITE SHIRTS? YOU WILL FIND THE BIGGER PIGGIES STIRRING UP THE DIRT, ALWAYS HAVE CLEAN **SHIRTS** TO PLAY AROUND IN —

BRIDGE

IN THEIR STYES WITH ALL THEIR BACKING
THEY DONT CARE WHAT GOES ON AROUND
IN THEIR EYES THERES SOMETHING LACKING
WHAT THEY NEED'S A DAMN GOOD WHACKING.

(3) EVERYWHERE THERES LOTS OF PIGGIES — LIVING PIGGIES LIVES — YOU CAN SEE THEM OUT FOR DINNER WITH THEIR PIGGY WIVES — CLUTCHING FORKS AND KNIVES TO EAT THEIR ~~PORK CHOPS~~.
BACON

(4) EVERYWHERE THERES LOTS OF PIGGIES — PLAYING PIGGY PRANKS YOU WILL SEE THEM ON THEIR TROTTERS AT THE PIGGY BANKS — GIVING PIGGY THANKS TO THEE, PIG BROTHER.

The above lyrics to *Piggies* were transcribed by Beatles roadie Mal Evans at Abbey Road on the back of a blank EMI recording sheet. The fourth verse was crossed out and not recorded. George later added the verse to his live performances of the song. The lyrics to *Helter Skelter* appearing on page 163 were also transcribed by Evans.

On October 10, George Martin's orchestral score of four violins, two cellos and two violas was added to Take 12 using the same musicians who would later play on "Glass Onion." The mono and stereo mixes were completed the following night. *The White Album* deluxe edition contains an instrumental backing of the song.

Rocky Raccoon

Recorded: August 15 (Abbey Road Studio 2)
Mixed: August 15 (mono); October 10 (stereo)

Producer: George Martin
Engineers: Ken Scott & John Smith

Paul: Lead and backing vocals; acoustic guitar (D-28)
John: Backing vocal; bass guitar (Fender VI); harmonica; accordion
George: Backing vocal; bass guitar
Ringo: Drums
George Martin: Piano

"Rocky Raccoon" was written in India by Paul, with a bit of help from John and Donovan. The song was originally titled "Rocky Sassoon," but was changed to "Rocky Raccoon" because "it sounded more cowboyish." According to Paul, "I like talking blues so I started off like that, then I did my tongue-in-cheek parody of a western and threw in some amusing lines."

The Esher demo lacks the talking blues intro as well as the verse about the doctor stinking of gin. The arrangement is similar to the finished master; however, the demo has more of a country and western feel to it, with George playing country-sounding lead fills after Paul's double-tracked vocal lines.

"Rocky Raccoon" was recorded in a single session held on August 15. The rhythm track, perfected in nine takes, features Paul on vocal and acoustic guitar, John on harmonica and Fender Bass VI, and Ringo on drums. As was the case with "Hey Jude," Paul did not want George playing lead guitar fills on the song, and Harrison was once again relegated to the control room.

The multiple outtakes of the song show that Paul was still formulating the words to the introduction and the doctor verse. Take 8, which is on *Anthology 3* and *The White Album* deluxe edition, has John proclaiming, "He was a fool onto himself." Paul uses this line early in his intro, in which Paul tells us that Rocky came from a little town in Minnesota. This is a tip of the hat to Bob Dylan, who grew up in Hibbing, Minnesota. During the start of the doctor verse, Paul flubs the lyrics, having the doctor "sminking" of gin. This causes Paul to laugh and ad-lib his way through the rest of the verse.

On Take 9, McCartney mimics Dylan's vocal style in his introduction. Paul was satisfied with this performance, so the group proceeded with overdubs. The first set wiped John's harmonica and bass track, which was replaced with George on bass and Ringo's snare drum giving a gun-shot effect following the line "Daniel was hot, he drew first and shot." Most of the instruments were given a reduction mix and bounced down to another tape to free up a track for additional overdubs. John re-recorded his harmonica part that had been previouslyrecorded over. George Martin provided the piano solos for the middle and end instrumental breaks, which were recorded on the Challen "jangle box" piano with the tape running at half-speed. When played back at the proper speed, the piano had a rollicking honky-tonk sound conjuring up images of a western saloon. John's accordion part was superimposed over the last verse. John, Paul and George added their backing harmony vocals. The song was mixed for mono at the end of the session, and for stereo on October 10.

Don't Pass Me By

Recorded: June 5 & 6; July 12 & 22 (Abbey Road Studio 2)
Mixed: October 11 (mono & stereo)

Producer: George Martin
Engineers: Geoff Emerick (June 5 & 6 & July 12); Ken Scott (July 22)
Phil McDonald (June 5 & 6); Richard Lush (July 12 & 22)

Ringo: Lead vocal; piano; sleigh bells
Paul: Drums; piano; bass guitar (Rickenbacker)
Outside musician: Jack Fallon (country-fiddle violin)

Ringo's "Don't Pass Me By" was the oldest song recorded for the album. Although the drummer had bits of the song completed back in 1963, he had to wait five years to get the Beatles to record his first solo composition. Oddly enough, EMI recording sheets initially listed the song as "Ringo's Tune (Untitled)" even though he had called the song "Don't Pass Me By" in a 1963 interview.

Paul and Ringo recorded the backing track, which consisted solely of Ringo's piano miked through a guitar amplifier and Leslie speaker, and Paul's drums, in three takes on June 5. Paul overdubbed a second piano part and Ringo added sleigh bells. Two reduction mixes were made, with Take 5 being the best. Ringo added a lead vocal, which was recorded over by one of two bass overdubs by Paul. Although a reduction mix (Take 6) was made, it was decided to go back to Take 5 when recording resumed the next day. Ringo's vocal was double-tracked and recorded at a slower tape speed to raise its pitch when played back at the normal speed. A new reduction mix was made and designated Take 7. Paul then added a new bass part on his Rickenbacker.

No additional work was done on the song until July 12, when Paul added bass, Ringo added piano and Jack Fallon played the tune's country-fiddle violin part. The song was then mixed for mono. The stereo mix was made on October 11. The mono version runs faster than the stereo version and has a different ending fiddle solo.

By the time Ringo entered Abbey Road on July 22 to re-record his lead vocal to "Good Night," a decision had been made to come up with an introduction for "Don't Pass Me By." On this date, two different edit pieces were recorded. Paul ran through four takes of tinkling around on piano, with the 45-second Take 4 being considered the best. George Martin taped a 48-second instrumental passage, previously recorded for the *Yellow Submarine* cartoon, using the same musicians present for the orchestral overdub for "Good Night." The two recordings met different fates. An eight second segment of McCartney's piano piece was edited to the mono and stereo mixes of "Don't Pass Me By" on October 11. Martin's orchestral piece was not used, but later appeared as the opening track on *Anthology 3* (retitled "A Beginning").

Anthology 3 contains the first 2:40 of the instrumental backing track of Take 3 with a Ringo vocal from Take 5. This stark version of the song has some later-mixed-out vocal ad-libs by Ringo and is missing the song's yet-to-be-recorded fiddle passages. *The White Album* deluxe edition contains the orchestral introduction followed by an early take of the song with a different vocal. At the end, Ringo says "This is some friendly." That ad lib led to the song being temporarily titled "This Is Some Friendly."

Why Don't We Do It In The Road?

Recorded: October 9 (Abbey Road Studio 1)
Mixed: October 16 (mono & stereo)

Producer: None
Engineer: Ken Townsend

Paul: Lead vocal; acoustic guitar (slapping of soundboard); piano; bass guitar (Rickenbacker); hand claps; electric guitar (Casino)
Ringo: Drums

According to Paul, "Why Don't We Do It In The Road?" was "a primitive statement to do with sex or...freedom." The idea for the song came from Paul observing a male monkey hop on the back of a female monkey for sex in the Indian jungle.

The song was recorded by Paul, with Ken Townsend serving as engineer, at Abbey Road on October 9. McCartney sang and played acoustic guitar on five takes. All solo performances start with Paul tapping out the beat on the sounding board of his guitar. Although the finished master is an all-out raunchy rocker, the early takes consist of Paul alternating between gentle, high-pitched vocals and his gritty rocker voice. Take 4 is on *Anthology 3*. Towards the end of the performance, Paul changes the line "No one will be watching us" to "People will be watching us." As the song ends, Paul asks Ken, "What do you think of all that; do you think I can do it better?" Apparently he thought Paul could do better because a fifth and final take was recorded, which is included on *The White Album* deluxe edition prior to overdubbs. Paul added piano to Take 5 that evening.

The next night, while George and John were involved with George Martin's string overdubs to "Piggies" and "Glass Onion" in Abbey Road's Studio Two, Paul had Ken and Ringo join him in Studio Three to complete his song. Vocals, hand claps, Rickenbacker bass and Ringo's drums were recorded onto Take 5, which was given a reduction mix to form Take 6. Paul then added an electric guitar part played on his Epiphone Casino. The song was mixed for mono and stereo on October 16.

I Will

Recorded: September 16 (Abbey Road Studio 2)
Mixed: September 26 (mono); October 14 (stereo)

Producer: Chris Thomas
Engineers: Ken Scott and Mike Sheady

Paul: Lead and backing vocals; acoustic guitar (D-28); acoustic 12-string guitar; sung bass part
John: Temple blocks (wooden instrument a/k/a "skulls"); maracas
Ringo: Drums (selected use of cymbals, snare, kick drum and tom)

Paul's raunchy rocker is followed by his gentle love song "I Will." Paul recalls having the melody for the song prior to his stay in Rishikesh. While in India, he tried collaborating with Donovan, but was not satisfied with the lyrics they came up with. Because the song was incomplete, it was not rehearsed at Kinfauns.

The song was recorded on September 16 at an Abbey Road session attended by Paul, John and Ringo, and produced by Chris Thomas. The trio went through 67 takes of the song with Paul on vocal and acoustic guitar, Ringo on drums and John on skulls and maracas. *Anthology 3* contains Take 1, showing that Paul had the basic arrangement worked out prior to entering the studio.

During the session, Paul drifted into a few spontaneous performances. One of these (Take 19) was a 2:21 ad-lib containing the words "Can you take me back where I came from, can you take me back?" A 28-second segment from the end of this recording was used as an uncredited link track between "Cry Baby Cry" and "Revolution 9." Other songs included: "Step Inside Love," a tune Paul wrote for Cilla Black in 1967; "Los Paranoias," a madcap jam with silly made-up-on-the-spot lyrics; an impromptu jam of Elvis Presley's version of "Blue Moon;" and "The Way You Look Tonight," whose lyrics came almost exclusively from "I Will." The first three are included on *The White Album* deluxe edition, along with Takes 13 and 29 of "I Will."

At the end of the session, it was decided that Take 65 was the best performance. The four-track tape was copied to another tape to allow for overdubs and was designated Take 68. The following evening, Paul overdubbed additional vocals, including an imitation of a bass guitar, and an acoustic 12-string guitar part. Paul's lead vocal was treated with ADT (artificial double tracking) when the song was mixed for mono on September 26 and for stereo on October 14.

Julia

Recorded: October 13 (Abbey Road Studio 2)
Mixed: October 13 (stereo & mono)

Producer: George Martin
Engineers: Ken Scott & John Smith

John: Lead vocal; acoustic guitar

The final track on Side Two is John's beautiful ballad, "Julia," which was written primarily in India. Julia was John's mother, who died when he was 17 years old. The song's depiction of Julia as an "ocean child" is a reference to Yoko, whose name means "child of the ocean" in Japanese. In his Playboy interview, John described the song as "a combination of Yoko and my mother blended into one."

Some of the song's lyrics, including its opening couplet, were adopted from *Sand And Foam*, a collection of writings and drawings by Kahlil Gibran, a Lebanese poet and philosopher who moved to America. Gibran's words "Half of what I say is meaningless, but I say it so the other half may reach you" became "Half of what I say is meaningless/But I say it just to reach you, Julia." Gibran's "When Life does not find a singer to sing her heart she produces a philosopher to speak her mind" was changed to "When I cannot sign my heart/I can only speak my mind." The song's imagery was inspired by Yoko, who sent letters to John while he was in India. According to John, "She

would write things like 'I am a cloud. Watch for me in the sky." This blending of people and nature probably influenced John's use of phrases such as "seashell eyes," "windy smile," "hair of floating sky," "sleeping sand" and "silent cloud."

John learned the finger-picking guitar style used on the song from Donovan and/or Gypsy Dave while in Rishikesh. Donovan recalls that "John was keen to learn the finger-style guitar I played and he was a good student." This style was also used by John on "Dear Prudence," as well as some of his post-Beatles recordings such as "Look At Me" and Yoko's "Remember Love."

The Esher demo shows that John had completed "Julia" prior to the start of the sessions; however, he did not record the song until October 13, making it the last new selection recorded for the album. It is John's first and only solo recording for a Beatles record. *The White Album* deluxe edition contains a rehearsal in which John initially strums the song because it's hard to sing while finger-picking. "Julia" was completed in three takes featuring John on lead vocal and acoustic guitar (with a capo on the second fret). *Take 2*, which is on *Anthology 3*, is a mostly instrumental run through that breaks down past the midway point. On his third attempt, John plays the tune perfectly. His lead vocal was then recorded twice to allow for overlapping of the word "Julia" at the end and start of the verses. Afterwards, the track was mixed for mono and stereo.

SAND AND FOAM

By

KAHLIL GIBRAN

Author of *The Prophet*

Alfred A. Knopf

The reality of the other person is not in what he reveals to you, but in what he cannot reveal to you.

Therefore, if you would understand him, listen not to what he says but rather to what he does not say.

Half of what I say is meaningless; but I say it so that the other half may reach you.

A sense of humor is a sense of proportion.

My loneliness was born when men praised my talkative faults and blamed my silent virtues.

14

When Life does not find a singer to sing her heart she produces a philosopher to speak her mind.

A truth is to be known always, to be uttered sometimes.

The real in us is silent; the acquired is talkative.

The voice of life in me cannot reach the ear of life in you; but let us talk that we may not feel lonely.

15

Birthday

Recorded: September 18 (Abbey Road Studio 2)
Mixed: September 18 (mono); October 14 (stereo)

Producer: Chris Thomas
Engineers: Ken Scott & Mike Sheady

Paul: Lead vocal; bass guitar; piano
John: Backing vocal; guitar (Casino)
George: Backing vocal; electric guitar; tambourine
Ringo: Drums; hand claps
Embellishments: Yoko Ono & Pattie Harrison (backing vocals);
Mal Evans (hand claps)

The album's third side opens with "Birthday," a powerful 12-bar blues rocker that was made up in the studio on September 18. Chris Thomas, who served as producer, recalls that the session began two hours earlier than the normal 5:00 p.m. start to accommodate the group's desire to break in time to watch the 9:00 p.m. BBC broadcast of *The Girl Can't Help It* at Paul's nearby Cavendish Avenue home. The 1956 rock 'n' roll film stars Jayne Mansfield and contains performances by Little Richard, Fats Domino, Eddie Cochran, Gene Vincent and the Platters. Paul was the first to arrive and quickly came up with the song's memorable riff. As the others arrived, the song began to take shape. The basic instrumental backing was recorded on a four-track tape machine and featured Paul on bass guitar and George on electric guitar hammering out the song's riff, with John on his Casino and Ringo on drums. *The White Album* deluxe edition contains Take 2, which is missing the riff leading into the middle eight. By the 20th take, the backing track was completed, and the gang headed for Paul's house to watch the film.

Upon their return, Take 20 was copied onto the eight-track to form Takes 21 and 22. The following overdubs were added: Paul's piano and scorching lead vocal; John's occasional matching lead vocal; George's harmony vocal in spots; backing vocals on the "birthday" refrain in the middle eight by Yoko Ono and George's wife Pattie; George playing tambourine with a gloved hand to avoid getting blisters; and Ringo and Mal Evans providing hand claps. The unique sound of the piano was achieved by miking it through a Vox Conquer amp and having balance engineer Ken Scott turning the amp's mid-range boost knob in time with the song to give it a wah-wah sound. The party ended around 4:30 a.m. Paul considers it one of his favorites on the album because it was instantaneous and good to dance to.

Yer Blues

Recorded: August 13 & 14 (Abbey Road Studio 2)
Mixed: August 14 (mono); October 14 (stereo)

Producer: George Martin
Engineers: Ken Scott & John Smith

John: Lead vocal; guitar (Casino)
Paul: Backing vocal; bass guitar (Fender Jazz)
George: Lead guitar
Ringo: Drums

"Yer Blues" is another song written in India by John, who later described it as a case of being "up there trying to reach God and feeling suicidal." With its opening line "Yes I'm lonely, wanna die," the song is full of anguish and foreshadows the tone of Lennon's early solo recordings.

The Esher demo, which has a Delta Blues feel, is lyrically similar to the finished master, but there are subtle differences. In the demo, he sings "My mother was of the earth, my father was of the sky, but I am of the universe and that's the reason why." By the time the song was recorded at Abbey Road, he had reversed the roles of his parents by singing "My mother was of the sky, my father was of the earth, but I am of the universe and you know what it's worth." There is also a change in the line about Mr. Jones, the central character of Bob Dylan's "Ballad Of A Thin Man" (from his 1965 LP *Highway 61 Revisited*). In the demo, John sings "I feel so insecure, just like Dylan's Mr. Jones." In the finished master, he feels suicidal.

At the request of John, "Yer Blues" was recorded in a small storage room next to the control room of Abbey Road's Studio Two. Lennon got the idea to record there when engineer Ken Scott jokingly complained to John about all the unconventional things the group was doing in the studio. Scott remarked, "Bloody hell, the way you lot are carrying on you'll be wanting to record everything in the room next door!" John thought it was a great idea and had the studio crew set up the band's amplifiers, microphones and instruments in the control room's tiny annex.

The session took place on August 13 with John on his Epiphone Casino, George on electirc guitar, Paul on his Fender Jazz Bass and Ringo on drums, with each instrument recorded on a separate track. The group ran through 14 takes before being satisfied with the basic backing. As John and George thought their guitar solos could be improved, new solos were punched into the two guitar tracks at the 2:28 mark, wiping the original solos (which can be heard

20th CENTURY-FOX
presents

TOM EWELL
JAYNE MANSFIELD
EDMOND O'BRIEN in

THE GIRL CAN'T HELP IT!

COLOR by DE LUXE

CinemaScope®

WITH GUEST STARS

JULIE LONDON • RAY ANTHONY • BARRY GORDON

AND FEATURING HENRY JONES • JOHN EMERY JUANITA MOORE

PRODUCED AND DIRECTED BY FRANK TASHLIN

SCREEN PLAY BY FRANK TASHLIN AND HERBERT BAKER

BASED ON A STORY BY GARSON KANIN

AND INTRODUCING THE FOLLOWING **ROCK 'N' ROLL STARS**
FATS DOMINO • THE PLATTERS • LITTLE RICHARD AND HIS BAND
GENE VINCENT AND HIS BLUE CAPS • THE TRENIERS • EDDIE FONTAINE
THE CHUCKLES • ABBEY LINCOLN • JOHNNY GLENN • NINO TEMPO • EDDIE COCHRAN

Copyright 1956 20th Century-Fox Film Corp.

56-559

in the left channel due to leakage into other microphones). Upon further review, the group decided that they liked Take 14 through the end of the solos and wanted to add Take 6 for the remainder of the song. Take 6 was given two reduction mixes of the guitars to one track numbered 15 and 16, with Take 16 deemed the best. Take 14 was also given a guitar reduction mix numbered Take 17 during which the guitars were heavily flanged with oscillator wobbling, particularly towards the end. The four-track tapes were then joined together with the opening minute or so of Take 17 being edited onto the end of Take 16 at the 3:17 mark of the finished master.

The following evening, John recorded his lead vocal over the Take 16 part of the song. Paul added his backing vocal on the line "girl you know the reason why" beginning with the second verse. Ringo double-tracked his snare drum during the guitar solo and the drum fill opening to Take 16 that was edited on after the solo. John chose not to re-record his lead vocal over the Take 16 ending part of the song, instead allowing his bleed-through guide vocal of the previous evening to stand alone in the background. The song was then mixed for mono. A brief edit piece was recorded on August 20 featuring Ringo's slow "two, three" vocal and hi-hat count-in. This was then edited to the start of the mono master, which fades at the 4:10 mark. When the song was mixed for stereo on October 14, it was faded out ten seconds earlier.

While John viewed the words to the song as "pretty realistic," he felt self-conscious about singing it in the idiom of American blues artists. Musically, "Yer Blues" became a parody of the English blues scene, particularly evident in its swing-time boogie-guitar instrumental passage and its simplistic guitar fills and solos.

The White Album deluxe edition contains Take 5, which is similar to the finished master, but with an extended jam after the solo.

Mother Nature's Son

Recorded: August 9 & 20 (Abbey Road Studio 2)
Mixed: October 12 (stereo & mono)

Producer: George Martin
Engineers: Ken Scott & John Smith

Paul: Lead vocal; acoustic guitar (Martin D-28); bass drum; bongos; timpani; percussion (Paul tapping a book cover)

Outside musicians: Two trumpets and two trombones (musicians unknown)

The album's next track, "Mother Nature's Son," may have also had its origin in India. John recalls a Maharishi lecture on nature that prompted him to write "I'm Just A Child Of Nature." The song, with its opening line "On the road to Rishikesh," was given demo treatment at Kinfauns, but was not recorded during the White Album sessions. Lennon later resurrected the song's melody and rewrote the lyrics for "Jealous Guy" (which is on his Imagine album).

While John believed the same lecture inspired Paul to write "Mother Nature's Son," McCartney remembers writing the song at his father's Liverpool home and that it was inspired by "Nature Boy," one of Paul's favorite standards. Nat "King" Cole's recording of "Nature Boy" was a U.S. million-seller that topped the charts for eight weeks in 1948. Paul describes "Mother Nature's Son" as a "heartfelt song about my child-of-nature leanings."

Although Paul had completed the lyrics and music to "Mother Nature's Son" by the time the Esher demo was recorded, he had neither worked out the opening or closing of the song nor refined its scat vocal passages.

The song was recorded at Abbey Road as a solo McCartney piece on the evening of August 9 after the other Beatles had all gone home. Paul went through 25 live performances of the song, each featuring his vocal and his Martin D-28 acoustic guitar. Take 24 was selected as the best, although many of the other performances could have served as the basic track. Anthology 3 contains Take 2. The White Album deluxe edition contains Take 15. Paul's vocal is more tentative than on the take selected for the master. At the end, he has a discussion with George Martin to obtain input during which he sarcastically asks, "Is there no one listening up there?"

On August 20, additional instruments were added to Take 24. After adding bass drum, Paul decided he wanted a distant drum sound for the latter part of the song. A bass drum was set up at the basement level of an Abbey Road stairwell with a microphone two stories higher. As Paul hit the drum, the microphone picked up the sound reverberation caused by the stairwell. This is first heard at the 1:54 mark. He also added bongos and timpani. Additional percussion was provided by Paul tapping the cover of the book The Song of Hiawatha by Henry Wadsworth Longfellow. Paul double-tracked his vocal at the end of the song. These overdubs were then given a reduction mix that was designated Take 26. The newly created open track was filled with George Martin's brass arrangement featuring four horns and Paul on a second acoustic guitar. The song was mixed for mono that evening, and for stereo on October 12.

Everybody's Got Something To Hide Except Me And My Monkey

Recorded: June 26 & 27, July 1 & 23 (Abbey Road Studio 2)
Mixed: July 23 (mono not used); October 12 (stereo & mono)

Producer: George Martin
Engineers: Geoff Emerick (except July 23) & Ken Scott (July 23); Richard Lush

John: Lead vocal; guitar (Casino)
Paul: Shouts; bass guitar (Rickenbacker); cowbell; chocalho
George: Backing vocal; lead guitar (Gibson SG)
Ringo: Drums
Embellishments: Hand claps

John's exuberant rocker "Everybody's Got Something To Hide Except Me And My Monkey" was written shortly after John began his relationship with Yoko in May 1968. In his Playboy interview, John described the song as: "a nice line that I made into a song. It was about me and Yoko. Everybody seemed to be paranoid except for us two, who were in the glow of love." The song's opening line "Come on is such a joy" was, according to George Harrison, a favorite saying of the Maharishi.

The Esher demo shows that although John had not come up with the song's introduction, the tune was essentially complete. Even at this early stage, the song's infectious nature is apparent. One can sense that the group was looking forward to recording this one.

On June 26, the Beatles ran through several takes of the song, but these were considered rehearsals, and the tape was recorded over. Fortunately, part of this rehearsal survived and is included on *The White Album* deluxe edition. The next evening, the backing track was recorded in six takes, with John on his Epiphone Casino, George on his Gibson SG, Paul on percussion (alternating between cowbell and chocalho) and Ringo on drums. During the song's mixdown to Takes 7 and 8, the tape was run at 43 cycles per second rather than the usual 50. Thus, upon playback at the normal speed, the song was in a higher pitch and considerably shorter. On July 1, Paul overdubbed two Rickenbacker bass parts. The song was given additional mixdowns to form Take 10, over which John added his lead vocal.

Although the track was thought to be complete, John apparently believed it could be improved. On July 23, he re-recorded his lead vocal onto Take 10. After reduction mixes formed Takes 11 and 12, backing vocals and hand claps were superimposed onto Take 12. The song was then mixed for mono, although it would receive an improved mono mix on October 12, when the stereo mix was made.

Sexy Sadie

Recorded: July 19 & 24, August 13 & 21 (Abbey Road Studio 2)
Mixed: August 21 (mono); October 14 (stereo)

Producer: George Martin
Engineers: Ken Scott; Richard Lush (July) & John Smith (August)

John: Lead and backing vocals; guitar
Paul: Backing vocals; piano; bass (Rickenbacker); organ; guitar
George: Backing vocals; lead guitar (Les Paul); tambourine
Ringo: Drums

"Sexy Sadie" dates back to India. In his Rolling Stone interview, John stated that the song was about the Maharishi, adding that he "copped out and wouldn't write 'Maharishi what have you done, you made a fool of everyone.'" John's disenchantment with the Maharishi started when he heard rumors that the holy man had made sexual advances towards some of the women at the compound. After John and George had heated discussions about this, they confronted the Maharishi. When John told the Maharishi they were leaving, he asked why. John curtly told him, "Well, if you're so cosmic, you'll know why." Because the Maharishi was never told what he had supposedly done, he was unable to deny the allegations. John interpreted the Maharishi's non-denial as an admission of guilt. John reportedly wrote the song just before leaving Rishikesh.

Although John's initial lyrics were crude and mentioned the Maharishi by name, by the time the Esher demo was recorded, Lennon had cleaned things up at George's request and replaced "Maharishi" with "Sexy Sadie." On July 19, the group ran through 21 takes of the song ranging in length from five and a half to eight minutes with John's lead vocal, electric guitars, organ and drums. *Anthology 3* contains the first 4:05 of Take 6. *The White Album* deluxe edition contains Take 3. John wasn't satisfied with the performances, so the group returned to the song on July 24. This time 23 takes (designated Takes 25 through 47) were recorded. Although Take 47 was deemed the best, John still was not satisfied.

The band tried a new approach to the song on August 13, with John on guitar and lead vocal, Paul on piano (with echo), George on his Les Paul through a Leslie speaker and Ringo on drums. The group recorded eight takes, designated Takes 100 through 107. The final version was considered the best and given four reduction mixdowns. On August 21, additional reduction mixes were made to allow for the overdubbing of an additional lead vocal by John, Rickenbacker bass and organ by Paul, tambourine by George and two sets of backing vocals by John, Paul and George.

Helter Skelter

Recorded: July 18 & September 9 & 10 (Abbey Road Studio 2)
Mixed: September 17 (mono); October 12 (stereo)

Producer: George Martin (July); Chris Thomas (September)
Engineers: Ken Scott; Richard Lush (July) & John Smith(September)

Paul: Lead vocal; guitar (Casino)
John: Backing vocal; bass guitar (Fender Jazz); saxophone
George: Backing vocal; lead guitar (Les Paul)
Ringo: Drums
Embellishments: Mal Evans (trumpet); piano (barely heard in mix)

"Helter Skelter" was the product of Paul's desire to record a song with "the most raucous vocal, the loudest drums." Paul claims he was inspired to make such a record after reading an interview with the Who's Pete Townshend in which the guitarist described his band's new single, "I Can See For Miles," as the loudest, rawest, dirtiest and most uncompromising song the band had ever recorded. While this story may have been embellished a bit by Paul, it demonstrates McCartney's competitive nature, in this case wanting to out do the Who at their own game. Paul took the symbol of a helter skelter (a spiral slide at a British fairground) as a "ride from the top to the bottom...and this was the fall, the demise, the going down."

The Beatles first attempt to record the song took place at Abbey Road on July 18. The band jammed its way through three extended performances featuring the standard lineup of two guitars, bass and drums backing Paul's lead vocal. The first two takes were over ten minutes each. Take 3 lasted an incredible 27:11, making it the group's longest recording by far. *The White Album* deluxe edition contains all of Take 2, a slow, deliberate, pounding version with some different lyrics ("I give you a thrill" and "Hell for leather").

Realizing that none of the July 18 takes were of a suitable length, the group re-recorded the song on September 9 utilizing the eight-track. The session marked Chris Thomas' baptism of fire as producer. The band ran through 18 chaotic takes of the song (designated Takes 4 through 21) before Paul was satisfied. The basic instrumental track consisted of Paul's rhythm guitar on his Epiphone Casino, George's distorted lead guitar on his Les Paul, John on Fender Jazz Bass and Ringo on drums. Overdubs were added to Take 21 the next night. Paul added a gritty, powerful lead vocal, and John and George supplied backing vocals. Ringo added a drum track with repeat echo applied to his snare, as well as an additional snare part. George's original guitar was recorded over with a new guitar part with Paul joining him for the descending notes following Paul

singing the words "Helter Skelter." Ringo added more snare drum to the descending notes section. In an unusual move, John added saxophone, and Mal Evans played trumpet. Piano was also added, though it can only be faintly heard in the stereo mix. The final result was just what McCartney had been aiming for: his "most raucous" vocal and Ringo coming through with his "loudest drums." After pounding away for 18 unrelenting performances of the song, Ringo shouted "I've got blisters on my fingers!" at the end of the final take. Ringo's immortal words are preserved on the 4:29 stereo mix of the song, but not on the shorter mono mix. The deluxe edition contains Take 17, which has Paul whooping it up and Ringo drum rolls. When it was over, Paul said, "Keep that one, mark it fab." Fab indeed!

Long, Long, Long

Recorded: October 7, 8 & 9 (Abbey Road Studio 2)
Mixed: October 10 (stereo); October 12 & 14 (mono)

Producer: George Martin
Engineers: Ken Scott & Mike Sheady

George: Lead vocal; acoustic guitars
Paul: Backing vocal; Hammond organ; bass guitar (Rickenbacker)
Ringo: Drums
Chris Thomas: Piano

The loudest song on the album is followed by the set's softest selection, "Long, Long, Long." Although on the surface its lyrics are about lost and regained love, George insists that the "you" in the song is God. He admits the chords were taken from Bob Dylan's "Sad Eyed Lady Of The Lowlands" from his 1966 LP *Blonde On Blonde*.

The song, initially titled "It's Been A Long Long Long Time," was recorded on October 7 in 67 takes with George on vocal and his Gibson J-200 acoustic guitar (capo on the third fret), Paul on Hammond organ and Ringo on drums. During one of the takes, Paul hit an organ note that caused a bottle of Blue Nun wine sitting on top of the Leslie speaker cabinet to rattle. The group liked the effect, so microphones were set up to capture the sound for use at the end of the song. While this was being recorded, George took a microphone and used it to strum his guitar, creating an abrasive sound, and Ringo added some drums. The next day, Harrison added a second vocal and acoustic guitar part, and Paul overdubbed his Rickenbacker bass. On October 9, Paul added his backing vocal, and Chris Thomas added a piano part on the bridge. John did not participate in the sessions. *The White Album* deluxe edition contains Take 44, which has different dynamics and a more intimate feeling.

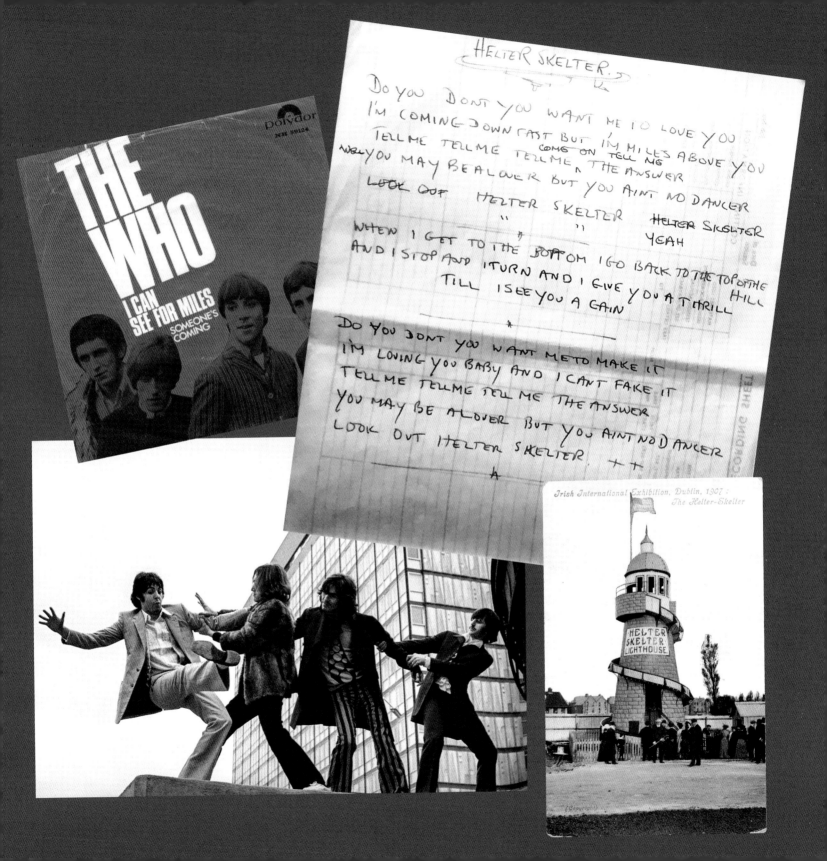

Revolution 1

Recorded: May 30 & 31, June 4 & 21 (Abbey Road Studio 2, May 30 & June 21; Studio 3, May 31 & June 4)
Mixed: June 4 (mono not used); June 21 & 25 (stereo mix and edit)

Producer: George Martin
Engineers: Geoff Emerick (except June 4) & Peter Bown (June 4); Phil McDonald (except June 21) & Richard Lush (June 21)

John: Lead vocal; acoustic guitar (Jumbo); lead guitar (possibly Stratocaster); mellotron (flute setting)
Paul: Backing vocals; piano; bass guitar (Rickenbacker); organ
George: Backing vocals; lead guitar (Stratocaster and/or SG)
Ringo: Drums; percussive clicks (at beginning)
Yoko: Voice on tape; electronic sound effects
Outside musicians: Derek Watkins & Freddy Clayton (trumpet); Don Lang, Rex Morris, J. Power & Bill Povey (trombone)

The fourth and final side of the album opens with the first song recorded for the disc, "Revolution." John wanted the song released as a single to serve "as a statement of the Beatles' position on Viet Nam and the Beatles' position on revolution." According to John, the lyrics expressed his feelings about politics: "I want to see the plan....Count me out if it's for violence. Don't expect me on the barricades unless it is with flowers."

John began work on the song while in India. By the time the Esher demo was recorded, John had only completed the first two verses. After singing the completed verses, John simulates an instrumental passage with scat vocals before repeating the first verse. John's anti-violence stance is clear as he sings the line "But when you talk about destruction, don't you know that you can count me out." The demo features acoustic guitars, hand claps, tambourine (on the last verse), John on lead vocal, Paul sometimes joining him on the verses, and Paul and George on the "Don't you know it's gonna be" backing vocals. The demo's tempo is faster than the initial recording of the song that would appear on the album, but slower than the fast version recorded for the single.

The rhythm track for the song, with John on acoustic guitar, Paul on piano and Ringo on drums, was recorded in 16 takes at the first *White Album* session on May 30. All of the performances, with the exception of the final take, were about five minutes long. Take 18 (there were no takes numbered 11 or 12) ran for 10:17. Its final six minutes consisted of jamming, electronic effects and John singing, screaming and moaning "All right" and "right" various ways. Midway, John says, "OK, I've had enough," but they keep playing.

Yoko's voice, from a pre-recorded tape, enters towards the end of the song. As the extended jam concludes, Yoko's talk about nakedness and exposure is heard. In the background, there are various sound effects, including an opera singer. This culminates with piano notes and Yoko, on tape, saying, "If...you become naked." After this sequence and the song comes to an end, Yoko comments, "That's too much." John replies "It's gonna be great." This remarkable take is included on the *White Album* deluxe edition.

On May 31, John added two vocal parts and Paul overdubbed his Rickenbacker bass onto Take 18. In rehearsal, John's stance on destruction alternated between "you can count me out" and "you can count me in." Although the lyric sheet included with the album reads "you can count me out," John actually sings "you can count me out, in." After a reduction mix created Take 19, Paul and George added their "shoo-be-do-wop-bow" backing vocals, which start during the first chorus and continue throughout the extended jam.

On June 4, John re-recorded his lead vocal. In an effort to alter the sound of his voice, Lennon sang while lying on his back on the floor of Abbey Road's Studio Three. He continued singing, and at times screaming, differing phrasing of "all right" and "right" throughout the extended jam. Another backing vocal overdub was added by Paul and George, who at 4:17 into the song begin singing "Mama...Dada...Mama...Dada" over and over again through the end. Other overdubs included percussive clicks (heard during the song's intro) and a second drum part by Ringo, a tone-pedal distorted lead guitar by John and organ by Paul (not heard in the final mix). The song was given another reduction mix (Take 20) to accommodate the additions.

Take 20 would serve as the master for "Revolution 1" after additional overdubs of brass by outside musicians and a lead guitar line by George on June 21. The song would also be edited down with a fade out 4:12 into the song.

Although Take 20 has yet to be officially released, it circulates among collectors, providing a fascinating look at John's creative mind at work. The track opens with an engineer stating "Revolution RM1 [for Remix 1] of Take..." As he hesitates, apparently forgetting what take it is, John says, "Take your knickers off and let's go." The engineer replies, "As you said...Revolution Take 20..." A few organ notes are heard, confirming that Paul had superimposed an organ part that was left out of the mix or recorded over. When the song "Revolution" begins, it sounds similar to the final version appearing on the album, containing the instrumental overdubs from the June

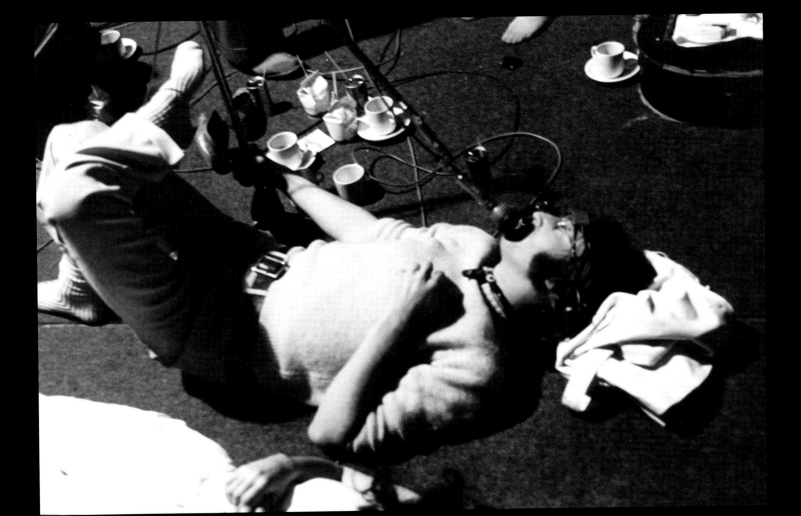

4 session, but missing those from the June 21 session, including Harrison's electric guitar part during the song's introduction and the brass overdubs. While the album track fades out at 4:12, this version continues as a song for an additional five minutes. John's differing phrasing of "all right" and "right" are heard throughout the extended jam, as are Paul and George's "shoo-be-do-wop-bow" and "Mama...Dada...Mama...Dada" backing vocals. Tape loops of phasing sounds are brought into the mix at various places. Take 20 retains the ending of Take 18, with Yoko's conversation about nakedness and exposure, along with the opera singer, piano notes and Yoko's "That's too much" and John's "It's gonna be great."

The naked conversation, along with its sound effects, is heard in its entirety beginning at the 7- minute mark in "Revolution 9." The main difference between the two versions of the passage comes early, as Yoko mumbles, "It's not that..." On "Revolution 9" there is silence; on Take 20, Paul emphatically replies, "It is that!"

John's vision for "Revolution" went beyond a mere rock 'n' roll song with an extended jam. "Tomorrow Never Knows" had been embellished with various tape loops to create otherworldly sounds. Towards the end of the June 4 session, John prepared two tape loops, one with the four Beatles singing "Aaaaaaaah" at a very high register and the other with a manic guitar phrase played on the high part of the fretboard. Neither of these tapes were used.

During sessions held on June 6, 10, 11, 20, and 21, John prepared tape loops and recorded voices, superimposed the tapes and voices over the extended jam portion of "Revolution" and mixed it all down to a sound collage titled "Revolution 9" (see below).

By the time work resumed on the rock part of "Revolution" on June 21, John had done substantial work on "Revolution 9." It was at this time that the song's title was changed to "Revolution 1" to distinguish it from "Revolution 9." After Martin's brass arrangement (two trumpets and four trombones) was recorded, and the song was given another reduction mixdown (Take 22), Harrison superimposed electric guitar. The song was edited and mixed for stereo on June 21 and again on June 25. The mono mix is a fold-down of the stereo.

John's push to have "Revolution" issued as the next Beatles single met resistance from Paul and George, who were concerned that the recording's slow tempo would prevent it from being a hit. A compromise was reached when John agreed to record the song as a rocker (as detailed in the recording information for the "Revolution" single). Although the re-recorded fast-tempo version made it suitable for single release, it ended up as the B-side to Paul's "Hey Jude."

Honey Pie

Recorded: October 1, 2 & 4 (Trident Studios)
Mixed: October 5 (mono & stereo); October 7 (EQ changed)

Producer: George Martin
Engineers: Barry Sheffield & unknown

Paul: Lead vocal; piano
John: Guitar (Casino)
George: Bass guitar (Fender VI)
Ringo: Drums (with brushes)
Sound effects: Scratchy record

Outside musicians: Dennis Walton, Ronald Chamberlain, Jim Chester, Rex Morris & Harry Klein (saxophones); Raymond Newman & David Smith (clarinets)

"Honey Pie" is a nod to the vaudeville tradition Paul was raised on, following in the footsteps of Paul's "When I'm Sixty-Four" and "Your Mother Should Know." It is also another of Paul's fantasy songs; this time written for a woman who sails to America and becomes a legend of the silver screen.

The Esher demo features Paul backed by acoustic guitars, percussion and tambourine. The recording lacks the song's spoken intro, although it has most of the lyrics of the finished master and some backing vocals, including some ad libs by John.

The backing track for "Honey Pie" was recorded in one take at Trident Studios on October 1 with Paul on piano, George on Fender Bass VI and Ringo on drums (with brushes). The next day, Paul superimposed his lead vocal. John added a jazzy lead guitar solo. During the instrumental break, Paul ad-libs "Yeah, like it like that, aah, ooh, I like this kinda hot kinda music, hot kinda music, play it to me, play it to me, Hollywood Blues." More overdubs were added on October 4, including George Martin's score of five saxophones and two clarinets. Paul recorded the line "Now she's hit the big time" in a manner mimicking the low fidelity recordings of the 1920s. To drive home the point, his vocal is backed by the sound of a scratchy record, duplicating the effect of listening to an old worn-out 78-rpm shellac disc. (Michael Nesmith of the Monkees had used the same scratchy record sound on his tune, "Magnolia Simms," from the group's May 1968 album, *The Birds, The Bees & The Monkees*.) "Honey Pie" was mixed for mono and stereo at Trident on October 5, although both mixes were copied and converted to a different equalization system two days later at Abbey Road. *The White Album* deluxe edition has an instrumental version of the song.

Savoy Truffle

Recorded: October 3 & 5 (Trident Studios); October 11 & 14 (Abbey Road Studio Two)
Mixed: October 14 (mono & stereo)

Producer: George Martin
Engineers: Barry Sheffield & unknown (October 3 & 4);
Ken Scott & John Smith (October 11 & 14)

George: Lead vocal; electric and acoustic guitars
Paul: Bass guitar (Rickenbacker)
Ringo: Drums
Chris Thomas: Electric piano; organ
Embellishments: Tambourine and bongos

Outside musicians: Ronald Ross & Bernard George (Baritone saxophone); Art Ellefson, Danny Moss, Harry Klein & Derek Collins (tenor saxophone)

George's fourth selection on the album, "Savoy Truffle," was inspired by Eric Clapton's addiction to chocolate. The lyrics jokingly warn Harrison's friend that he'll have to have his decaying teeth pulled out if he doesn't cut back on the sweets. Most of the candies mentioned in the song, including Creme Tangerine, Montelimart, Ginger Sling, Coffee Dessert and Savoy Truffle, are taken from Mackintosh's Good News double centre chocolate assortment box. Cherry Cream and Coconut Fudge are Harrison creations. The lyrics contain a cryptic reference to "Ob-La-Di, Ob-La-Da," with George singing "We all know Ob-La-Di-Bla-Da/But can you show me where you are?"

The song's backing track, featuring George on electric guitar, Paul on his Rickenbacker bass and Ringo on drums, was recorded in one take at Trident Studios on October 3. Two days later, Harrison returned to Trident to add his lead vocal and acoustic guitar. Chris Thomas' score of two baritone and four tenor saxophones was recorded on October 11 at Abbey Road. At Harrison's request, the saxes were given a distorted sound. The song's final overdubs, consisting of lead guitar played by George, electric piano and organ by Thomas, tambourine and bongos, were added on October 14. These would be the last instruments recorded for the album. Ringo was not present because he had left that morning for a two-week family vacation in Sardinia. The song was mixed for mono and stereo later that evening. The deluxe edition of *The White Album* contains the instrumental backing of the song.

Cry Baby Cry

Recorded: July 15, 16 & 18 (Abbey Road Studio 2)
Mixed: October 15 (stereo & mono)

Producer: George Martin
Engineers: Geoff Emerick (July 15 & 16) & Ken Scott (July 18);
Richard Lush

John: Lead and backing vocals; acoustic guitar (Jumbo)
Paul: Backing vocals; bass guitar (Rickenbacker); piano
George: Lead guitar (Les Paul)
Ringo: Drums
George Martin: Harmonium
Embellishments: Tambourine
Sound effects: Tea party

John's "Cry Baby Cry" dates back to 1967. His inspiration for the song came from an ad, "Cry baby cry, make your mother buy." While in India, John refined the lyrics, which have a nursery-rhyme quality. By the time the Esher demo was recorded, the song was essentially complete.

On July 15, the Beatles recorded two hours of unnumbered takes of the song. As these were considered rehearsals, the tapes were recorded over. Fortunately, one of the later-recorded rehearsal takes was not taped over and is on the deluxe edition of *The White Album*. Prior to getting started, John says a silly little poem. The song is taken at a slow pace and has a bluesy feel to it. John plays organ, along with George on guitar, Paul on bass and Ringo on drums.

The next day, the group began the proper recording of the song. *Anthology 3* contains Take 1, which features John's excellent guide vocal and acoustic guitar, Paul on his Rickenbacker bass, Ringo on drums and George with occasional lead fills. The tenth and final take was deemed "best" and given a mixdown reduction to form Take 12. During the mixing, John's acoustic guitar was given ADT treatment with variable tape speed to produce a phasing effect. Paul then added piano and George Martin contributed harmonium.

After taking a day off to attend the *Yellow Submarine* premiere, the group completed its work on the song on July 18, with additional overdubs onto Take 12. These included John's lead vocal, backing vocals by John and Paul, an additional harmonium part by George Martin heard during the opening chorus, Harrison's lead guitar lines on a Gibson Les Paul, tambourine and tea party sound effects. The song was mixed for stereo and mono on October 15.

Can You Take Me Back (Uncredited link)

Recorded: September 16 (Abbey Road Studio 2)
Mixed: October 16 and/or 17 (mono & stereo)

Producer: Chris Thomas
Engineers: Ken Scott

Paul: Lead vocal; acoustic guitar (Martin D-28)
John: Maracas
Ringo: Drums

The final chord of "Cry Baby Cry" is followed by an uncredited link track, Paul's "Can You Take Me Back." The ad-lib tune was recorded during the September 16 session that produced "I Will." The 2:21 performance, which was logged in as Take 19 of "I Will," features Paul on vocal and acoustic guitar, John on maracas and Ringo on drums. When the album was banded on October 16 and 17, a 28-second segment from the end of the song was placed immediately after "Cry Baby Cry," giving listeners the impression that it was part of the song. Its words, "Can you take me back where I came from, can you take me back?," are not included on the album's lyric sheet.

The complete version of "Can You Take Me Back" is included on the deluxe edition of *The White Album*. Paul's ad libbed vocals include: "I am happy here my honey, can you take me back?" "I ain't happy here my honey, can you take me back?" "Are you happy living here?"

Revolution 9

Recorded: May 30 & 31, June 4 (Abbey Road Studio 2, May 30; Studio 3, May 31 & June 4) (recording of *Revolution 1*)
June 6, 10, 11, 20 & 21 (Studio 3, June 6, 10, 11 & 20; Studio 1, June 20; Studio 2, June 20 & 21) (effects and prose)
Mixed and edited: June 21 & 25 (stereo); August 20 (mono)

Producer: George Martin
Engineers: Geoff Emerick (except June 4) & Peter Bown (June 4); Phil McDonald(except June 20 & 21) & Richard Lush(June 20 & 21)

John: Lead vocal ("all right" and "right" from *Revolution 1*); prose
George: Prose
Yoko Ono: Prose
Sound effects: Detailed below

"Revolution 9" is the most controversial track ever to appear on a Beatles album. It is not really a song, but rather a sound collage of multiple tape loops put together by John. In his Playboy interview, John recalled, "Yoko was there for the whole thing and she made decisions about which [tape] loops to use. It was somewhat under her influence." Although Paul had produced a random-sounding sound collage with the group on January 5, 1967 (an unreleased track that is known as "Carnival of Light"), he did not participate in the making of "Revolution 9" and thought it inappropriate for a Beatles LP. At John's insistence, the track ended up on *The Beatles* despite objections from the other Beatles and George Martin.

The track took on a life of its own, springing out of the six minute instrumental jam at the end of Take 18 of "Revolution 1." As detailed above, the extended ending of the song has John singing and sometimes screaming "all right" and "right." These words are often brought up to the front of the mix in "Revolution 9." In addition, the one-minute segment tagged on to the end of the song featuring the conversation between Yoko and John about nakedness remains part of "Revolution 9" with only minor alterations.

On June 6, John began assembling tapes and loops of various sound effects, some of which would be incorporated into "Revolution 9." Lennon prepared more tapes of sound effects on June 10 and 11.

The master version of the track was compiled during a 7:00 p.m. through 3:30 a.m. session held on June 20. According to John, "There were about ten machines with people holding pencils on the loops — some only inches long and some a yard long. I fed them all in and mixed them live. I did a few mixes until I got one I liked." To accommodate the simultaneous inclusion of multiple tape loops into the mix, all three of Abbey Road's studios were used. Prior to compiling the master version, John prepared several different tape loops that could be brought into the mix whenever it suited his fancy.

The most memorable sound was lifted from the start of a Royal Academy of Music tape. It consists of an unknown engineer repeating the phrase "number nine." The "number nine" loop is brought into the mix nine separate times during the piece, with the phrase itself heard a total of 43 times. George Harrison was the only other Beatle present at the session. He joined John on the studio floor to record a bizarre series of phrases and bits of strange conversation that were faded into the mix at various times. The master version was completed by the end of the session, although additional sound effects were superimposed onto the master tape the following evening. The stereo mix was also made that night, with

John panning many of the sound effects across the left and right channels. On June 25, the 9:05 stereo master was edited down to 8:12. The mono mix, which was merely a mixdown of the stereo master, was made on August 20.

"Revolution 9" is preceded by a bit of a conversation (secretly recorded by John) in which Apple office manager Alistair Taylor apologizes to George Martin for forgetting to bring him a special claret. After Alistair asks, "Will you forgive me?," Martin replies, "Mmm...yes," to which Alistair retorts, "cheeky bitch."

The track begins calmly enough with the "number nine" voice panning from left to right over a slow piano theme in B minor, which is also faded in and out of the mix throughout the piece. The serenity quickly yields to chaotic sound effects, including bits of symphonic music (some normal and some reverse looped), choral passages, crowd noises and crashing cymbals. John's dialog is brought to the front of the mix, revealing that "as time went by they'd get a little bit older and a little bit slower." The swirling symphonic sounds continue, leading into laughter, a crying baby, the "number nine" loop and George asking "Who wants to know?" Additional confusion persists and John's repeated screaming of "right" from the extended ending to Revolution 1 is brought to the forefront of the mix. This is followed by the "number nine" loop, a ringing bell and the blended sounds of a choral passage, an unintelligible conversation, crowd noise, symphonic instruments, honking horns and other various effects.

The voices of George and John come forward to reveal George saying "with the situation," John adding "they are standing still" and George mentioning a telegram. John's moans from the Revolution 1 jam and the "number nine" voice return, leading into the following dialog from John: "Who could tell what he was saying; his voice was low and his mind was high...." As the conversation fades, an "all right" from John leads into crowd noise and the return of "number nine" and chaotic music. John can be heard saying "so the wife told him he'd better go to see a surgeon" as the crowd noises and effects build up. John continues his prose with "so anyhow he went to see the dentist instead, who gave him a pair of teeth, which wasn't any good at all, so, so instead of that he joined the fookin' navy and went to sea." A tape loop of a crowd chanting "hold that line" and "block that kick" also enters the mix.

After the choral passage returns, John can be heard saying "Here I sit in my broken chair, my wings are broken and so is my hair, I am not in the mood for wearing blue clothing" over the sound of crackling flames. John's voice from Revolution 1 returns amid gunfire and other sound effects. As the choir returns, George says "only to find the night watchman unaware of his presence in the building."

The return of the "number nine" loop leads to more audible prose, including John's "industrial output, financial imbalance" and George's "thrusting in between your shoulder blades." As things calm down, the piano theme returns, and John continues with "the Watusi, the Twist" and George adds "El Dorado." John then commands, "Take this brother, may it serve you well," apparently a reference to a mind-altering drug.

The mood of the piece abruptly changes and Yoko's soft conversation about exposure and nakedness competes with an operatic tenor and various sound effects. As the piano theme returns, the piece gets quiet for a brief moment to expose Yoko saying "If you become naked." (This one-minute segment was part of the extended version of Take 18 of "Revolution 1" discussed above.) This leads into a crowd chanting "hold that line" a few times before switching to "block that kick." The track ends with "block that kick" panning between the left and right channels before moving to the center and fading away.

For most listeners back in 1968, "Revolution 9" was unlike anything they had ever experienced. Had the track appeared on a John and Yoko album, the piece would have been heard by a relatively small audience. But being part of a Beatles album meant that millions of listeners would hear the experimental recording whether they wanted to or not.

Critics and fans alike were deeply divided on their feelings towards the track. Many found it to be noisy, boring and pointless, or even worse. Others found it to be thought-provoking and narcotic. For those who weren't initially turned off, the track made for fascinating listening. It is truly a recording that reveals new things with each listen. Like it or not, "Revolution 9" is part of what makes The White Album so unique.

The famous "number nine" loop gained notoriety beyond the song, with many listeners mimicking its sound. In addition, the number nine later took on significance to Beatles fans. During the height of the Paul McCartney death rumor, the tape loop was a major clue supposedly pointing to Paul's death. By some incredible coincidence, when the record is played backwards, the phrase "number nine" sounds like "turn me on, dead man." The author remembers hearing its eerie sound and nearly ruining his turntable in the process!

169

LIFE

The
Days in
the Lives
of

THE beatLes

*They call it
their authentic
biography*

SEPTEMBER 13 · 1968 · 50¢

Good Night

Recorded: June 28, July 2 & 22 (Abbey Road Studio 2 except July 22; Studio 1, July 22)
Mixed: October 11 (mono and stereo)

Producer: George Martin
Engineers: Geoff Emerick (June 28), Pete Bown (July 2) & Ken Scott (July 22); Richard Lush

Ringo: Lead vocal

Outside musicians: 12 violins, 3 violas, 3 cellos, 3 flutes, clarinet, horn, vibraphone, harp and double bass (identities unknown)
Mike Sammes Singers: Ingrid Thomas, Pat Whitmore, Irene King, Val Stockwell, Ross Gilmour, Mike Redway, Ken Barrie & Fred Lucas

The album's final selection, "Good Night," was written by John for his then five-year-old son, Julian. Perhaps believing the tender lullaby would harm his image, John turned the song over to Ringo. Paul fondly recalls John teaching the song to Ringo. "[I]t was fabulous to hear him do it, he sang it great...he sang it very tenderly."

The Beatles first attempt at the song took place on June 28, with rehearsals featuring John on guitar or piano, George Harrison on percussion and Ringo on vocals. Five early takes were recorded, each starting with a different spoken introduction by Ringo. The *Anthology* video contains a segment of Ringo reciting the following prose over John's finger-picking-style guitar: "Come on, now, it's time you little toddlers are in bed. I'm having no more messing. You've been out to the park all day, you've had a lovely time. Now it's time for bed. Are we ready? Daddy'll sing." *The White Album* deluxe edition has another of these takes, which breaks down and causes Ringo to say, "Daddy went a bit crazy."

On July 2, Ringo re-recorded his lead vocal onto Take 5. Ten numbered takes, also featuring harmony backing vocals from John and Paul, were recorded. The deluxe edition contains Take 10, featuring John's finger-picking guitar on his Casino. George Martin had copies of Take 15 made to enable him to write an orchestral score.

The deluxe edition also contains a version with Ringo backed by Martin on piano and Harrison on a shaker. The song's lush orchestral backing was recorded on July 22 in 12 takes, designated Takes 23 through 34. George Martin conducted the orchestra detailed above. Backing vocals by the Mike Sammes Singers were then recorded over Take 34. Finally, Ringo recorded his charming solo lead vocal, which ends with him whispering, "Good night, good night everybody, everybody, everywhere, good night."

Banding of the Album

At 5:00 p.m. on October 16, John, Paul, George Martin and engineers Ken Scott and John Smith met at Abbey Road to determine the running order of the 30 plus songs available for the album. Neither Ringo, who was on family vacation in Sardinia, nor George, who was in Los Angeles producing Jackie Lomax's album *Is This What You Want?*, was present for what would be the Beatles only 24-hour session.

Although Harrison's "Not Guilty" was mixed for mono, it was not given a stereo mix and was quickly passed over. John lobbied for both of his experimental tracks, "What's The New Mary Jane?" and "Revolution 9," but in the end only "Revolution 9" was included.

The wide variety and number of the songs presented a sequencing challenge. Following the producer's practice of opening a record with a "potboiler," Sides One and Three open with powerful rockers. Three of the songs with animals in their titles are together on Side Two. Many of the hardest rocking songs are on Side Three. Each of George's four songs is on a different disc. By coincidence, the record's first two tracks feature Paul on drums rather than Ringo. "Revolution 9," which is both a challenging listen and a difficult song to follow, appears where it belongs, towards the end of the LP. And Ringo's charming "Good Night" is the perfect way to close the set.

As with the group's previous British LP, *Sgt. Pepper*, the songs run together without the normal three to six second gap between tracks. This was accomplished with cross-fades ("Back In The U.S.S.R." into "Dear Prudence"), tight edits and an uncredited link track ("Cry Baby Cry" to "Can You Take Me Back" to "Revolution 9").

Additional Songs

As was often the case with Beatles recording sessions, the group recorded a pair of songs for release only as a single. The initial choice for the A-side was the up-tempo version of "Revolution," but it was relegated to the B-side when Paul came up with "Hey Jude."

Although the group ran through over 100 numbered takes of "Not Guilty," it did not make the cut. Nor did John's "What's The New Mary Jane?" The Abbey Road engineers also recorded a handful of impromptu performances by Paul of songs and song fragments, including "St. Louis Blues," "Step Inside Love," "Los Paranoias" and two Elvis songs, "Blue Moon" and "(You're So Square) Baby I Don't Care." There is also part of an early rehearsal of "Let It Be." All are included on the *White Album* deluxe edition and detailed below.

Hey Jude

Recorded: July 29 & 30 (Abbey Road Studio 2); July 31 & August 1
(Trident Studios)
Mixed: August 2 (stereo); August 3 & 8 (mono)

Producer: George Martin (except July 29)
Engineers: Ken Scott & John Smith (July 29 & 30); Barry Shefield
(July 31 & August 1)

Paul: Lead vocal; piano; bass guitar
John: Backing vocal; acoustic guitar (Jumbo)
George: Backing vocal; electric guitar
Ringo: Drums; tambourine

Embellishments: John Perry (backing vocals)
Outside musicians: Of the 36 classical musicians, all are unknown
except Bobby Kok and Peter Halling on cello and Bill Jackman and
Brian Warren on flute. The instruments were: ten violins; three
violas; three cellos; two flutes; one contra bassoon; one bassoon; two clarinets; one contra bass clarinet; four trumpets; four
trombones; two horns; two string basses; and one percussion.
Most of the musicians added backing vocals and hand claps during
the songs extended refrain

Paul got the idea for "Hey Jude" while driving in his car to visit
Cynthia and Julian Lennon. Although John had recently divorced
Cynthia, Paul thought it wrong to end his friendship with her and
John's son, Julian, so he decided to visit and see how they were
doing. At the time, Cynthia was still living in John's Kenwood house,
so Paul was used to writing songs on the way to Kenwood, where he
and John had collaborated on many songs in the past. In Barry Miles'
Paul McCartney Many Years From Now, Paul explained:

"I started with the idea 'Hey Jules,' which was Julian, don't
make it bad, take a sad song and make it better. Hey, try and deal
with this terrible thing. I knew it was not going to be easy for him. I
always feel sorry for kids in divorce. The adults may be fine but the
kids...I had the idea by the time I got there. I changed it to 'Jude'
because I thought that sounded a bit better."

Although Paul was probably not aware of it, the name change
also fit in nicely with the theme of the song — Saint Jude is the
patron saint of desperate cases.

Shortly thereafter, Paul finished the song at his Cavendish
home. When John and Yoko visited him on July 26, 1968, he played
the song for them. Although Paul had completed the lyrics, there
was one line he viewed as filler that he intended to replace. When
he got to the line "The movement you need is on your shoulder," he

looked at John and told him he would fix it. Much to Paul's surprise,
John told him to leave the words alone, calling it the best line in the
song. In the *Anthology* video, Paul commented:

"So that was the great thing about John, where as I would
have definitely knocked that line out, he said 'it's great,' I could see
it through his eyes and go 'oh, OK.' So that is the sorta line now
when I do that song, that's the line when I think of John, you know,
sometimes I get a little emotional during that moment."

While John knew Paul had written the song for his son
Julian, he thought Paul had subconsciously written it for him. In his
interview for Playboy magazine, John stated:

"I always heard it as a song to me. If you think about it...Yoko's
just come into the picture. He's saying, 'Hey Jude — hey, John.'
I know I'm sounding like one of those fans who reads things into it,
but you *can* hear it as a song to me. The words 'go out and get her'—
subconsciously he was saying, 'Go ahead, leave me.' On a conscious
level, he didn't want me to go ahead. The angel in him was saying,
"Bless you." The devil in him didn't like it at all, because he didn't
want to lose his partner."

John viewed the song as one of Paul's masterpieces, as did
millions of others. For many, the song is a message of inspiration:
to adjust to a bad situation and make it better and to have the
confidence to go out and do what you want to do.

Paul and John both recognized the song's potential, so it
was destined from the start to be a single. This decision was made
despite the song's length, which would ultimately stretch past seven
minutes due to its long anthem-like sing-along ending. At a time
when singles normally ran between two and three minutes long,
the idea of a single shattering the conventional time barrier was
indeed revolutionary. But the Beatles never let rules interfere with
their music.

Recording on "Hey Jude" began July 29, 1968, at Abbey Road.
While Ken Scott served in his usual function as engineer, George
Martin did not attend. As Paul was feeling his way through his latest
composition, the six takes recorded that evening sound more like
magnificent rehearsals rather than serious attempts to capture a
master recording. The lineup for the live recordings featured Paul
on piano and lead vocal, John on acoustic guitar and backing vocal,
George on electric guitar and backing vocal and Ringo on drums.
Although the song's glorious sing-along ending was in place from
the start, the three completed takes were not as long as what would
later become the finished master. Take 1 lasted 6:21, while Takes 2

and 6 ran for 4:30 and 5:25. *The White Album* deluxe edition has Take 1, complete with Paul warming up his vocal chords with "hey"s. Paul sings one of the lines differently than the finished master with "She has found you, now go and get her" instead of "you have found her." Paul also adds some extra "better"s in the song's midsection. George plays some lead guitar lines towards the end. *Anthology 3* contains an edited version of one of the latter takes from this session. Between takes, Paul performed a snippet of "St. Louis Blues."

The following evening, the Beatles were joined by George Martin at Abbey Road for more recorded rehearsals of the song. Takes 7 through 23 were performed without George Harrison, who was stationed in the control room with George Martin and Ken Scott. Harrison had wanted to add lead guitar fills to the song, an idea that was shot down by Paul in a less than diplomatic manner.

The Beatles had earlier agreed to be filmed for a documentary by the National Music Council of Great Britain. This session, which was really a rehearsal, provided the perfect opportunity for the Beatles to keep their promise. The crew, led by producer James Archibald, shot several hours of film. The finished show, titled *Music!*, featured two segments (running 2:32 and 3:05) of the Beatles performing and talking about the new song. The color documentary was shown in British theaters on the same bill with Mel Brooks' comedy classic, *The Producers*, in October 1969. The film was broadcast in the U.S. as part of the NBC network television show Experiment In Television on February 22, 1970.

Although the Beatles had previously been filmed in the studio, this was the first time that a camera crew was allowed to capture the group running through take after take of a new song. The idea of filming the group's rehearsals appealed to Paul, who would soon come up with the concept of having the band perform a concert for television. As part of the program, the group would be shown rehearsing new songs for the concert. During the month of January 1969, the group was filmed rehearsing and recording new songs and old favorites. Although the planned television concert never took place, the film of the group's rehearsals eventually evolved into the movie *Let It Be*.

On July 31, the Beatles were ready to record "Hey Jude." The session was booked at Trident Studios, a facility familiar to George and Paul, who had each produced Apple sessions there. Trident's main attraction was its then state-of-the-art eight-track recorder Although EMI had purchased an eight-track recorder, it had yet to be installed.

The Beatles, with Paul on piano, John on acoustic guitar, George on electric guitar and Ringo on drums, ran through four takes of rhythm tracks designated Takes 1 through 4. Take 1 was deemed the best and was subjected to overdubs.

The Beatles completed the single on August 1 at a follow up session also held at Trident. Paul overdubbed a bass part and lead vocal. He was then joined by John, George and Ringo for the backing vocals. Ringo also added a tambourine part. Just before the first part of the song comes to an end at the three-minute mark, an expletive is heard. Although John credited the naughty word to Paul after he hit a clunker on piano, Grapefruit singer John Perry claims he was in the studio and was responsible. During the last verse, Paul signaled Perry to join them at the mic for the song's extended vocal refrain ("nah, nah nah nah nah nah nah, nah nah nah nah, Hey Jude"). Following Paul's gesture, Perry put on a pair of headphones and was caught off-guard. "They were SO LOUD that I shouted out 'F#@*ing Hell!' to my eternal shame or glory depending on your standpoint!" Perry then nervously sang along with the Beatles to the end of the song. During the song's ending mantra, Paul gets carried away with his vocal, adding excitement with all his "Judy, Judy, Judy, woooh!" improvisations, which he later described as "Cary Grant on heat!"

After the Beatles completed their vocals, 36 classical musicians were brought in to add George Martin's score to the song's ending mantra. The instruments consisted of ten violins, three violas, three cellos, two flutes, one contra bassoon, one bassoon, two clarinets, one contra bass clarinet, four trumpets, four trombones, two horns, two string basses and a percussionist. The latter portion of Paul's bass part was recorded over by the strings during this orchestral overdub session. After the music was completed, the orchestra members were asked to participate in the recording of additional hand claps and the ending vocal refrain. Although most were happy to join in and get extra pay, one musician thought himself above it all and reportedly stormed out the studio mumbling, "I'm not going to clap my hands and sing Paul McCartney's bloody song!"

On August 2, three stereo mixes were made of McCartney's "bloody song" at Trident. Although stereo Remix 3 was collapsed to form a mono mix, this mix was not used. Three new mono mixes from the eight-track tape were made on August 8 at Abbey Road. The final mix, Remix 4, became the master for the mono single.

In Miles' *Many Years From Now*, Paul tells an amusing story about the recording of what turned out to be the master take of "Hey Jude." Just prior to the start of recording, Ringo sneaked off to the bathroom. Paul was unaware that the drummer was not behind his set, so he started the song. Because the drums are not used in the first verses of the song, Paul was unaware of Ringo's absence until he noticed the drummer tiptoeing behind him, trying to get to his drums. According to Paul:

"And just as he got to his drums, boom boom boom, his timing was absolutely impeccable. So I think when those things happen, you have a little laugh and a light bulb goes off in your head and you think, 'This is the take!' and you put a little more into it...what just happened was so magic! So we did that and we made a pretty good record."

Although the Beatles selected "Hey Jude" to be the A-side, Ken Mansfield, who served as manager of Apple Records' American operations, remembers Paul having serious misgivings about the acceptability of the song due to its length. In his book *The Beatles, the Bible, and Bodega Bay*, Mansfield tells of Paul's artistic insecurity and how he put Paul at ease. Mansfield, who was in London at the time, told Paul he would take an advance of the record with him and visit several key radio stations on his way back to Los Angeles. He would play the song for respected DJs to get their opinion on the single and phone Paul with the results upon arriving back at the Capitol Tower. As expected, the music directors were extremely enthusiastic about "Hey Jude," so Paul could relax about Apple's first release.

To promote their new single, the Beatles recruited Michael Lindsay-Hogg to direct performance videos of the two songs. The director had put together the promotional clips for "Paperback Writer" and "Rain," and would later direct the *Get Back/Let It Be* project. The promo clips were taped after the single's release at Twickenham Film Studios in St. Margaret's, London on September 4, 1968.

The Beatles ran through three performances of "Hey Jude," with the most commonly shown video consisting of the first part of the first performance edited with the second part from the third. The set consisted of a stage containing Paul's piano, three microphones and a Fender speaker cabinet. Ringo's drum kit and a Fender amplifier were on a separate and higher platform. George, armed with a Fender Bass VI, sat on the top edge of the speaker cabinet, while John, with his Epiphone Casino hollow body electric guitar, sat on the drum riser with his feet resting on the top of the cabinet to the left of George's body. A 36-piece orchestra was set up on three successively higher-raised rows in the background.

Behind and to the left of the platforms were 300 lucky extras, some of whom were fans invited by Beatles assistant Mal Evans. The Beatles and the orchestra played over the recorded single, with Paul singing along with his prerecorded lead vocal. During the second part of the song, Paul's vocal was recorded live for the video. For the extended mantra during the second part of the song, many of the extras climbed on the platforms, singing and swaying with the Beatles. Although really not a live performance, the video captured the excitement of the event.

Because the "Hey Jude" video was scheduled to make its debut on the September 8 Frost On Sunday, David Frost stopped by Twickenham Film Studios to introduce the song and give the impression the Beatles were appearing exclusively on his show. With Frost looking on, the Beatles performed a jazz version, complete with John and Paul vocals ("hear the beat of David Frost"), of the show's theme song, "By George! It's The David Frost Theme." The song actually was "by George" because was composed by George Martin. Frost then commented:

"Beautiful. Absolute poetry. Welcome back to part three, as you can see with the greatest tearoom orchestra in the world.... Making their first audience appearance for over a year, ladies and gentlemen, the Beatles."

John then gives a salute to the host and George Harrison lowers his microphone to say "Thank you, David." The introduction was then edited to the front of the "Hey Jude" clip for broadcast on Frost's show. The performance video of the song, without the Frost intro, was shown three times (September 12 and 26, and December 26) on the BBC's Top Of The Pops. All British broadcasts were in black and white. The video was shown in America in color on the October 6, 1968 Smothers Brothers Comedy Hour. The Frost intro-duction and the performance of the song appear on the *Anthology* video, although the second half of the song is interrupted three times—twice by comments from George and Paul superimposed over the video, and once by a Lennon voice-over. Ringo follows the song by comparing the group's eventual break up to a divorce. Unfortunately the negative comments of the individual Beatles diminish the exuberance and excitement of the original unaltered video. *The Beatles 1+* video has a different Frost intro followed by a quick vamp of "It's Now Or Never" leading into the promotional video of the song. The bonus disc has a new edit of "Hey Jude" performances preceded by another Frost intro and John singing the opening line to "You Are My Sunshine."

Revolution

Recorded: July 10, 11 & 12 (Abbey Road Studio 3 except Studio 2 on July 12)
Mixed: July 12 & 15 (mono); December 5, 1969 (stereo)

Producer: George Martin
Engineers: Geoff Emerick; Richard Lush (except July 11) & Phil McDonald (July 11)

John: Lead vocal; lead guitar (Casino)
Paul: Backing vocal; bass guitar
George: Backing vocal; guitar (Les Paul)
Ringo: Drums
Embellishments: Hand claps
Outside musician: Nicky Hopkins (piano)

The song initially selected for the A-side to the Beatles first Apple single was "Revolution." John's political statement set to music was the first song recorded by the Beatles after their return from India in the spring of 1968. John had pushed for the song to be the next Beatles single, but Paul and George objected, fearing that the song's slow tempo would prevent it from being a hit. A compromise was reached by John agreeing to re-record the song as a rocker. The story behind the original version of the song, later renamed "Revolution 1," appears above.

On July 9, 1968, the band recorded several takes of the fast version of "Revolution" after working on "Ob-La-Di, Ob-La-Da." As these runthroughs were rehearsals, the tape from this session was recorded over. Fortunately, an incomplete rehearsal survived and is included on *The White Album* deluxe edition. It rocks out at the end, with George playing a riff he would later use in "Old Brown Shoe. "

The following evening, the group went through ten takes of the song, with John and George on highly distorted guitars, Paul on bass and Ringo on drums. The guitars' unique, hard-biting fuzz sound was achieved by running the guitars directly through the recording console. This overloaded the channels and caused tremendous distortion. Ringo's drums were highly compressed, adding to the song's hard and heavy sound. Hand claps and a second drum part were then superimposed over Take 10, which was given three reduction mixes (Takes 11 through 13), with Take 13 being the best. The deluxe edition contains this instrumental take. John then added his no-nonsense lead vocal to form Take 14. Another Lennon lead vocal, as well as the scream heard during the song's hard hitting introduction, was added as part of Take 15.

Work continued on the song the following night, with Nicky Hopkins adding an electric piano solo to the song's instrumental break and another bit of fast-paced piano to the song's ending coda. This was then mixed down to form Take 16.

The fast and loud single version of "Revolution" was completed the following evening, on July 12, with the addition of another lead guitar part by John and a second bass part by Paul. The song was then mixed for mono; however, neither John nor Paul were satisfied with the results, so two more mono mixes (designated Remixes 20 and 21) were made on July 15. Mono Remix 21 was selected as the master. As the song was intended for release only as a mono single, no stereo mix was made at the time. The song was not mixed for stereo until December 5, 1969, when a stereo mix was needed for the American *Hey Jude* album.

In addition to having a totally different sound than the original "Revolution 1," the single version of the song has a slight change in the lyrics. On the album version of the song, John is ambivalent about his stance on revolutionary violence so he sings, "But when you talk about destruction, don't you know that you can count me out/in." For the single John removes the ambiguity by singing "don't you know that you can count me out."

The "Revolution" promotional video is a straightforward performance, with the Beatles shown on stage with Ringo in the rear on a raised platform. John is with his Casino guitar, George with a red Gibson Les Paul guitar and Paul with his Hofner bass. Although the Beatles play over a backing instrumental track of the single, the vocals are entirely live and different from the released single. Paul handles the song's introductory scream and sings harmony with George on some of the lines to the verses. In addition, Paul and George sing the "shoo-be-do-wop-bow, shoo-be-do-wop-bow" refrains heard on the album version of the song. John also draws from his initial rendition of the song by singing "But when you talk about destruction, don't you know that you can count me out/in." This exciting performance combines the best elements of the album and single versions of the song.

The "Revolution" promo clip was shown in England in black and white on the September 19 Top Of The Pops. In America, it appeared in color on The Smothers Brothers Comedy Hour on October 13, a week after the "Hey Jude" film. The "Revolution" performance is in the *Anthology* video; however, the song is briefly interrupted by a Lennon voice-over during the second chorus. *The Beatles 1+* video has the complete unaltered performance on its bonus disc.

DSOE 16.740

EMI
ODEON

THE BEATLES

hey jude revolution

Foto: John Kelly

Not Guilty

Recorded: August 7, 8, 9 & 12 (Abbey Road Studio Two)
Mixed: August 12 (mono) [Stereo mixes made in 1984 & 2018]
Producer: George Martin
Engineers: Ken Scott & John Smith

George: Lead vocal; rhythm & lead guitar (Les Paul)
John: Harpsichord; electric piano (earlier takes)
Paul: Bass guitar (Rickenbacker)
Ringo: Drums

"Not Guilty" was written by George in response to the grief he received from John and Paul over the Beatles involvement with the Maharishi. In an interview with Timothy White for Musician magazine, George explained, "I said I wasn't guilty of leading them astray in our all going to Rishikesh to see the Maharishi." The song also appears to be a commentary on George's desire to have his songs placed on Beatles albums. Harrison sings "Not guilty of getting in your way, while you're trying to steal the day" and "I only want what I can get." It also has a clever pun with "I won't upset the apple cart."

This would be the first song in which a Beatle took aim at his band mates. George would strike again with "Wah-Wah," introduced during the *Get Back* sessions, but not properly recorded until his *All Things Must Pass* LP, and "Sue Me Sue You Blues" on *Living In The Material World*. Paul got into the act with "You Never Give Me Your Money" and "Carry That Weight" from *Abbey Road*. Paul's "Too Many People" from *Ram* was viewed by John as a personal attack. He responded with "How Do You Sleep?" Ringo took a nostalgic view with "Early 1970," but his "Back Off Bugaloo" may be aimed at Paul.

"Not Guilty" was written shortly after George's return from India and was recorded in demo form at Kinfauns. On August 7, the Beatles recorded 46 takes (only five complete) with George on his Les Paul guitar, John on electric piano, Paul on his Rickenbacker bass and Ringo on drums. The next evening the group ran through Takes 47 through 101, this time with John on harpsichord. Take 99 was judged the best and was given a reduction mix (designated Take 102) the following night to allow for overdubs, which included additional drums by Ringo, bass by Paul and rhythm guitar by George. Harrison then recorded his solo played on his Les Paul through a Fender Twin-Reverb amplifier placed in an echo chamber, with the microphone placed across the room to pick up the ambient sound. George sat in the control room and had his guitar cord run to the echo chamber. Harrison also recorded his lead vocal from the control room on

August 12. Although given a mono mix that evening, the song was not mixed for stereo and was not selected for the album. In 1984, Geoff Emerick made an edited stereo mix of the song for the aborted *Sessions* LP. This mix is on *Anthology 3*. *The White Album* deluxe edition has an unedited stereo mix that rocks out at the end. George rerecorded "Not Guilty" for his 1979 LP *George Harrison*.

What's The New Mary Jane

Recorded: August 14 (Abbey Road Studio Two)
Mixed: August 12 (mono) & October 14 (stereo)
Producer: George Martin
Engineers: Ken Scott & John Smith

John: Lead vocal; piano
George: Acoustic guitar (J-200)
Yoko Ono: Vocals; percussion
Mal Evans: Vocals; percussion

Embellishments: Harmonium; tin whistles; xylophone; hand bells and piano strings being plucked and scraped

Although "What's The New Mary Jane" is credited to Lennon-McCartney, it was written by John with an assist from self-proclaimed electronic genius Alex Mardas, the madcap inventor who headed Apple Electronics. The song, like many of Magic Alex's inventions, doesn't work. Its "hook" consists of little more than John singing "What a shame Mary Jane had a pain at the party."

"What's The New Mary Jane" was recorded on August 14, 1968, in a session with John and George as the only Beatles in the studio. Although the song sounds improvised, the Esher demo shows that John had actually worked out its arrangement months in advance. Four backing tracks, featuring John on vocal and piano and George on his Gibson J-200 acoustic guitar, were recorded. Take 4, which rambled on for over six and one-half minutes, was deemed the best and embellished with a second vocal and piano part from John and more acoustic guitar from George. Also present in the studio were Mal Evans and Yoko, who each contributed vocals and percussion. Additional overdubs included harmonium, tin whistles, xylophone, hand bells and piano strings being plucked and scraped. At the end of the tape, John says "Let's hear it, before we get taken away." The song was mixed for mono at the end of the session. A stereo mix was made on October 14, thus indicating that John wanted the track on the album. Fortunately, Paul and George Martin were able to convince John there wasn't space for the song.

In November 1969, John decided that if the Beatles wouldn't release "What's The New Mary Jane" or "You Know My Name (Look Up The Number)," he would put them out as a Plastic Ono Band single. On November 26, John, serving as co-producer with Geoff Emerick, remixed and edited the songs at Abbey Road. During the second stereo remix of Take 4 of "What's The New Mary Jane," John and Yoko added vocals and sound effects to the two-track stereo tape. This was designated Remix 5, which was later edited to form Remix 6. Although Apple announced that the songs would be released in England as APPLES 1002 on December 5, the single was never issued. In 1984, Geoff Emerick made a new stereo mix of the song for the aborted Sessions LP. Emerick's *Anthology* remix is similar to his *Sessions* mix. *The White Album* deluxe edition contains Take 1, which has John's laughter and lasts under two minutes.

St. Louis Blues

Recorded: July 30, 1968, during the "Hey Jude" sessions

Between takes of "Hey Jude," Paul (on piano joined by John on acoustic guitar) warmed up with a few lines of W.C. Handy's jazz standard "St. Louis Blues" ("I hate to see that evening sun go down").

Step Inside Love

Recorded: September 16 (Abbey Road Studio 2)

Producer: Chris Thomas
Engineers: Ken Scott and Mike Sheady

Paul: Lead vocal; acoustic guitar (D-28)
John: Temple blocks
Ringo: Percussion (snare drum rim)

During the recording of "I Will," Paul would occasionally drift into spontaneous numbers between proper takes of the song. "Step Inside Love" was written by Paul in 1967 to serve as the theme song for Cilla Black's TV series. The initial recording of the song, consisting of a verse and refrain, took place on November 21, 1967. After the show's debut on January 30, the song proved so popular that Paul was asked to write a bridge and additional lyrics so the song could be issued as a single. This expanded version of "Step Inside Love" was recorded on February 28, 1968, with George Martin producing, and issued as Parlophone R 5674 on March 8. The song charted at number eight in the U.K. This stripped down recording highlights the song's bossa nova flavor and runs about 90 seconds.

Los Paranoias

Same recording session and personnel as "Step Inside Love"

At the end of "Step Inside Love," Paul blurts out the name of a fictional lounge band, Joe Prairies and the Prairie Wallflowers. After John shouts out "Los Paranoias," Paul laughs and ad-libs a song to match, with lyrics such as "Baby, come on and join the Los Paranoias/ Just enjoy us Los Paranoias." John joins in on the fun, singing "I can't make it" in the middle of the song. John also plays maracas.

Blue Moon

Same recording session and personnel as "Step Inside Love"

"Blue Moon," written by Richard Rodgers and Lorenz Hart in 1934, became a pop standard. The Beatles were familiar with the song through Elvis Presley's 1954 recording of the song for Sun Records. When released as a single by RCA in 1956, "Blue Moon" charted at number 55 in Billboard, 42 in Cash Box and 36 in Music Vendor. In the U.K., the song peaked at number nine when issued by HMV. This impromptu version breaks down after a few verses.

(You're So Square) Baby I Don't Care

Recorded: September 9 (Abbey Road Studio 2)

Producer: Chris Thomas
Engineers: Ken Scott; John Smith

Paul: Lead vocal; guitar (Casino)
John: Bass guitar (Fender Jazz)
George: Lead guitar (Les Paul)
Ringo: Drums

"(You're So Square) Baby I Don't Care," written by Jerry Leiber and Mike Stoller for the film *Jailhouse Rock*, was recorded by Elvis Presley in 1957. The song was included on the *Jailhouse Rock* EP, which peaked at number 14 on the U.K. Record Retailer EP chart. Paul led the group through a bit of the song during the September 9 "Helter Skelter" recording session.

Let It Be

During the sessions for "While My Guitar Gently Weeps," the group jammed on a new song by Paul, "Let It Be." In addition to Paul's vocal and piano, the track has organ, guitar and drums.

White Mono, White Stereo, White Sellers

by Pascal Lambini

By 1968, attitudes toward mono and stereo were changing all around the world. Stereo record players were now outselling monaural ones in almost every country. As a result of shifting preferences, German Odeon had already switched to stereo-only for albums in the fall of 1964. In the United States and Canada, Capitol Records had just eliminated the mono/stereo option for LPs and was considering switching to stereo for singles as well. Great Britain would hold on for a few more months before deciding not to release new albums in mono. By the end of 1969, the worldwide transition was nearly complete, with only a few countries around the EMI world still pressing more albums in mono than in stereo.

Rock 'n' roll records in general were becoming far more complex than the 1950's "guitar and drums" sound. As the Beatles worked on *The White Album*, George Martin found that many songs required more than four tracks.

In late June, George Harrison produced a session at Trident Studios for Apple artist Jackie Lomax that yielded "Sour Milk Sea." The year-old London studio that had an eight-track recording machine. The following month Paul produced Mary Hopkin's "Those Were The Days" at Trident. When it came time to record Paul's anthem sing-along "Hey Jude," their familiarity with Trident and its advanced recorder led to the decision to leave the confines of Abbey Road and record the song at Trident (although recorded rehearsals were held in Studio Two). And so, on July 31 and August 1, 1968, the Beatles recorded "Hey Jude" at Trident using an eight-track console for the first time. As if to herald the demise of mono, a stereo mix was made of a song destined for single release first (August 2) and folded down into mono (August 6), although a proper mono mix was made two days later.

Although EMI Studios had purchased a 3M eight-track recorder earlier in the year, it was still being held for quality review. When the Beatles learned of its existence, they persuaded engineer Ken Scott to have it installed in Studio Two. The first song recorded on the eight-track was the remake of "While My Guitar Gently Weeps."

The shift from four- to eight-track recording greatly affected *The White Album*. Some songs that had been recorded on four-track consoles were dubbed down to an eight-track console and finished there. Some songs were already complete and were not remixed later. In the case of *Revolution 1*, the mono mix was made by combining the channels of the stereo mix, but a number of songs received distinct mono mixes. Sometimes these mono mixes were made before the stereo mixes, while at other times the stereo mixes were made first. This was certainly a break from the days when George Martin viewed the stereo mix as being for hi-fi freaks only or as an interim step to the final product – a mono mix. The transition to an eight-track machine located at EMI seems to have stabilized the process somewhat.

180

For all songs begun on or after October 8, 1968, the stereo and mono mixes were usually made on the same day. *The White Album* was the last album that was given a dedicated mono mix (the mono U.K. *Yellow Submarine* LP is a fold-down of the stereo mix). Some of the songs on *The White Album* sound quite different in mono than they do in stereo.

Although *The White Album* was not issued in mono in the United States, some Americans heard mono mixes of some of the songs on the radio a few weeks ahead of the album's release. These recordings came from a source known as the Peter Sellers Tape, which consisted of early mono mixes of a dozen songs recorded during the album sessions. Ringo had given a tape of early mixes to Sellers, who, at the time, was best known for his radio performances as part of Goon Show and as the bumbling Inspector Clouseau from the movie *The Pink Panther*. In early 1969, Ringo would appear with his friend in the film *The Magic Christian*.

The Peter Sellers Tape contains the following songs: "Back In the U.S.S.R.;" "Rocky Raccoon;" "Wild Honey Pie;" "Mother Nature's Son;" "Sexy Sadie;" "Don't Pass Me By;" "Yer Blues;" "Good Night;" "Everybody's Got Something To Hide Except Me And My Monkey;" "Ob-La-Di, Ob-La-Da;" "Blackbird;" and "Not Guilty." The last song was not included on *The White Album*.

Back In The U.S.S.R. The airplane sound effects are placed differently in the mono mix (October 23, 1968) than in the stereo mix (October 13, 1968). The introduction in the mono mix has screaming sounds and louder piano than the stereo mix, which has additional guitar notes during the solo, as well as more shouting and louder piano. The Peter Sellers Tape version is the same as the mono mix, but the fade is longer as the song does not fade into "Dear Prudence."

Dear Prudence Both stereo and mono mixes were made on October 13, 1968. The fade-out in the stereo mix drops to a lower volume.

Glass Onion Both mixes were made on October 10, 1968. There are slight differences at the end of the instrumental break. In the mono mix, Paul can be heard joining John as he sings "oh yeah," whereas in the stereo mix, John's voice is alone.

Ob-La-Di, Ob-La-Da Both mixes were made on October 12, 1968. The stereo mix has hand-clapping during the introduction, whereas the mono does not. The Peter Sellers Tape version opens earlier with some laughing and a false start and has hand claps during the introduction. It also has a slightly longer ending.

Wild Honey Pie Paul's vocal is double-tracked in both mixes. The vocal that is louder in the mono mix (August 20, 1968) is softer in the stereo mix (October 13, 1968) and vice versa. The Peter Sellers Tape version is the same as the mono mix, but has four taps at the beginning to set the beat.

The Continuing Story Of Bungalow Bill Both the mono and stereo mixes were made on October 9, 1968. There are no noteworthy differences.

While My Guitar Gently Weeps Both mixes were made on October 14, 1968. In the mono mix, Eric Clapton's weeping guitar remains at full volume throughout, whereas in the stereo mix, Clapton's guitar returns to a lower volume after his solo. The stereo mix, which ends earlier than the mono mix, has repeated "yeah"s sung by George during the fade.

Happiness Is A Warm Gun The organ heard during the song's intro continues until the drums enter in the mono mix (September 26, 1968), whereas the organ is mixed out earlier in the stereo mix (October 15, 1968). The mono mix has louder bass during the second section ("I need a fix") than the stereo mix. It also has a laugh near the end of the song that is not heard in the stereo mix. During the second section, the word "down" is heard by itself during the instrumental line in the stereo mix.

Martha My Dear Both mixes were made on October 5, 1968. There are no noteworthy differences.

I'm So Tired Both mixes were made on October 15, 1968. Paul's backing vocal on "you'd say" is louder in the mono mix than in the stereo mix.

Blackbird Both mixes were made on October 13, 1968. The bird sounds differ between the mixes. The Peter Sellers Tape version is the same as the mono mix, but without the bird sound effects and a bit of reverb added to Paul's voice.

Piggies Both mixes were made on October 11, 1968. The pig sounds differ between the mixes and the guitar is louder in the mono mix than in the stereo mix.

Rocky Raccoon There are no noteworthy differences between the mono mix (August 15, 1968) and the stereo mix (October 10, 1968). The mix on the Peter Sellers Tape is the same as the mono mix.

Don't Pass Me By Both mixes were made on October 11, 1968. The tape was sped up for the mono mix, making the song faster and in a higher pitch than the stereo mix. The mono mix also has the country fiddle throughout the mix, whereas it is more limited in the stereo mix. The mono and stereo mixes have different endings. The version on the Peter Sellers Tape is similar to the final mono mix, but there is quite a bit more that was later edited out. There are some stray bass notes at the beginning and the bass seems stronger throughout. There is a reprise of the first verse after the eight-count near the end.

At the end of the song, there is some clapping for Ringo, and then he says "What a show!" and "Wonderful" followed by mock dog-barking and "Bravo." After that,

Ringo adds a teaser that if Sellers wants to hear more, "You've got to turn the tape over."

Why Don't We Do It In The Road? Both mixes were made on October 16, 1968. The stereo mix has hand clapping during the intro, whereas the mono mix does not.

I Will Paul's vocal imitation of a bass starts after the first verse in the mono mix (September 26, 1968), whereas it starts at the beginning of the song in the stereo mix (October 14, 1968).

Julia Both mixes were made on October 13, 1968. There are no noteworthy differences.

Birthday In the mono mix (September 18, 1968), in the middle of the song where Paul yells "dance... dance," the second "dance" is at a lower volume, making it difficult to hear. In the stereo mix (October 14, 1968), the entire "dance...dance" is at the same volume and is easily audible.

Yer Blues The mono mix (August 20, 1968) has a longer fade-out than the stereo mix (October 20, 1968). On the Peter Sellers Tape, the song is preceded by African-sounding music, Ringo saying "It's a raid" and a bit more music that overlaps with the opening count in to the song.

Mother Nature's Son Both mixes were made on October 12, 1968. There are no noteworthy differences. The mix on the Peter Sellers Tape is the same as the mono mix.

Everybody's Got Something To Hide Except Me And My Monkey Both mixes were made on October 12, 1968. The ad libbed screaming at the end of the song differs between the mono and stereo mixes. The mix on the Peter Sellers Tape sounds like a different take. It may be Take 11.

Sexy Sadie In the mono mix (August 21, 1968), the bass does not begin until when the lead vocal starts, whereas in the stereo mix (October 14, 1968), the bass is present from the start of the song. The mono mix also has one less drumstick tap during the intro than in the stereo mix. The mix on the Peters Sellers Tape is the same as the mono mix, but has a longer fade-out.

Helter Skelter The distorted guitar noises and Paul's lead vocal and bass are more pronounced in the mono mix (September 17, 1968) than in stereo mix. The mono mix also has beeping sounds that randomly appear. More notably, on the mono mix, when the song fades out, it does not return, whereas in the stereo mix it fades back in to the end of the take, where Ringo shouts "I got blisters on my fingers!" The mono mix is nearly a minute shorter with a running time of 3:37 compared to the 4:29 stereo mix.

Long, Long, Long In the mono mix (October 10, 1968), the double-tracked vocals come in at the third "long," whereas in the stereo mix (October 14, 1968), the double-tracked vocals begins on the first "long." In addition, the rhythm guitar is louder toward the end of the song in the stereo mix.

Revolution 1 Although an initial mono mix of the song was made on June 4, 1968, the mono mix used for the album is a fold-down of the stereo mix made on June 25.

Honey Pie Both mixes were made on October 5, 1968. The guitar fills after the third verse last longer in the mono mix than in the stereo mix, enabling the listener to hear the guitar over the other instruments and vocals until the second chorus begins.

Savoy Truffle Both mixes were made on October 14, 1968. The mono mix has additional guitar during the chorus after the instrumental bridge and additional sounds during the bridge that are not audible in the stereo mix, which has organ during the last verse not heard in the mono mix.

Cry Baby Cry Both mixes were made on October 15, 1968. There are no noteworthy differences between the mono and stereo mixes. There is an anomaly on the U.S. pressings, specifically an audible warble during the line "by the children" that is not in the master tape or on the U.K. discs.

Revolution 9 The mono mix (August 20, 1968) is a fold-down of the stereo mix made on June 25. The voices heard at the beginning of the track are louder than on the stereo mix.

Good Night Both mixes were made on October 11, 1968. The mono mix starts at full volume, whereas the stereo mix fades in at the beginning. The mix on the Peter Sellers Tape seems incomplete. The backing vocals are louder and the overdubs are different during the instrumental buildup just before the repeat of the second verse. Ringo's voice also seems louder at the end when he is whispering.

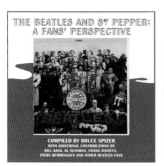

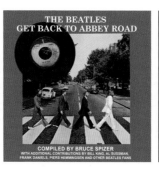

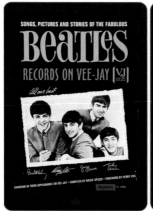

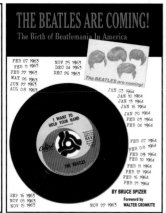
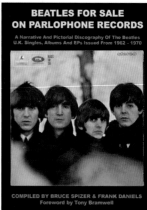